DEVELOPING YOUR LEADERSHIP COMPETENCE

Integrating Leader Development Principles
&
Biblical Perspectives

Benson Katulwa, Ph.D.

Leadership development principles &Biblical Perspectives

Copyright © 2018 Benson Katulwa

Published by Centre for Christian Discipleship

All rights reserved worldwide. No part of this publication may be replicated, redistributed, or given away in any form without the prior written consent of the author

ISBN-13: 9781717841261

All scripture quotations, unless otherwise indicated are taken from THE HOLY BIBLE, NEW KING JAMES Version®. Copyright © 1982 by Thomas Nelson, Inc.

Dedication

I dedicate this book to my sons; Abraham Mumo, and Philip Kyama; and to my darling daughter Shalom Mbete Muteti. For in you guys, I see a great potential to be great leaders and to change the World

Acknowledgments

A good book is rarely the work of one person. I, therefore, wish to acknowledge the support and the encouragement I received from my family and friends as I worked on this book.

First and foremost, I wish to thank my wife and my sons for proofreading the book and helping to fix the typos and misspelled words. Thanks for supporting and encouraging me to go on with the project.

Many thanks to Professor Wariara Kariuki for taking the time out of her very tight schedule to write the Foreword and provide suggestions for improvement, and, to my colleagues and dear friends; Dr. Titus Mwanthi, Joseph Nzioki, and Ms. Gertrude Obwoge for writing an objective and yet, a very encouraging endorsement for this book. Your constructive suggestions added much value to this work.

Then there was my MA in Theology and MALM 2018 classes at Scott Christian University who read the manuscript from an academic perspective and provided constructive criticism and improvement issues. Thanks to Pastor Stephen Kioko, Tony Nzoka, Oscar Kamula, Joseph Mutua, Richard Owuor and Yusuphu Konzongwe for your valuable ideas. I do appreciate.

Finally to my friend and graduate student, Mr. Benson Kithuka who edited and wrote a powerful review of the book, I am indebted to you. Thanks for your valuable technical assistance regarding the book structure and its organization.

Table of Contents

Dedication iii
Acknowledgments iv
Endorsements vi
Foreword 1
Preface 3
Chapter 1. Understanding the Leadership Context 5
Chapter 2. Understanding Leadership Character 39
Chapter 3. Developing Your Character 57
Chapter 4. Clarifying Your Vision 91
Chapter 5. Achieving Your Goals 121
Chapter 6. Developing Your Emotional Intelligence 133
Chapter 7. Improving Competence Though Feedback 147
Chapter 8. Developing Your Leadership Style 157
Chapter 9. Developing Your Administrative Competence 183
Chapter 10. Take It Home 213
About the Author 229

Endorsements

This is a must-read book for every leader. I have enjoyed reading all the chapters and in particular, I like the chapters on developing Your Character, Clarifying Your Vision, and, Achieving your goals. This book will be of great benefit to many.

Dr. Titus N. Mwanthi, Registrar, Catholic University of East Africa

A major challenge in leadership is striking the delicate balance between developing one's leadership ability and building the capacity of followers to effectively contribute to the achievement of the organizational vision. In *Developing your Leadership Competence*, Dr. Katulwa provides practical approaches towards the achievement of this balance. Any executive, leader, or aspiring leader will find substantive insights for effective leadership in this book.

Gertrude Obwoge, CEO, Top-View Consultants & the Founder Dean, School of Professional Studies, Scott Christian University, Kenya

Dr. Katulwa highlights some of the most overlooked yet pivotal tenets of leadership. In this pragmatic and practical approach, the book presents both the principles of leadership and Biblical worldview of equipping, empowering and guiding the 21st-century leaders in their leadership journey. The author provides leaders with knowledge, insights and critical leadership skills to their success. Summative, informative and holistic, the book cuts across all the spheres of influence making it applicable to leaders from all manner of organizations and Industry.

Joseph Nzioki MA in Leadership., Ph.D. Cad. – E. Africa Director for Global Learning and Partnerships, Beulah Heights University

Going through this book on *Developing Your Leadership Competence*, you will find it a one stop shop for useful information that will put you on a pedestal of an exemplary leader. Since we have noted that everyone can be a leader, Dr. Katulwa's ideas revolve around the notion of trying to make leaders more efficient and effective in their work.

Benson Kithuka, Deputy Principal, Kwakukui Secondary School

Foreword

"He also chose David His servant and took him from the sheepfolds, from following nursing ewes. He brought him to shepherd Jacob His people, and Israel His inheritance. So He shepherded them with the integrity of His heart and led them with His skillful hands" (Psa 78:70-72)

There are many examples of good leaders in the Bible and my favorite is King David. He exemplified effective leadership and at the core of his leadership were the 'heart' of leadership and skillfulness in leadership. In the scripture above we see that David was chosen by God to lead His people. The statement about skillfulness supports the need for leadership development. Further interrogation of David's life reveals how he developed his leadership. In many aspects of life including leadership, a lot of information and opinions exist on 'what' along with great chasms of 'how'. It is gratifying and of great significance to the Church and academia that a book has been written to address the 'how' of leadership development: *Developing Your Leadership Competence: Integrating Leader Development Principles and Biblical Perspectives*

I am very glad that Dr. Benson Katulwa has written this book which reflects his passion and mission in life. He has many years' experience in raising and developing leaders as a pastor and teacher (Ephesians 4: 11). Many students and other people in Kenya and beyond have benefitted from the services of this Spirit-filled, humble and knowledgeable teacher and pastor and I am one such beneficiary.

I first met Dr. Katulwa when I enrolled as a student in the Master of Arts in Leadership program at the Pan Africa Christian University in Nairobi, Kenya. He made a lasting impression on me and encouraged me to use my experience as an academic to enrich my own learning experience and that of fellow students in my class. I have continued to interact with him (albeit in somewhat reversed roles!), and I continue to draw from his heart as a servant leader.

I am confident that many more people including students, teachers, leaders, laity, and clergy will benefit from the collection of his wisdom, knowledge, and skills in leadership in the form of this book. The book is a must-read for any serious leader, especially those who profess the Christian faith and/or those in Christian organizations and ministries. The book combines theory and practice in leadership and the Biblical case studies enrich the content for those in Christian leadership. For readers who have prior leadership training, the book is a good recap of leadership theories and practical application of the theories. For those who have not had such training or a new in leadership, this book is a good starting point in developing your leadership skills. The Biblical examples will enhance the readers' appreciation and application of the Bible and show that truly the Bible has answers to every sphere of human life.

I believe that any leader who reads and applies the knowledge in this book including the biblical principles of leadership from the case studies will greatly enhance their leadership roles, tasks and experience. I am glad that this book has been written for a worldwide readership and does not necessarily focus on the African context. This then enhances its reach among scholars and leaders.

I highly recommend this book to my fellow leaders, within the whole continuum of leadership, whether at the family, community or organizational level.

Professor. Wariara Kariuki, Deputy Vice-Chancellor, Academic Affairs. Scott Christian University, Machakos, Kenya.

Preface

Welcome to the World of 21st Century and beyond, where, leaders have joined the class of endangered species. Every day, somewhere in the world, a leader is haunted out of office by angry followers. 'The Leader Must Go,' has become the clarion call of frustrated followers. The people's tolerance for unable leaders has become less and less over the years. They want competent leaders, who understand their priorities and are able to mobilize and redirect all the available resources towards the implementation of real solutions to real problems.

Leading people and organizations in the 21st Century has become a tough challenge for many leaders. The leader is sandwiched between demanding followers on one hand, and, a dynamic global environment where knowledge doubles every year and skills have a half-life of 2.5 to 5 years on the other hand.

To overcome these challenges, the leader must continually learn new ways of getting things done through the people. The leader must understand what motivates people, be skilled at assessing their capabilities, matching their abilities with appropriate responsibilities and inspire them to action. Above all else, the leader must deliver the expected results.

I wrote this book to provide both the potential and the practicing leaders with the tools and the handles they need to navigate the muddy waters of leadership in a dynamic global environment, where the leader's competence must be matched with the right character.

In writing this book, I had in mind, the needs of the potential and aspiring leader, practitioner, leadership student and the academic instructor who may be looking for a suitable textbook to use. I, therefore, tried to integrate both the motivational and academic approaches to meet the needs of the two worlds.

As you read this book, expect to:
- Find out what you need to know and do to become a more competent leader,
- Discover how your character draws people to you or

repels them, and what you can do to develop it,
- Learn how to build a winning strategy by aligning your mission and vision for your life purpose and by, setting and achieving your goals,
- Gauge the level of your emotional intelligence, its impact on your people skills, and how you can use feedback to reinforce your people skills,
- Identify your default leadership style and learn how to use the right style in any given situation, and,
- Recognize where administration fits within the leadership equation and how to develop your administrative ability.

Leadership is a complex and dynamic process that requires a multifaceted approach. The book is a good starting point for leader's personal leadership development journey.

Benson Katulwa

Chapter One

Understanding the Leadership Context

Introduction

Close to a thousand years before the birth of Christ, Solomon, the wisdom guru and the author of the Biblical books of wisdom made an observation that stands valid up to today. He said, "The race is not to the swift or the battle to the strong, nor does food come to the wise, or wealth to the brilliant or favor to the learned; but time and chance happen to them all" (Ecc 9:11).

Solomon's observation makes even more sense when applied to leadership practice. Everyone is born a leader, but not everyone leads. Everyone gets the opportunity to make a difference, but not everyone makes a difference. Everyone gets a chance to lead, but effective leadership does not happen by chance. Only the prepared can see and seize the opportunity to make a difference in their lives and the lives of those around them.

Having a leadership position without the capacity to lead equals frustration and failure. That is where personal leadership development comes in. Personal leadership development is the process of enhancing the capacity to lead oneself and effectively carry out leadership roles in organizations.[1] It is a strategic investment in a structured learning process that provides individuals with the opportunities, training, and experiences to become better leaders[2] in their sphere of influence.

Why Develop Your Leadership Ability?

Leadership development is not an optional indulgence for leaders who want to make a difference. On the contrary, "Leadership and learning are indispensable to each other."[3] The need for leadership development is urgent for the 21st-century global environment because what worked in the past is no longer working.

Traditional leadership ideas and practices are outdated, and leaders need new approaches to influence people. For this to happen, the leader must continue growing.

The following are eight reasons every person should invest in personal leadership development:

1. The global environment needs dynamic leaders

Before the 1970's, the global environment was relatively stable and predictable. More emphasis then was on management as opposed to leadership development. Business scholars treated leadership as a function of management alongside planning, organizing and controlling.

That is no longer the case. The 21st-century leadership environment has changed substantially. Changes in technology and globalization are taking place at an accelerated rate[4] affecting every aspect of human life and endeavor. That includes; people's attitudes, their expectations, perspectives, reasoning and the way they do things. The world has now become a global village where happenings in one part of the globe have a real-time impact on what is happening in other parts of the world.

Accelerated changes in science, technology, and globalization present a constant challenge to leaders and their organizations. To overcome these challenges, the leader must continually learn new ways of getting things done through the people. The leader must understand what motivates people, be skilled at assessing their capabilities, matching their abilities with appropriate responsibilities and inspire them to action.

2. Traditional leadership approaches are inadequate

Emerging global trends have rendered traditional leadership styles irrelevant and inadequate. We live "in a world where knowledge doubles every year and skills have a half-life of 2.5 to 5 years."[5] Advanced information communication technology, fast happening changes combined with globalization have led to the emergence of global trends that have rendered the traditional approach to leadership obsolete. Some of the notable global trends necessitating the need for leadership development include:[6]

- Growing internationalization of organizations,
- The increasing number of knowledge workers,
- Pressure from the civil society on organizations to be drivers of social change,
- Increased networking nature of multinational organizations,
- Increasing reduction of borders and, trade barriers,

- Increasing the role of information and telecommunication technologies in networking,
- Changing organizational structures from the top down to flat structures,
- Decentralization of power, and
- The growing number of remote workers among others trends.

The 21st-century leader must keep ahead of, and leverage on these global trends to maximize the opportunities they present besides mitigating the challenges created by the same trends.

3. Empowered followers demand effective leadership

In the past, people treated the leader with respect and accorded him unqualified cooperation. The leader's respect emanated from his position. He knew the way, and the people took his directions at their face value. That is no longer the case.

Today's followers are more empowered. They are educated, exposed and well informed. The leader no longer has the monopoly of knowledge, power, and resources. The followers look at him just as 'one of us' who must prove he is worthy of the trust given to him by the people. They well understand that the leader enjoys the power which they have donated to him. Thus, the leader no longer enjoys the unqualified right to give directions but often needs to consult and accommodate divergent ideas and views of the people.

Based on the current perceptions, the leader's role has shifted from that of:

a. Giving orders to facilitating collaboration. The leader must be skilled at spotting opportunities for collaboration and making partnerships with other people and organizations.

b. Declaring performance to capacity building. The successful leader is seen as the one who empowers stakeholders to make decisions and take action without waiting for the leader's permission.

c. Firefighting to proactive leadership style. In the years to come, success will go to leaders who can anticipate and pre-empt challenges before they become emergencies. Such leaders will understand the immediate and long-term consequences of their decisions, appraise trends and discern where the world is going.

a) Know it all answer provider to a listener. Whereas the successful leaders of past appeared to the solution provider, future leaders will spend more time asking questions and listening to their followers to tap from their resourcefulness.

The role of the 21st-century leader is that of a facilitator and an enabler rather than the command and control manager of the 1970s.[7] Leaders who fail to understand this changing perception of their role will needlessly spend more time and resources addressing conflicts and dealing with rejection from their followers.

To avoid falling into this pitfall, wise leaders will invest in developing their leadership competence to keep up with the fast-changing demands associated with their role.

4. Non-growing leaders lose their position

In this time and age, people do not follow a leader simply because he or she holds a high position within the organizational structure. As the saying goes, it is not the size of the dog that matters; rather, it is the size of the fight in the dog. Likewise, it is not the size of the leader or, how long he has held a position. It is his or her capacity to get results that matter.

In the law of the lid, Maxwell compares leadership ability to a lid in the leader's life that determines the leader's level of effectiveness.[8] In Maxwell's words,

> If the leadership is strong, the lid is high. But if it is not, then the organization is limited. That is why in times of trouble, organizations naturally look for new leadership. When the country is experiencing hard times, it elects a new president. When a company is losing money, it hires a new CEO. When a Church is floundering, it searches for a new senior pastor. When a sports team is losing, it looks for a new coach.

The 21st-century leader must continually grow to increase her effectiveness through leadership development.[9] Non-growing leaders are likely to be overthrown by their followers, soon or later.

5. Effective leaders develop social skills

To lead effectively, the leader must build and demonstrate interpersonal competence including social awareness and social skills.[10] Only then will the leader be able to show social awareness through service orientation, ability to empathize, and develop others.

The leader must invest in leadership development because it supports the development of both social awareness and social skills, which enable the leader to manage conflict, foster a spirit of collaboration and cooperation and through relationship building. A leader without social skills will watch helplessly as minor conflicts escalate to unmanageable levels and threaten to tear the organizations part.

6. Character development produces authentic leaders

Leadership development is a worthy investment whose benefits outweigh its costs. Numerous research findings indicate that leaders with character build competitive and supportive organizations, which inspire people to do their best to contribute to the organizational goals. Besides, successful leadership development produces authentic leaders who:

- Know who they are and what they believe in;
- Show consistency between their values, ethical reasoning, and actions;
- Develop positive psychological states such as confidence, optimism; hope, and resilience in themselves and their associates;
- Are widely known and respected for their integrity.

Developing the ability to lead is necessary for the development of the characteristics that make up authentic leaders such as integrity, listening skills, transparency and consistency among others.

7. Growing leaders build sustainable organizations

Organizational continuity largely depends on the leader's ability to develop other leaders. Harvey Firestone was right when he said, "It is only as we develop others that we permanently succeed."[11] This point is best illustrated in the life of Jesus Christ who founded the church, which has continued to impact the world more than 2000 years later. Unlike many leaders who focus on gaining followers, Jesus focused on developing the twelve disciples. For about three years, Jesus intensely invested in these men and prepared them to take over his work after he was gone. The rest is history.

Leaders who do not focus on developing other leaders to take over from them cannot promise continued impact of their organizations. In most cases, their organizations disintegrate within the next generation of leaders after they are gone. The only way to ensure continued growth and impact of your organization is to be deliberate in preparing other leaders to carry the mantle when you are gone. After all, there is no success without a successor.

8. Leaders are not merely born, they are made

Are leaders born or made? Can leadership be taught and learned? These questions have been subjects of debate for many decades.[12] Two schools of thought emerged on both sides of the divide with the supporters of the "great man" theory holding that some people are born with leadership qualities that qualify them to perform as leaders and hence there is little that can be done to develop leaders.[13]

On the other hand, there are those who have argued that leadership ability can be developed.[14] Among the advocates of this school of thought is Kotter who argued that dozens of people could play important leadership roles in the business organization if they were carefully selected, nurtured, and encouraged.[15]

To date, the majority of authors, researchers and scholars seem to agree that leadership can be developed.[16] Accordingly, leadership is not an exclusive club for those born with leadership qualities but is a skill that can be taught. "Leaders aren't born, they are made. And they are made just like anything else, through hard work. And that's the price we'll have to pay to achieve that goal or any goal."[17] That should motivate many leaders to take the initiative to develop their leadership ability.

Warren Bennis describes the need for leadership development in these words:

> The most dangerous leadership myth is that leaders are born -- that there is a genetic factor to leadership. This myth asserts that people simply either have certain charismatic qualities or not. That's nonsense; in fact, the opposite is true. Leaders are made rather than born."[18]

Case Study 1. 1: Joshua – a leader who learned to lead

Joshua takes the credit for leading the Israelites across River Jordan and for distributing the land to the twelve tribes of Israel. His leadership legacy is summed up in these words: "Israel served the Lord all the days of Joshua, and all the days of the elders who outlived Joshua, who had known all the works of the Lord which He had done for Israel,"(Jos 24:31).

But, was Joshua born a great leader or did he develop his ability to lead over time? Well, he may have been a born leader but, he definitely learned a lot from Moses his mentor and master. The following are three key observations about Joshua's growth journey as a leader:

a. **Joshua was a competent professional**
Initially, Joshua was a competent soldier but not a great leader. As a soldier, he fought and defeated the Amalekites decisively as recorded by Moses:

> Now Amalek came and fought with Israel in Rephidim. And Moses said to Joshua, "Choose us some men and go out, fight with Amalek. Tomorrow I will stand on the top of the hill with the rod of God in my hand." So Joshua did as Moses said to him, and fought with Amalek. And Moses, Aaron, and Hur went up to the top of the hill. So Joshua defeated Amalek and his people with the edge of the sword (Ex 17:8-10, 13).

b. **Joshua failed the leadership test on several occasions**
Joshua's major test as a leader came when he was appointed among other 12 clan representatives to go and spy the land before the nation could cross to occupy it. Joshua's attempt to motivate the people to cross and take possession of the land was a disaster. Here is the story as recorded in Numbers 14:6-10:

> And Joshua the son of Nun and Caleb the son of Jephunneh, who were among those who had spied out the land, tore their clothes and said to all the congregation of the people of Israel, "The land, which we passed through to spy it out, is exceedingly good land. If the Lord delights in us, he will bring us into this land and give it to us, a land that flows with milk and honey. Only do not rebel against the Lord. And do not fear the people of the land, for they are bread for us. Their protection is removed from them, and the Lord is with us; do not fear them." Then all the congregation said to stone them with stones. But the glory of the Lord appeared at the tent of meeting to all the people of Israel.

Joshua watched helplessly as his appeals to the people fell on deaf ears and the people turned back in rebellion and wandered for forty years in the desert.

c. **Joshua was intentional**

Being an assistant Moses' gave him many opportunities to learn by observation and experience as Moses provided leadership to the nation of Israel. Here are some defining milestones in his leadership development:

> d. **Joshua served Moses faithfully,** (Num 11:28.)
> Joshua's service to Moses began as a youth when he became a personal assistant to Moses and continued until Moses died. He shared the hard times with Moses and would not let go of his mentor.
>
> e. **Joshua stuck with Moses through good and bad times**
> Joshua traveled with Moses to the Mountain to meet with God and waited for forty days and nights until Moses finished talking to God. At the tent of meeting, Joshua would wait until Moses finished his work before he could leave (Ex 24:13-18).
>
> f. **Joshua was obedient to Moses.**

Joshua learned leadership hands-on as Moses delegated leadership roles to him. He not only selected the men who went out to battle the Amalekites but also led the team as instructed by Moses, (Ex 17:9-13.

As a result, Joshua enjoyed these benefits for his commitment to growing as a leader:

- Received encouragement from Moses (Deu 3:28).
- Learned vital lessons from Moses (Ex 17:14).
- Shared most intimate leadership experiences with Moses and,
- He was most qualified to succeed Moses.

Reflection questions

> a) Is it possible to be a competent professional and a poor leader at the same time? Explain giving examples where possible.

b) What are some of the things Joshua did that helped him become a better leader? Be specific

Becoming the Leader People Want to Follow

Leadership is a voluntary relationship between the leader and the followers. As Maxwell points out, "The key to becoming an effective leader is not to focus on making other people follow but on making yourself the kind of a person they want to follow."[19]

Getting people to want to follow you is important because there is little you can do if they choose not to follow! The wise leader understands this and channels his or her energy towards becoming that kind of a person that will inspire people to walk alongside him or her in pursuit of shared goals.

Leadership is about who you are as well as what you do. Who you are, determines what you do and greatly influences how you relate to others. The way you relate to others will either draw people to you or drive them away from you.

People follow leaders for various reasons. Different studies[20] have identified different factors that influence followers to choose to follow one leader and not the other. Here are a few of these factors,

1. **People follow leaders who serve their interest**

Leading people is like taking them on a journey. People do not just get into any moving bus. Rational people first confirm where the bus is going. They also want to know when it will arrive and how much it will cost them. In the same way, people do not just follow leaders because leaders ask them to. They follow leaders likely to help them reach their destination.

When you ask people to follow you, their first concern is whether following you will benefit them in any way. Becoming the kind of person others want to follow begins with understanding their concerns and genuinely wanting to help reach their goals.

Jesus understood and demonstrated this principle well. The disciples were looking for a king who would overthrow the Romans and reestablish the Jewish earthly kingdom. Jesus had a different agenda- the kingdom of heaven. Matthew.19: 27-29 in the case below reveals this conflict of agenda in these words:

Case Study 1. 2: What is in it for us?

Then Peter answered and said to Him, "See, we have left all and followed you. Therefore what shall we have?" So Jesus said to them, "Assuredly I say to you, that in the regeneration, when the Son of Man sits on the throne of His glory, you who have followed me will also sit on twelve thrones, judging the twelve tribes of Israel. And everyone who has left houses or brothers or sisters or father or mother or wife or children or lands, for my name's sake, shall receive a hundredfold, and inherit eternal life. Matthew 19:27-29

Reflection questions

a) What did Peter ask?

b) How did Jesus respond to their concern?

c) What do you think the disciples would have done if Jesus had failed to address their concern?

Peter's question reveals a fundamental leadership principle; people do not commit to following the leader until they know the leader cares for them. "Behold we have left everything and followed you; what then will be there for us?" they asked.

It is interesting to note here that Jesus did not rebuke them for asking the question. Instead, he gave them the assurance they needed. First, they would rule with him in his eternal kingdom and, second, they would receive a hundredfold of their investment.

Peoples' needs fall into two categories, first their real needs and second, their felt needs. Felt needs are not always the real needs. Instead, they are the symptoms their real needs. The disciples' real needs were spiritual while their felt needs were material cares. Jesus addressed both.

Many leaders fail to attract followers because their visions are selfish and do not take care of the follower's concerns. If you want people to follow you, then answer their question: "what is there for us?"

2. **People follow leaders they like**

Leadership is about relationships. People do not follow leaders they do not like. Effective leaders understand this well and spend time building healthy relationships. Consider the acronym RELATE below to identify specific steps you can take to build positive relationships:

- Respect differences
- Encourage others to do their best
- Listen actively
- Appreciate the contribution of other people
- Take time to relate
- Empathize

To improve your relationship with the people you lead, spend more time with them, get to know them better, and seek to understand what matters to them.

3. People follow caring leaders

Genuine leaders show concern for their people. Jesus attracted multitudes to his ministry because he sincerely cared for the people. The gospel according to Matthew records that; "When he saw the crowds, he had compassion on them because they were confused and helpless, like sheep without a shepherd, (Mat 9:36)." People who care identify with the aspirations, dreams, joys and the pains of their people.

Showing concern is both an action and a motive issue. It involves what you say, why you say it and what you do about the issue. The journey to becoming a worthy leader following begins by checking your motive for being a leader.

Good leaders frequently examine their motives by asking questions such as; why did I accept this position? Is it because of the benefits? If there was no allowance, prestige, power or the title, would I still accept it?

You can become the leader people want leaders to follow by showing interest in what matters to them. This may include visiting them in hospital, supporting their wedding plans, and attending the burial of their loved ones among many other things. When people realize you care, they will be attracted to you and will want to follow your leadership.

4. People follow leaders they trust

Trust is the glue that holds people and their leaders' together.[21] It is the foundation of leadership. "Men of genius are admired, men of wealth are envied, men of power are feared, but only men of character are trusted."[22]

Your ability to inspire people depends on trust. People will have confidence in your decisions and follow you to the extent to which they trust you.

Effective leaders know how to build and sustain trust.[23] They understand and practice behaviors that reinforce trust. You can also build and establish trust among your people by:

- Leading by example
- Communicating effectively
- Admitting mistakes and acknowledge mistakes,
- Fulfilling promises and commitments,
- Trusting group members
- Asking for their opinion
- Treating everyone fairly

Building trust does not happen overnight. It is a hard and long process. The longer the leader practices the trust-building behaviors, the more their people trust them.

5. People follow leaders they respect

The Merriam-Webster dictionary defines respect as "a feeling of admiring someone or something that is good, valuable, important, etc."[24] Like trust, respect is earned by respecting oneself and others.

People like working with leaders who are sensitive to their feelings. A survey conducted by the Centre for Creative Leadership found that treating people with respect on a daily basis was considered among the most helpful things a leader can do to address conflict or tension.[25]

Practicing the golden rule pays good returns for leaders. Treating others as you would have them treat you triggers a reciprocal response from your group members (Luk 6:31). No one likes to be treated with disrespect. No one likes being made fun of, ridiculed, put down or made the subject of negative jokes.

While it is true there is a place for public rebuke; it should be done carefully and only as a last resort measure. Effective leaders earn their respect by valuing members' opinions, views and perspectives, listening attentively to them as they speak, being considerate to their preferences, likes and dislikes, and by being sensitive to their feelings.

Effective leaders treat their members with respect. They avoid words and actions that insult and interpreted to show disrespect for their members such as:

- Insulting or making fun of them,
- Teasing or mocking them,
- Talking about them behind their backs or gossiping about them,
- Pressuring them to do something they don't like,

The list is long! However, instead of trying to remember everything, it would help remember Jesus' version of the golden rule which goes like, "So in everything, do to others what you would have them do to you, for this sums up the Law and the Prophets (Matt. 7:12).

1. People follow leaders who add value to them

When you appreciate people, you add value to them. Effective leaders know how to make their followers feel important regardless of their age, gender, education, economic, social status and ethnicity. Leaders add value to their followers by opening their eyes to see opportunities beyond their reach, they challenge them to become better and help them get out of their comfort zones.

As a leader, you can add value to your followers by deliberately making everyone in your organization feel needed and appreciated. Select your words carefully and focus on what your followers have in common instead of dwelling on the differences. Avoid the temptation of giving special treatment to some people just because of their status.

In today's world, organizations diversity has become a key feature, making it easy for a leader to make some people feel insignificant and hence, hindering them from feeling part of the team. For instance, some people may feel devalued when the leader:

- Uses own mother tongue in the presence of people from other cultures
- Looks down upon the poor

- Speaks disrespectfully about the other gender
- Appoints leaders based on ethnic affiliation or other unfair criteria

2. People follow better leaders than themselves

People follow better and stronger leaders than themselves. To attract followers, the leader must be more competent and should demonstrate a stronger character than the followers. Competence comes from the right knowledge, the right skills, and the right values. People identify with competent leaders because they promise a better chance of victory and success.

People are attracted to competent leaders because they demonstrate the necessary knowledge, values, and skills, and hence, offer a better chance of taking the people where they ought to be. A leader's competence is greatly enhanced by experience and a record of accomplishment of success. Such a leader can focus on expected outcomes and deliver them

Competent leaders demonstrate the following competencies:

- Technical knowledge of their field,
- A clear vision and goals of their organization,
- Good people skills – ability to relate well to people,
- Positive attitude,
- Ability to empower others,
- Good understanding of leadership,
- Ability to influence others,
- Ability to adapt to changing circumstances, and,
- Building and supporting teams.

Expectations of the Leadership Role

Leadership is "An exchange relation in which the followers surrender some of their status and autonomy in return for the services of the leader in maintaining goal direction and unity of action for the group."[26] In exchange for their status and autonomy, followers consciously or unconsciously expect their leaders to perform certain functions the benefit of the people involved.

Failure to deliver on those expectations leave the followers feeling short-changed and unobligated to continue following the leader. Wise leaders, therefore, do not hesitate to invest their time and resources in search of the knowledge, values, and skills to meet their followers' expectations.

While the leader may not fulfill all that people expect of him or her, studies[27] have identified several minimum functions every leader should do well to be effective. Below is a discussion of 8 functions performed by competent leaders:

1. Leaders provide direction

Effective leaders set the direction for their organization. That involves developing a clear vision, setting goals and determining effective strategies to translate their goals into reality. That is not all; good leaders share the vision and ask their members to commit to it.

Real leaders enlist members to a shared vision by raising the hope and expectation of a better tomorrow. They help members see how their dreams can be realized by supporting the leader's vision.

Jesus started his leadership by asking the disciples to follow him. He challenged them, "Follow me, and I will make you fishers of men". You have not started leading until you ask people to follow you. Remember, "The very essence of leadership is that you have to have a vision. It's got to be a vision you articulate clearly and forcefully on every occasion. You can't blow an uncertain trumpet."[28]

2. Leaders align people

The leader and the people are brought together by different needs. The leader gets a vision and then looks for people to help him realize that vision. At the entry point, the average employee cares less about the mission and vision of the organization. He joins the organization because he has bills to pay, so he looks for a job to make money to pay his bills. The business owner, on the other hand, starts the business to make money – so he hires the employee to help him reach his vision of making money.

What applies to the business also applies to other types of organizations. The Pastor, for instance, needs to fulfill God's call in his life, so he starts a church. The church member needs prayers to get a job, healing, prosperity and so on. The member goes to the church to fulfill his spiritual needs.

Effective leaders do not just set the direction; they ensure their followers understand where the organizations headed and are inspired to pursue the vision. Aligning people involves getting them to believe in the vision and adjust their priorities to match those of the organization.[29]

The key to aligning people with the organizational direction lies in understanding their needs and aspirations and then, leveraging on those needs to secure the peoples' commitment to the vision. Case 1.3 below illustrates how leaders align people to their vision.

Case Study 1. 3. Jesus aligns his disciples with his vision
The conflict of interest between the vision of Jesus and the disciples' expectations becomes obvious as you read the four Gospels. Despite Jesus' attempt to explain his focus, every time he talked about the kingdom of heaven, they took it to mean the earthly kingdom of Israel. In the course of his teachings Jesus taught them:

> It is easier for a camel to go through the eye of a needle than for someone who is rich to enter the kingdom of God." When the disciples heard this, they were greatly astonished and asked, "Who then can be saved?" Jesus looked at them and said, "With man this is impossible, but with God all things are possible."

> Peter answered him, "We have left everything to follow you! What then will there be for us? "Jesus said to them, "Truly I tell you, at the renewal of all things, when the Son of Man sits on his glorious throne, you who have followed me will also sit on twelve thrones, judging the twelve tribes of Israel. And everyone who has left houses or brothers or sisters or father or mother or wife or children or fields for my sake will receive a hundred times as much and will inherit eternal life (Mat 19:24-29).

Reflection questions
a) What does Peter's answer to Jesus tell you about the disciple's priorities?

b) Did Jesus' response adequately address the disciples' expectations? Explain

3. **Leaders lead change**

The longer an organization lasts, the more it tends to traditions and the old ways of doing things. If not checked, those old ways become defense mechanisms for resisting change.

Former US Senator Robert F. Kennedy was one good leader at challenging processes. He said, "Some men see things as they are and say, why; I dream things that never were and say, why not."[30] Effective leaders do not allow the status quo to limit their thinking. They try out new things or do the same things differently. They scrutinize their methods, procedures, and practices to identify improvement issues. They challenge their followers to be creative, innovative and to experiment with new ideas.

Stagnant groups and dying organizations on the hand, hold back from trying new ideas. They resist change. Though they may not admit it, they believe in the maxim "We have always done it that way." To keep thriving and breaking into new frontiers, the organization must constantly look for new ways of approaching issues. Kouzes and Posner call this practice 'Challenging the processes'.[32]

Effective leaders constantly question basic beliefs and assumptions to find better ways of doing things. They question operating procedures and systems to ensure continuous improvement.

Behind the greatest discoveries and breakthroughs in human history were courageous leaders who from challenged limiting ways of seeing and doing things! Jesus was good at challenging traditions. A greater part of the Sermon on the Mount was a typical challenge on popular understanding and practice of religion. The case below attests to this fact:

Case Study 1. 4: Jesus Challenges the Status Quo
a. Anger
You have heard that it was said to those of old, you shall not murder; and whoever murders will be liable to judgment.' But I say to you that everyone who is angry with his brother will be liable to judgment; whoever insults his brother will be liable to the council; and whoever says, 'You fool!' will be liable to the hell of fire. So if you are offering your gift at the altar and there remember that your brother has something against you, leave your gift there before the altar and go. First, be reconciled to your brother, and then come and offer your gift (Mat 5:21-24).

b. Lust

You have heard that it was said, you shall not commit adultery.' But I say to you that everyone who looks at a woman with lustful intent has already committed adultery with her in his heart. If your right eye causes you to sin, tear it out and throw it away. For it is better that you lose one of your members than that your whole body is thrown into hell. And if your right hand causes you to sin, cut it off and throw it away. For it is better that you lose one of your members than that your whole body goes into hell (Mat 5:27-30).

c. Divorce

It was also said, whoever divorces his wife, let him give her a certificate of divorce.' But I say to you that everyone who divorces his wife, except on the ground of sexual immorality, makes her commit adultery, and whoever marries a divorced woman commits adultery (Mat 5:31-32).

d. Oaths

"Again you have heard that it was said to those of old, you shall not swear falsely, but shall perform to the Lord what you have sworn.' But I say to you, do not take an oath at all, either by heaven, for it is the throne of God, or by the earth, for it is his footstool, or by Jerusalem, for it is the city of the great king. And do not take an oath by your head, for you cannot make one hair white or black. Let what you say be simply 'Yes' or 'No'; anything more than this comes from evil (Matt 5:33-37).

e. Retaliation

You have heard that it was said, an eye for an eye and a tooth for a tooth.' But I say to you, do not resist the one who is evil. But if anyone slaps you on the right cheek, turn to him the other also. And if anyone would sue you and take your tunic, let him have your cloak as well. And if anyone forces you to go one mile, go with him two miles. Give to the one who begs from you, and do not refuse the one who would borrow from you (Mat 5:38-42).

Reflection questions

a) In this case study, how many times did Jesus challenge the status quo?

b) In each case, identify the status quo and the new

perspective Jesus introduced.

In this passage, Jesus challenged his disciples' old way of thinking while provoking them to think differently. He understood the power of the traditional way of thinking and practice to limits God's working in peoples' lives! For that reason, He told the Pharisees "Thus you nullify the word of God by your tradition that you have handed down. And you do many things like that" (Mar 7:13, NIV).

Every time Jesus challenged a tradition, he provided an alternative way of thinking and doing things. It is not enough to point out what is wrong, always provide a better way of doing things.

4. Leaders empower others

Unlike average leaders who lead followers, effective leaders empower and raise other leaders. They strongly believe that "Two people are better off than one; for they can help each other succeed" (Ecc 4:9, NLT). Great leaders understand what average leaders fail to; that organizational success depends on maximum utilization of everyone's abilities. Such leaders create a climate of teamwork and trust where members contribute their ideas and resources to support the goals of the organization.

Successful organizations are made up of empowered members with the freedom to make decisions. Such members have the confidence to take the initiative to further the organizational agenda without fear of being reprimanded.

Effective leaders take deliberate steps to empower their people. For instance they:

- Involve them in decision-making,
- Equip them with knowledge, values, and skills,
- Delegate critical tasks,
- Share power and authority, and
- Offer visible support.

Most leaders complain about their followers who do not perform as expected. They wish their followers were more proactive, skilled and productive. Unfortunately, there is no ready market for empowered followers. You have to empower the one you already have.

Even Jesus did not start with ready-made disciples. He had to develop the ones he had. Shortly after He ascended to heaven, his disciples faced stiff opposition from their rulers, elders, and scribes who tried to stop them from preaching the gospel.

In Acts 4:13 we read, "Now when they saw the boldness of Peter and John and perceived that they were uneducated and untrained men, they marveled. And they realized that they had been with Jesus."

Anyone familiar with the life of Jesus and His disciples will confirm that the disciples were not always that bold. When Jesus was arrested at the Gethsemane, the disciples ran and abandoned him. Peter denied him three times.

After Jesus resurrected and went up to heaven, the disciples locked themselves in the upper room fearing the Jews. Where then did they get this boldness? The answer – Jesus empowered them.

Case Study 1. 5: Jesus; the empowering leader

Jesus spends about three years training his disciples. During that period, Jesus used several methods to equip and empower them. The following are five things Jesus did to empower his followers:

    a. He shared his expectations for them.

    From the beginning, Jesus made it very clear what he expected of his disciples. In Mark 1:17 Jesus said to them, "Follow Me, and I will make you become fishers of men."

    When people know in advance what you expect of them, they adjust their conduct to match your expectations. Unclear expectations disempower people and produce passive followers.

    b. He taught them

    The Gospels, refer to Jesus by many names including Master, Lord, Savior, and teacher. Out of the ninety times, Jesus is referred to directly, called the teacher 60 times.[33] And that is what Jesus spent most of his time doing. He taught his disciples.

    In Matthew 5:1-2 we read: "And seeing the multitudes, He went up on a mountain, and when He was seated His disciples came to Him. Then He opened His mouth and taught them…"

In Luke 6: 40 Jesus taught, "Students are not greater than their teacher. But the student who is fully trained will become like the teacher", (NLT).

Effective leaders are teachers. They teach their people how to serve and by so doing empower them.

c. He emphasized application
Jesus held his disciples accountable to do what he taught them. In John 13:17 he told his disciples: "Now that you know these things, you will be blessed if you do them," (NIV). Effective leaders understand that people gain more confidence by practicing what they learn. They, therefore, expect their people to do what they teach them.

d. He allowed opportunities to internalize their learning
The disciples of Jesus like most of us were slow learners. Because Jesus understood this, he was patient with them. He allowed them time and provided opportunities to internalize his teachings.

e. He facilitated their performance
In Matthew 28:19-20, Jesus gave his disciples their final assignment. He told them: "Go therefore and make disciples of all the nations, baptizing them in the name of the Father and of the Son and the Holy Spirit, teaching them to observe all things that I have commanded you; and lo, I am with you always, even to the end of the age." But then the disciples were discouraged because he told them that he would be leaving them.

To encourage them Jesus commanded them to wait for the gift of the Holy Spirit who would empower them to fulfill the great assignment that he had given them. This happened in Acts 2:1*ff* when the Holy Spirit empowered them to carry out their mission.

Effective leaders empower their people by providing whatever they need to carry out their mandate.

5. Leaders show the way
Another practice shared by effective leaders is that they lead by example. They know the way, go the way and show the way. They model the way. Jesus modeled this practice well before his

disciples. He never asked the disciples to do anything they had not seen him do. In Luke 11: 1 we read: "Now it came to pass, as He was praying in a certain place, when He ceased, that one of His disciples said to Him, "Lord, teach us to pray, as John also taught his disciples…"

Apostle Paul had such a great impact on his followers because he modeled what he expected from his followers. He was not afraid to challenge people to follow his example as we see in 1 Cor. 11:1 where he exhorts the Corinthian Church to" Follow my example, as I follow the example of Christ". To the Philippians Paul instructs; "Whatever you have learned or received or heard from me, or seen in me—put it into practice. And the God of peace will be with you" (Phi 4:9).

Great leaders practice this principle in their lives by modeling the expected behavior to their people. That way they empower them to act. Like Paul and Jesus, you will be a more effective leader when your followers can confirm that you have been consistent in practicing what you are asking them to do.

6. Leaders inspire people.

Leaders are good at encouraging others. They remain in touch with life challenges that could discourage and demotivate them even to the point of giving up. They take time to encourage their people to uplift their spirits. In the process of pursuing organizational goals, people get worn out, tired and burned out.

Jesus was a great encourager. In John 14:1-4 uses these words to encourage his disciples: "Let not your heart be troubled; you believe in God, believe also in me. In my Father's house are many mansions; if it were not so, I would have told you. I go to prepare a place for you. And if I go and prepare a place for you, I will come again and receive you to myself; that where I am, there you may also be. And where I go you know, and the way you know."

- Leaders use different methods and approaches to encourage their followers: Here are some things you could do to encourage your people:
- Recognize and appreciate their contribution,
- Look for opportunities to praise their abilities,

- Pray for them and let them know you are doing it,
- Celebrate achievements regularly, and
- Be there for them at their lowest moments,

7. Leaders raise other leaders

Developing other leaders is an important task for every leader. Ultimately, "The final test of a leader is that he leaves behind him in other men the conviction and the will to carry on." - Walter Lippmann

Case Study 1. 6: Great leaders raise leaders

The Bible contains a few examples of who raised leaders developing other leaders in the perhaps you mentioned some of the following:

- Moses mentored Joshua
- Elijah mentored Elisha
- King David mentored his son Solomon
- Jesus mentored the twelve apostles
- Paul mentored Timothy and Titus among many others

Raising leaders is important for two reasons:

a. Leadership is for a season

Whatever position you hold as a leader, a time will come when you will hand over and move on to your next assignment. Before you are a leader, success is all about growing yourself. When you become a leader, success is all about growing others. —Jack Welch

Many leaders enjoy watching their organizations flourish under their watch. For many, this joy turns into regrets and disappointment as they watch the same organization flounder and decline after they have left. Founder leaders who fail to prepare other leaders to take over after them often fall victim to this tragedy as they watch their life work decline and eventually collapse due to poor leadership.

Dale Carnegie once said, "No man will make a great leader who wants to do it all himself, or to get all the credit for doing it."[35]

b. It takes more leaders to manage growth.

The number one hindrance to growth in any organization is lack of ready leaders. An organizational expansion is almost impossible without capable leaders. It takes able leaders to open new branches, to venture into new horizons and to diversify investment. Effective leaders understand this principle and make deliberate efforts to mentor, disciple and prepare other leaders to take up leadership roles.

1. Leaders pursue desired results

Leadership comes with high expectations. A leader's most important job is to get results. As Sharma points out, "Leadership is not about a title or a designation. It is about impact, influence, and inspiration. Impact involves getting results, influence is about spreading the passion you have for your work, and you have to inspire team-mates and customers."[36]

Every organization exists to fulfill a given mandate. Results are the key indicators of the fulfillment of that mandate. Leaders who are not getting results are not leading.[37] Leaders, therefore, define the desired results and do everything within their power to ensure the organization is reaching its results.

Case Study 1. 7: God's expects results

The God of the Bible expects leaders to get results. In Isaiah 5:1-7 the prophet expresses God's disappointment with his people for failure to produce expected results. These are his words:

> Now let me sing to my Well-beloved
> A song of my Beloved regarding His vineyard:
> My Well-beloved has a vineyard
> On a very fruitful hill.
> He dug it up and cleared out its stones,
> And planted it with the choicest vine.
> He built a tower in its midst,
> And also made a winepress in it;
> So He expected it to bring forth good grapes,
> But it brought forth wild grapes.
> "And now, O inhabitants of Jerusalem and men of Judah,
> Judge, please, between Me and my vineyard.
> What more could have been done to my vineyard
> That I have not done in it?
> Why then, when I expected it to bring forth good grapes,
> Did it bring forth wild grapes?
> And now, please let Me tell you what I will do to my vineyard:
> I will take away its hedge, and it shall be burned;

And break down its wall, and it shall be trampled down.
I will lay it waste;
It shall not be pruned or dug,
But there shall come up briers and thorns.
I will also command the clouds
That they rain no rain on it."
For the vineyard of the Lord of hosts is the house of Israel,
And the men of Judah are His pleasant plant.
He looked for justice, but behold, oppression;
For righteousness, but behold a cry for help.

To whoever much is given, much is required. In the above scripture passage, the vineyard owner did everything for his vineyard expecting a good return from his vineyard. Instead, he got wild grapes. The consequences were dire. He threatened to lay it waste, neglect it, break down its wall and let it be trampled down.

In John 15:16 Jesus reminds his disciples of his expectations. He tells them: "You did not choose me, but I chose you and appointed you that you should go and bear fruit and that your fruit should remain, that whatever you ask the Father in my name He may give you."

How People Learn Leadership

Leadership is a difficult discipline to teach and learn. Due to this challenge, leadership scholars have wrestled with the question of how leadership develops for decades. Are leaders made or born? Can leadership be taught and, can it be learned?

These questions have been subjects of debate for many decades. Two schools of thought emerged on both sides of the divide with the supporters of the "great man" theory holding that some people are born leaders and that all they need is the right environment to spur them to heights of exemplary leadership.[38]

On the other hand are those who believe everyone has the potential to be a great leader provided he is willing to develop his leadership skills. According to this school of thought, dozens of people could play important leadership roles in organizational life if they were carefully selected, nurtured, and encouraged.

To date, the majority of authors, researchers and scholars favor the position that leadership can be developed. They point out that leadership is not an exclusive club for those born with leadership qualities, but is a skill that can be taught.

As Vince Lombardi pointed out, "Leaders aren't born, they are made. And they are made just like anything else, through hard work. And that's the price we'll have to pay to achieve that goal or any goal."[39] Here are six ways leaders develop their leadership ability:

1. Observation

Many prominent leaders developed their leadership ability by closely working with and observing their successors. Nelson Mandela narrates how his political interest was stirred as he first listened to the elders of his tribe in his village as a youth. The elders would tell how their ancestors fought in defense of their country and the acts of courage performed by generals and soldiers during those heroic days.

As he served his guardian chief David Dalindyebo, Mandela observed as the Chief presided over days-long tribal meetings through which the chief would lead the people to consensus. Through these observations, Mandela developed the conviction that he would serve his people and make his humble contribution to their struggle for freedom.[40] The rest is history. Mandela grew up to be one of the greatest leaders that ever lived in modern Africa and the world.

2. The lecture

Many institutions rely on the lecture method as the principal means for transferring knowledge from the teacher to the student. Through this method, the instructor verbally communicates the subject matter to passive learners seated in a classroom whose major role is to listen and observe the instructor.[42]

In spite of its popularity, research rates the method poorly regarding effectiveness when used as the main leadership development method. For instance, one study found the lecture method to be inferior to the experiential learning and public instruction.[43]

The use of the traditional lecture method is ineffective in facilitating knowledge gain and retention. Research indicates that people learn at most 20% of what they hear.[44] The lecture method's ineffectiveness is understandable given the lack of engagement on the part of the learner who plays the role of a passive spectator in the learning process.[45]

3. **Case study analysis**

Case study analysis is a useful tool for developing problem-solving skills in leadership. Through this method, learners analyze real or hypothetical leadership cases to provide workable solutions to the presented challenges. The method has been used for decades in social sciences and other disciplines.[46]

Numerous studies on the effectiveness of case studies indicate increased student motivation and enhanced ability to internalize course material when used within the classroom setting.[47] When combined with other learning activities, case study analyses are more effective.

If you are considering using this method, you can increase its effectiveness by combining it with group activities such as[48]

- Reflection journals covering the course readings, group discussions, and reactions to lectures and assignments;
- Developing personal and professional codes of ethics;
- Reading, analyzing, and discussing ethical dilemmas;
- Writing and presenting one's ethical dilemma; and,
- Reviewing oral and written analyses of ethical dilemmas of at least two other classmates.

4. **Group discussions**

The discussion learning method is a "strategy for achieving instructional objectives that involve a group of persons, usually in the roles of moderator and participant, who communicate with each other using speaking, non-verbal and listening processes."[49] The method involved a greater degree of interaction between the instructor and learners than the lecture method.[50]

It affords learners a greater opportunity and freedom to express their opinions and ideas while at the same time listening to those of their peers and the teacher.

The discussion method has more flexibility and greater potential to help both the instructor and the learners achieve several learning objectives. When well facilitated, group discussions can lead to:

- A better grasp of the subject matter,[51]
- Issue-oriented discussions leading to attitude change,[52]

- Better problem solutions,[53]
- Improved discussion skills by students,[54]
- Improved student motivation and,
- Better instructor evaluation of students' understanding of the subject matter content.[55]

Experiential learning

Experiential learning is the process of learning through experience by reflection and doing. It is an activity designed to generate experiences and "live" data to teach concepts, ideas, and behavioral insights.[56] It is one of the most effective leadership development learning methods due to its advantages over the traditional approach.

The purpose of experiential learning is to bridge the gap between classroom learning and practical knowledge needed in the real world. The need for experiential learning in leadership development cannot be overemphasized. "There is a set of leadership skills that cannot be taught or lectured about, but that can be learned only experientially. You have to put people in an experiential situation, in small groups and have them work through leadership tasks"[57]

The adage "I hear, and I forget, I see, and I remember I do and I understand" sums up the benefits of experiential learning perfectly. Specific benefits include:

- Connecting learning to the real world. Experiential learning takes data and concepts and applies them to hands-on tasks
- Providing participants with opportunities to develop creativity
- Enhancing learning through reflection
- Makes use of mistakes as students learn through trial and error
- Leads to accelerated learning
- Prepares students for leadership in real life

5. **Action learning**

As a tool for leadership development, action learning has gained popularity especially with 'best practice' companies in Europe and the US.[58] Many researchers attribute the rapid adoption of the action learning to the realization that the only sustainable competitive advantage in a rapidly changing environment is the rate at which individuals and organizations learn.

It is a process of engaging people in solving real-life problems without solutions before the process.[59] It involves "learning from concrete experience and critical reflection on that experience – through group discussion."[60]

Action learning works best when the facilitator does not interact with the learners from an expert's position but instead starts from a position of not knowing with the other action-learners.

A Model for Personal Leadership Development

Figure 1.1 below shows the leader development model adopted in this book.

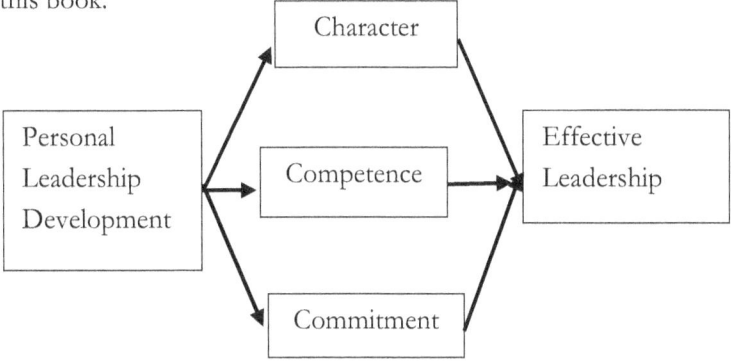

Figure 1. 1. Leader development model

Personal leadership development is an outcome of the interaction of 3 variables, namely; character competence, and commitment. Of these three, character lays the foundation for effective leadership. [61] Leadership character is the foundation on which commitment and competencies rest. It determines the quality of commitment, the degree and the quality of influence the leader exerts on the stakeholders. Without character, the leader is likely to commit to the wrong things and use unethical means to achieve his or her goals.

Competence entails technical know-how of one's chosen occupation. You are competent when you can deliver results without compromising the ethical standards of your profession. Leadership competencies comprise the knowledge of key concepts and facts, the understanding of how leadership works, and, the ability to relate well with other stakeholders to get the job done

Commitment is a measure of the degree of effort the leader is willing to invest in preparation for the leadership task and the ability to carry out the hard work effective leadership demands. The leader is committed when he or she demonstrates the ability to mobilize stakeholders and other resources to pursue and fulfill the mission and the vision of the organization.

Most leaders focus on developing their technical skills while neglecting character and commitment. The result of this neglect is usually technically competent leaders who are unethical and corrupt. For the best results, leadership development efforts should focus on these three elements with a lot more emphasis on character.

Conclusion

We live and work in a constantly changing world. To overcome the challenges brought about by changing times, technology and demanding empowered follower, the leader must continually learn new ways of getting things done through the people. The leader must understand what motivates people, be skilled at assessing their capabilities, matching their abilities with appropriate responsibilities and inspire them to action. Above all else, the leader must deliver the expected results.

Leaders need to ensure that their knowledge, skills, and experiences are evolving with changing demands. Consequently, committing to continuous learning and development crucial to remain relevant and effective.

References

1. Martineau, J., Hoole, E. & Patterson, T. (2009). Leadership de-development: is it worth the money? Center for Creative Leadership. EFMD Global Focus. Volume 03, Issue 03. Rommin Adl, R. (August 2013). How to Attack the Business Skills Mismatch, Chief Learning Officer Magazine
2. Lawson, K. (2009). Leadership Development Basics: A complete guide to guide you. Alexandria, Virginia. ASTD Press; 1 edition
3. Kennedy, J. F. (November 22, 1963). Speech prepared for delivery in Dallas the day of his assassination. http://www.quotationspage.com/quote/3225.html

4. Hitt, M. A., Black, J. S., & Porter, L. W. (2005). Management. Upper Saddle River, NJ: Prentice-Hall.
5. Gorman, C. (2014). The Urgent Need for Leadership Development. Talent Management and HR. https://www.tlnt.com/the-urgent-need-for-leadership-development/
6. De Meyer, A. (2010, February). Collaborative leadership: New perspectives in leadership development. (Cambridge Judge Business School, Working Paper Series.
7. Enterprising Nation. (1995). Report of the industry task force on leadership and management skills: Renewing Australia's managers to meet the challenges of the Asia-Pacific century. Canberra: Australian Government Publishing Service.
8. Maxwell, J. C. (1998). The 21 Irrefutable Laws of Leadership: Follow them and the People will Follow You. Nashville, TN: Thomas Nelson Publishers
9. Day, D. (2000). Leadership development: Review in context. Leadership Quarterly, 11(4), 581–613.
10. Gardner, J. W. (1990). On Leadership. New York, Free Press.
11. Soderquist, D. (2005). The Wal-Mart Way: The Inside Story of the Success of the World's Largest Company. Nashville TN: Thomas Nelson Inc.
12. Elmuti, D., Minnis, W., & Abebe, M. (2005). Does education have a role in developing leadership skills? Management Decision, 43(7/8), 1018-1031.
13. Carlyle, T. (2007). On heroes and hero-worship and the heroic in history. Whitefish, MT: Kessinger. Grint, K. (2000). The arts of leadership. Oxford: Oxford University Press. Nietzsche, F. (1969). The will to power. New York: Vintage.
14. Kakabadse, A. P., & Kakabadse, N. (1999). The essence of leadership. London: Thomson International.
15. Kotter, J. P. (2000, December 1). What leaders really do. Harvard Business Review, Best of HBR (R0111F).
16. Mostovicz, E. I., Kakabadse, N. K., & Kakabadse, A. P. (2009). A dynamic theory of leadership development. Leadership & Organization Development Journal, 30(6), 563-576.

17. Attributed to Vince Lombardi in Elkins, R. (2012). Leadership: Elevate Yourself and Those Around You- Influence, Business Skills, Coaching & Communication. LULU Press.
18. Attributed to Warren G. Bennis in Farlow, M. J. (2012). Leaders are made not born: 40 Simple Skills to Make You the Leader You Want to Be. St. Louis, Missouri: LinkUp Publishing.
19. Reina, D. S. & Reina, M. L. (1999).Trust and Betrayal in the work-place: Building Effective Relationships in Your Organisation. San Francisco, CA: Berret-Koehler.
20. Wikangas, L. & Okumura, A. (1997). Why Do People Follow Leaders? A Study of A U.S. and A Japanese Change Program Leadership Quarterly, 8(3), 313-337.
21. . Reina, D. S. & Reina, M. L. (Trust and Betrayal in the workplace: Building Effective Relationships in Your Organization. San Francisco, CA: Berret-Koehler.
22. Zig Ziglar, (1997). Over the Top: Moving from Survival to Stability, from Stability to Success from Success to Significance. Nashville, TN. Thomas Nelson;
23. Walter, E. (2015), 12 Leadership Behaviors That Build Team Trust. Forbes Media; ILM, (2003). Becoming more effective.
24. Centre for Creative Leadership (2015). The Power of Respect. https://www.ccl.org/articles/leading-effectively-articles/the-power-of-respect/Merriam-Webster Inc. (2016).
25. Homans, G.C. (1950). The Human Group. New York: Harcourt, Brace.
26. Kouzes, J. M., & Posner, B. Z. (1995). The leadership challenge: how to keep getting extraordinary things done in organizations. San Francisco: Jossey-Bass Publishers
27. Quoted in Maxwell, J. C. (2010). The Right to Lead: Learning Leadership Through Character and Courage. Nashville, Thomas Nelson, p.26
28. Kotter, J. P. (2000). What leaders really do. Harvard Business Review. Product number 3820.
29. Billington, J. H. (2010). Respectfully Quoted: A Dictionary of Quotations. Library of Congress

30. De Cagna, J., Gammel, C. D., Notter, J., Rops, M.; Smith, A. (2007). 101 Things About Associations We Must Change. Morrisville, North Carolina: Lulu Enterprises, Inc.
31. Kouzes, J. M., & Posner, B. Z. (1995). The leadership challenge: how to keep getting extraordinary things done in organizations. San Francisco: Jossey-Bass Publishers
32. Pritchard, R. (2011). Teacher. http://www.crosswalk.com/blogs/dr-ray.pritchard/teacher.html
33. Kassin, S., Fein, S. & Markus, H. R. (2010). Social Psychology. Belmont, CA: Cengage Learning.
34. Quoted in Hickey, J. P. (2016). Getting personal: A guide to Personal Development. Melbourne, Florida. Motivational Press, Inc.
35. Ulrich, D., Zenger, J. & D. & Smallwood, N. (1999). Results-Based Leadership: How Leaders Build Business and Improve the Bottom Line. Boston, MA: Harvard Business School.
36. Elmuti, D., Minnis, W., & Abebe, M. (2005). Does education have a role in developing leadership skills? Management Decision, 43(7/8), 1018-1031.
37. Carlyle, T. (2007). On heroes and hero-worship and the heroic in history. Whitefish, MT: Kessinger. Grint, K. (2000). The arts of leadership. Oxford: Oxford University Press. Nietzsche, F. (1969). The will to power. New York: Vintage.
38. Kakabadse, A. P., & Kakabadse, N. (1999). The essence of leadership. London: Thomson International. Mostovicz, E. I., Kakabadse, N. K., & Kakabadse, A. P. (2009). A dynamic theory of leadership development. Leadership & Organization Development Journal, 30(6), 563-576. Maxwell, J. C. (1998). The 21 irrefutable laws of leadership: Follow them and people will follow you. Nashville: Thomas Nelson Publishers.
39. Attributed to Vince Lombardi in Lussier, R. N. & Kimball, D. C. (Applied Sport-Management Skills, 2nd Ed. Champaign, IL: Human Kinetics,
40. Mandela, N. (1990). Nelson Mandela: The Struggle is My Life. Bombay. IDAF Publications Ltd.

41. Osakinle, E. O., Onijigin, E. O., & Falana, B. A. (2010). Teaching methods and the learners' environment in a Nigerian university. African Journal of Basic & Applied Sciences, 2(1-2), 7-10.
42. Curtin, J. L. (2002). Teaching versus facilitating leadership development: Trends in business. Journal of Leadership Education, 1(1), 58-67.
43. Williams, J., & McClure. (2010, Summer). The effects of teaching methods in leadership Knowledge retention: An experimental design of Lecture, experiential, and public pedagogy. Journal of Leadership Education, 9(2), 86-100.
44. Dale, Edgar. (1969, p. 108). Audio-Visual Methods in Teaching, 3rd ed., Holt, Rinehart & Winston, New York,
45. Young, M., Robinson, S., & Albert, (2009). Students pay attention! Combating the vigilance decrement to improve learning during lectures. Active Learning in Higher Education, 10(1), 41-55.
46. Barrows, H. S., & Tamblyn, R. M. (1996). Problem-Based Learning: An approach to medical education. New York: Springer.
47. McNair, M. P., & Hersum, A. C. (1954). The case method at the Harvard business school. New York: McGraw-Hill
48. Shapiro, J., & Stefkovich, J. A. (2005). Ethical leadership and decision making in education (2nd Ed.). Mahwah, NJ: Lawrence Erlbaum Associates.
49. Gall, M. D., & Gillett, M. (2001). The discussion method in classroom teaching. Theory into Practice, 12(2), p.99.
50. Osakinle, E. O., Onijigin, E. O., & Falana, B. A. (2010). Teaching methods and the learners' environment in a Nigerian university. African Journal of Basic & Applied Sciences, 2(1-2), 7-10.
51. McKeachie, W. J. (1965). Teaching tips: A guidebook for the beginning college teacher (5/e). Ann Arbor, MI: George Wahr Publishing.
52. Fisher, F. L. (1968). Influences of reading and discussion on the attitudes of fifth graders towards Indians. Journal of Educational Research, 62, 130-134.

53. Gall, M. D., & Gall, J. P. (1976). The discussion method, In The psychology of teaching methods. Gage 75th yearbook of the national society for the study of education (Ed.). N. L. (1976), pp. 166-216). Chicago: University of Chicago Press.
54. Gage, N. L., & Berliner, D. C. (1975). Educational psychology. Chicago: Rand-McNally.
55. Gall, M. D., & Gillett, M. (2001). The discussion method in classroom teaching. Theory into Practice, 12(2).
56. Warrick, D. D., Hunsaker, L., Cook, W., & Altman, S. (1979). Journal of Experiential Learning and Simulation, 1, 91-100.
57. Saloner, G. (2010, April 1). Building the next generation of business leaders. McKinsey Quarterly.
58. Fulmer, R. M., & Goldsmith, M. (2001). The leadership investment: How the world's best organizations gain a strategic advantage through leadership development. New York: American Management Association.
59. Revans, R. W. (1978). The A.B.C. of action learning: A review of 25 years of experience. Altrincham, Greater Manchester, Great Britain: R.W. Revans.
60. Zuber-Skerritt, O. (2002). The concept of action learning. The Learning Organization, 9(3), 114-124.
61. Crossan, M., Gandz, J., Seijts, G. (2016). Developing Leadership Character. New York, NY. Routledge, Taylor & Francis.

Chapter Two

Understanding Leadership Character

Introduction

The greatest lie one can believe in is that all one needs to succeed as a leader is a technical competence. That life was disapproved by Norman Schwarzkopf, a US General who observed; "Leadership is a potent combination of strategy and character. But if you must be without one, be without the strategy."[1] Schwarzkopf's words would be questionable if they had been uttered by an ordinary man. But not so. Schwarzkopf was a career soldier all his adult life. He served as a commander and strategist of the most powerful army in modern times both in the Vietnam War and the Operation Desert Storm in Iraq.[2] Schwarzkopf must have understood fully, the power of both character and strategy. Given his background, only a fool would doubt his wisdom.

Contrary to Schwarzkopf's wisdom, the world of the 21st century is a scene of contrasts as far as leadership is concerned. First, the society believes in a world where it is okay for people to have:

> Wealth without work,
> Pleasure without conscience,
> Knowledge without character,
> Commerce without morality,
> Science without humanity,
> Worship without sacrifice, and
> Politics without principle.[3]

Second, the same society that is character-deficient expects to get trustworthy leaders. In fact, the greater the moral decay in the society, the louder the cry for leaders of integrity. So, we match to the next elections with hope, that the next generation of leaders will be better. That hope is however short lived as the people soon discover, same forest, different monkeys.

Since character is the most powerful means of persuasion,[4] this chapter is devoted to character development as the foundation of leadership.

Defining Leadership Character

The Collins English Online Dictionary defines character as an "aggregate of features and traits that form the individual nature of some person or thing."[5] Other sources define a person's character as "The way someone thinks feels, and behaves."(Merriam-Webster online dictionary)

- The sum of those qualities of moral excellence that stimulate a person to do the right thing, which is manifested through right and proper actions despite internal or external pressure to the contrary."[6]

The following quotes shed more light on the essence of character:

- Character — the willingness to accept responsibility for one's own life — is the source from which self-respect springs. -Joan Didion
- Character is doing what you don't want to do but know you should do" — Joyce Meyer
- A man is literally what he thinks, his character being the complete sum of all his thoughts." — James Allen[8]

Character is what makes a person unique from others. A person's character is a complex combination of moral mental and emotional qualities. In other words, character is a combination of a multitude of features and human qualities that describe the person.

Character is like a meal whose flavor depends on the various ingredients used to prepare it. The final taste of that meal depends on the number of the ingredients used, the amounts, the proportions, and the cooking process used to prepare the meal.

A variety of these qualities of the human personality and learned attributes combine to produce one's character. Among these qualities are a person's intellect, thoughts, ideas, motives, intentions, temperament, judgment, behavior, imagination, perception, emotions, love, and hatred to mention but a few."[9]

A person's character traits combine to produce one's disposition which is defined by the most dominant quality displayed most frequently. For instance, when we say a person has a good character, we use terms like integrity, honesty, strong moral fiber, care and concern for others, and the like.

In this text, we define character as "The combination of inborn traits and learned attributes that subconsciously affects everything we do. The inborn traits, are passed on by our genes based on hereditary factors and are arranged at the time of conception."[10]

Case Study 2. 1: Character illustrated

The term character does not feature prominently in the Bible. However, the concept appears in several places using different illustrations. For instance, human character is personified by:

a. The natural man

The term 'natural man' in the Bible to refers to the human nature before the influence of the Holy Spirit. According to 1 Cor. 2:14, "The natural man cannot receive and understand the things of the spirit of God, for they are foolishness to him; nor can he know them, because they are spiritually discerned."

b. The Flesh

The word flesh as used in John 3:6 and several other scriptures refer to self-effort. Consequently, "That which is born of the flesh is flesh, and that which is born of the Spirit is spirit."

c. The old man

The old man refers to the natural tendencies as opposed to the new nature created in the image of God. Believers are thus urged to "…put off concerning the former conversation the old man, which is corrupt according to the deceitful lusts (Eph 4:22 (KJV).

All these terms refer to the human temperament, which lasts throughout your life even after conversion. It does not go away. However, some aspects of your temperament may soften or get more pronounced with time.

There are two wrong assumptions that believers can assume regarding their temperaments, the first assumption is that, once you become a Christian your temperament is totally changed, and your weaknesses go away. The underlying implication of this assumption is, if you are Choleric, you cannot get angry, and if you get angry, it is enough evidence, you are not a Christian. Similarly, a Christian Sanguine can no longer exaggerate, and if you do, you are not a Christian.

Those who prescribe to this assumption discourage other believers by questioning whether they are truly born again. As a result, genuinely born again believers get confused and often doubt their salvation which may lead some to give up.

The second assumption argues that you can do nothing about your temperamental weaknesses. People who take this stand excuse their failures with arguments like, "I was born like that" or "that is me,", and, there is nothing I can do about it. Others will say, "I am myself. Such arguments keep people from taking responsibility for their character weaknesses and so become a bad example of a believer.

Character is a Matter of the Heart

The word "heart," occurs over one thousand times in the Bible. The heart refers to the inner core of a man comprising the mind, the emotion, and the will. Below is a brief description of each of these heart components that make up the heart and ultimately determine your character.

a. The mind

The human mind describes the reasoning or intellectual ability of a person.[11] The mind exerts great influence on a person's character since as a man thinks in his heart, so is he (Prov 23:7).

Through the mind, the person knows, thinks, understands, meditates, plans, imagines, creates, reasons and performs other related functions that set him apart from lower forms of living organisms.

A person's character is a reflection of his or her persistent state of mind. For instance, a corrupt leader is an outcome of a corrupt mind. According to the Bible, the mind can assume various states including being:

- Anxious – Luke 12:29,
- Blinded - 2 Cor. 3:14, 4:4,
- Corrupt - 2 Cor 11:3 2Tim 3:8,
- Indecisive (Double-minded) - James 1:8
- Pure – 2 Peter 3:1,
- Sound – 2 Tim 1:7,
- Renewed – Rom. 12:2, Eph. 4:23

All these and many other mental attributes combine to define a person's character, which in turn affect his or her ability to influence others.

b. The emotion
Human emotion represents the subjective sensation, feeling, and excitement perceived by a person and expressed through the body. Emotion can be either negative or positive.

Through positive emotion, the heart expresses love, care, compassion, forgiveness, joy, makes merry, cheers, trusts, shows courage, encourages, delights, sings and makes music. Through negative emotion, the heart expresses anger, hate, wrath, bitterness, revenge, sorrow, despair, and grief among a long list of emotional expressions.

A leader's long-term emotional state exerts a great impact on his or her character because; there is a connection between emotion and every thought, perception, and expression of human life. Gentleness, humility, patience and many other related character traits are all expressions of one's prevailing emotional state.

c. The Will
The human will is a self-determining agent in that; it denotes the heart's ability to choose or decide upon a course of action purposely. The will includes the capacity to make meaningful moral choices.

God has given every person the freedom to choose, accept or reject external conditions and environmental influences thereby assuming responsibility for his or her choices. The capacity to make choices plays a major role in shaping the person's character which in turn affects his ability to influence others.

What Character Is Not
Though closely related, character goes deeper than mere outward appearance, reputation, and conduct. Before we proceed further, let us examine the distinction between character and these closely related terms:

4. Character is more than an outward appearance
A person's character is more than what he or she appears outwardly. Outward appearances can be deceptive. It is possible for a person with bad character to appear good outwardly. The priority of character over outward appearance comes alive as you read the

case below:

Case Study 2. 2: When good looks matter less

The story of Samuel the prophet as narrated in 1 Samuel 16:4-10 highlights the priority of character over outward appearance in leadership. After rejecting Saul as king over Israel, God sent Samuel to the house of Jesse to inaugurate the next king of Israel. Here are the details:

Samuel did what the Lord said. When he arrived at Bethlehem, the elders of the town trembled when they met him. They asked, "Do you come in peace?" Samuel replied, "Yes, in peace; I have come to sacrifice to the Lord. Consecrate yourselves and come to the sacrifice with me." Then he consecrated Jesse and his sons and invited them to the sacrifice. When they arrived, Samuel saw Eliab and thought, "Surely the Lord's anointed stands here before the Lord." But the Lord said to Samuel, "Do not consider his appearance or his height, for I have rejected him. The Lord does not look at the things people look at. People look at the outward appearance, but the Lord looks at the heart." Then Jesse called Abinadab and had him pass in front of Samuel. But Samuel said, "The Lord has not chosen this one either." Jesse then had Shammah pass by, but Samuel said, "Nor has the Lord chosen this one." Jesse had seven of his sons pass before Samuel, but Samuel said to him, "The Lord has not chosen these."

Reflection questions
a) How did Samuel reaction on seeing Eliab?
b) What reason did God give for rejecting the seven sons of Jesse?

You cannot tell a person's character by just looking at their outward appearance. People can appear holy and godly outwardly. They can raise their hands in worship, use the right language and even talk about their commitment to ethical conduct. However, that is not necessarily their true character. The seven sons of Jesse displayed an impressive outward appearance; God rejected them because their hearts were not right.

Notice what God told Samuel:

But the Lord said to Samuel, "Do not consider his appearance or his height, for I have rejected him. The Lord does not look at the things people look at. People look at the outward appearance, but the Lord looks at the heart (1 Sam 16:7).

5. Character is more than reputation

Thomas Paine pointed out the difference between reputation and character in these words: "Reputation is what men and women think of us. Character is what God and the angels know of us."

The temptation to be more concerned about reputation instead of one's character is real. Many leaders are good at presenting a wonderful image outwardly while their real character is wanting. This should not be so. If you watch your character, your reputation will take care of itself.

The need to watch one's character cannot be over-emphasized. A person's character is the reality of himself while his reputation is the opinion others have formed about him. Leaders should be more concerned about their character than their reputation. If you watch your character, your reputation will take care of itself.

Case Study 2. 3: When leaders care more about reputation

People are not always what others think they are. The religious leaders in the days of Jesus were more concerned about their reputation instead of their character. They did their best to create a positive image before the masses, but Jesus saw through their façade and confronted them publicly. Here is the story:

"Woe to you, teachers of the law and Pharisees, you hypocrites! You give a tenth of your spices—mint, dill, and cumin. But you have neglected the more important matters of the law—justice, mercy, and faithfulness. You should have practiced the latter, without neglecting the former. You blind guides! You strain out a gnat but swallow a camel. "Woe to you, teachers of the law and Pharisees, you hypocrites! You clean the outside of the cup and dish, but inside they are full of greed and self-indulgence. Blind Pharisee! First, clean the inside of the cup and dish, and then the outside will be clean.

"Woe to you, teachers of the law and Pharisees, you hypocrites! You are like whitewashed tombs, which look beautiful on the outside but the inside are full of the bones of the dead and everything unclean. In the same way, on the outside, you appear to people as righteous, but on the inside, you are full of hypocrisy and wickedness. "Woe to you, teachers of the law and Pharisees, you hypocrites! You build tombs for the prophets and decorate the graves of the righteous, (Mat 23:23-29).

Reflection questions
a) Identify four things the teachers of the law and Pharisees did which showed their preoccupation with reputation instead of their character
b) What two examples did Jesus use to show the gap between who they were and who they pretended to be?

Like the teachers of the law and Pharisees, the Church at Sardis had a good reputation but lacked good character. They had a name of being alive while indeed they were dead. As a result, they lost their power to bear witness for Christ. To correct this misplaced emphasis on reputation the angel of the church in Sardis wrote to them; "Wake up! Strengthen what remains and is about to die, for I have found your deeds unfinished in the sight of my God" (Rev 3:2).

When leaders focus more on reputation rather than their character, they lose their influence on those around them. Instead, they become repellants to the same people they are seeking to lead.

6. Character is more than conduct
Conduct refers to your behavior on a particular occasion or in a particular context. A person's conduct is not necessarily a true reflection of character. When a person's conduct and his or her real character match, we say he or she is a person of integrity. Integrity is a major building block of character.

The Impact of Character on Leadership
Research findings on leadership indicate that many failures in leadership are character related.[11] Here are nine ways character affects leadership performance:

1. Character determines influence
Montgomery defined leadership as "The capacity and the will to rally men and women to a common purpose and the character which inspires confidence."[12] From Montgomery' statement, the message is clear – there is a particular character which inspires confidence. On the reverse side, it is logical to conclude that one's

character can inspire loyalty, trust or rebellion.

For instance, consider this scenario: Two leaders give the same instructions to the same followers. One gets an enthusiastic response while the other is met with indifference. What makes this difference? Character.

Leadership is influence[13] and influence proceeds from your character. A leader's character affects his or her leadership ability in both direct and indirect ways. It determines the degree and the quality of influence wielded. The test of the leader's character is therefore not what he or she does and says but the reaction he or she elicits from the followers. Your character will either reinforce or weaken your influence with people.

2. Character determines your relationships

Character has a great influence on human relationships. It shapes how we engage the world, what we notice, what we reinforce, whom we engage, what we value, what we choose to act on and what we ignore.[14] Character affects the way you interact with customers, employees, suppliers among other stakeholders.

John Maxwell in his book, *The 5 levels of Leadership* describes the levels through which leadership effectiveness progresses.[15] At the bottom is the position level where the leader begins. At this level, people follow the leader because he has a positional power. The leader depends on his authority to move people to do what he wants. The longer the leader stays there, the more difficult it becomes to influence the people. The leader who depends on power and authority will only exert influence over them as long as he or she has something the people need desperately. Otherwise, they will not follow the leader.

The second level of influence according to Maxwell is the permission level. At this level, the people follow the leader voluntarily. The leader finds it easy to influence the people since they have already given him or her the permission to lead them.

Your character determines how you relate to people. Good character leads to quality relationships with people, who in turn give you the permission to lead them. Poor character leads to troubled relationships with people often characterized by conflicts, misunderstandings, and ugly confrontations. Troubled relationships greatly undermine the leader's ability to move people towards the organizational goals.

3. **Character influences the choices you make.**
There is a reciprocal relationship between character and choices. Your choices determine character, and your character influences your choices.[16] Different leaders facing the same challenges, in similar circumstances under the same conditions, will make different decisions. Why? The leader's choices reflect his or her values and priorities.[17]

The choices a leader makes under pressure reveals his character. The greater the pressure, the deeper the revelation and, the truer the choice to the character's essential nature.

Case Study 2. 4: Character has the strength to say 'No.'

The story of Daniel provides us with a good illustration here. Daniel was under much pressure to conform to the Babylonian culture. First, he was a young man in a foreign land where he had no connections, second, he was a slave boy in no position to negotiate with his masters, and third, he could have easily rationalized that God would understand given his difficult situation. In those circumstances, Daniel had to make a choice; to eat the king's food and wine which were ritually unclean and which would defile him, or to say no and risk the consequences. So what did Daniel decide?

Read on:

> But Daniel resolved not to defile himself with the royal food and wine, and he asked the chief official for permission not to defile himself this way. Now God had caused the official to show favor and compassion to Daniel, but the official told Daniel, "I am afraid of my Lord the king, who has assigned your food and drink. Why should he see you looking worse than the other young men your age? The king would then have my head because of you." Daniel then said to the guard whom the chief official had appointed over Daniel, Hananiah, Mishael, and Azariah, "Please test your servants for ten days: Give us nothing but vegetables to eat and water to drink. Then compare our appearance with that of the young men who eat the royal food, and treat your servants in accordance with what you see."

So he agreed to this and tested them for ten days. At the end of the ten days, they looked healthier and better nourished than any of the young men who ate the royal food. So the guard took away their choice food and the wine they were to drink and gave them vegetables instead (Dan 1:8-16)

Reflection questions
a) What situation was Daniel in that tested his character?
b) What options did Daniel have given his circumstances?
c) What choice did Daniel make that proved he was a person of character?
d) Was this an easy choice for Daniel to make?

The case of Daniel is a good illustration of character on parade. As Aristotle once said, "Character is that which reveals moral purpose, exposing the class of things a man chooses and avoids." Out of the many young men chosen to serve the Babylonian king, Daniel made a choice that distinguished him from the rest of his team.

What do we learn from Daniel about the power of leadership character? When under pressure it is more convenient to take shortcuts, compromise and justify our unethical actions. It is easier to give up on what we believe to be right. That is the leader's character test.

4. Character affects how you treat others
How you treat others says a lot about your character. Johann von Goethe was right when he said, "You can easily judge the character of a man by how he treats those who can do nothing for him."

Case Study 2. 5: The wicked servant
Jesus gave a parable of a servant who owed his master a huge sum of money. This servant could not pay his debt, so he pleaded with his master to give him more time to pay. The master was a compassionate person, so he forgave his servant's debt, but, as soon as the servant walked out of the master's presence, he met his fellow servant who owed him a few coins. Read the case below:

> Therefore, the kingdom of heaven is like a king who wanted to settle accounts with his servants. As he began the settlement, a man who owed him ten thousand bags of gold was brought to him. Since he was not able to pay, the master ordered that he and his wife and his children and all that he had be sold to repay

the debt. "At this, the servant fell on his knees before him. 'Be patient with me,' he begged, 'and I will pay back everything.' The servant's master took pity on him, canceled the debt and let him go. But when that servant went out, he found one of his fellow servants who owed him a hundred silver coins. He grabbed him and began to choke him. 'Pay back what you owe me!' he demanded. "His fellow servant fell to his knees and begged him, 'Be patient with me, and I will pay it back.' "But he refused. Instead, he went off and had the man thrown into prison until he could pay the debt. When the other servants saw what had happened, they were outraged and went and told their master everything that had happened.

"Then the master called the servant in. 'You wicked servant,' he said, 'I canceled all that debt of yours because you begged me to. Shouldn't you have had mercy on your fellow servant just as I had on you?'

Reflection questions
a) How much did the master owe the first servant?
b) What did the master do when the first servant begged for mercy?
c) How did the servant whose debt was canceled by their master treat his fellow servant who could not pay his debt?
d) How did the master describe the character of the servant who would not forgive his fellow servant?

It is interesting to note that the master of the unforgiving servant described him as a wicked servant. Leaders deal with people who offend, malign and do all manner of things to hurt them. You can tell a Leader's character by the way she treats those under her authority. A leader who cannot overcome resentment against others, hide hurt feelings, and forgive quickly is unlikely to lead effectively in the long run.

5. Character predicts your response to temptations.
Another way to judge a person's character is to observe what tempts him and how he handles temptations. When tempted, "Leaders always choose the harder right rather than, the easier wrong." — Orrin Woodward

The leadership role brings with it many temptations to the leader.

There is the temptation to abuse power, take advantage of the people you serve, convert public resources for personal gain and so on. It takes a strong character for a leader to resist all those temptations.

Case Study 2. 6: Character knows when to take off

Joseph was severely tempted to commit sex with the wife of his boss at Potiphar's house. The chances of being found out were almost nil. He had a nice opportunity to compromise his values and get away with it. Besides, he was bound to obey his master's wife as an employee. At least it would have been for a man of weak character. But Joseph said no. Instead, he fled and left his cloak in her hands. Read the details in the case below:

> Joseph found favor in his eyes and became his attendant. Potiphar put him in charge of his household, and he entrusted to his care everything he owned. From the time he put him in charge of his household and of all that he owned, the Lord blessed the household of the Egyptian because of Joseph. The blessing of the Lord was on everything Potiphar had, both in the house and in the field. So Potiphar left everything he had in Joseph's care; with Joseph in charge, he did not concern himself with anything except the food he ate. Now Joseph was well-built and handsome, and after a while, his master's wife took notice of Joseph and said, "Come to bed with me!" But he refused. "With me in charge," he told her, "my master does not concern himself with anything in the house; everything he owns he has entrusted to my care. No one is greater in this house than I am. My master has withheld nothing from me except you because you are his wife. How then could I do such a wicked thing and sin against God?" And though she spoke to Joseph day after day, he refused to go to bed with her or even be with her. One day he went into the house to attend to his duties, and none of the household servants was inside. She caught him by his cloak and said, "Come to bed with me!" But he left his cloak in her hand and ran out of the house.

Reflection questions
a) Based on Joseph's job description as given in this case study, what title would you give him in today's business context?

b) What job-related temptation did Joseph face at his workplace?
c) What made it easy or hard for Joseph to overcome this temptation?
d) What job-related temptations do you face in your workplace and,
e) What can you do to overcome those temptations?

Joseph understood what leaders of character do. "The measure of a man's character is what he would do if he knew he never would be found out."[18] When people know you can be trusted to do what is right despite the many temptations, they trust you more and continue to follow and honor you.

On the contrary, people will not continue to follow a leader who betrays their trust by succumbing to temptations, no matter how strong the temptations may be.

6. Character determines how you handle feedback

People react differently to the leader's attempts to move them towards the organizational goals. Some people embrace the leader's call and encourage him to go on; others disagree with the leader, his goal or his methods. Those who disagree may criticize, withdraw their support or even confront the leader only to leave him hurting. As a wise leader, understand that people will react to you as a result of their mindset, rather than as a reflection of your worth. Most people use others as mirrors for their darkness. If such people have hurt you, perhaps you can use these experiences to become a different kind of person—one who reflects the light within others instead of using them as mirrors. Maybe your experiences of pain can lead you to be a great leader, someone who lights up the world.[19]

How you react to feedback can reveal a lot about your character and affect your level of influence with the people. Leaders who handle feedback positively continue to increase their influence while those who fail to manage it well stand to see their influence declining.

Positive feedback like praise can reveal pride or humility on the part of the leader. A leader who allows pride to get into the head risks a waning influence while humility goes a long way to endear the people to the leader. Negative feedback like criticism, rebuke and correction can reveal the leader's insecurities when the leader gets defensive and fights back. Leaders who ignore or fight back those who provide negative feedback lose their influence very fast.

1. **Character influences your response to popular opinion**

Charles Spurgeon captured the impact of the popular opinion on character is in these words; "Character is always lost when a high ideal is sacrificed on the altar of conformity and popularity".[20]

The popular opinion is not always the right opinion. 'Everyone does it' is a common excuse for compromise and unethical conduct. What people do not realize is that their opinion of the world is also a confession of their character. [21] What everyone does or thinks is not necessarily right. Men and women of character gladly take their stand against popular opinion when it violates their ethical standards.

Leaders of strong character know what they believe and defend it regardless of public opinion. After all, "A conscious human is driven by their conscience, not popular opinion."[21]

Case Study 2. 7: Stop this hypocrisy, Paul tells Peter

Apostle Peter whose other name was Cephas presents a good example of a leader with a weak character, especially in his earlier days. As a disciple of Christ, he could not admit before a maid that he was one of the followers of Christ. Due to his fear of what people would say, think or do, he denied his master three times. Paul later confronted him about this weakness as narrated in the case below:

> When Cephas came to Antioch, I opposed him to his face, because he stood condemned. For before certain men came from James, he used to eat with the Gentiles. But when they arrived, he began to draw back and separate himself from the Gentiles because he was afraid of those who belonged to the circumcision group. The other Jews joined him in his hypocrisy, so that by their hypocrisy even Barnabas was led astray. When I saw that they were not acting in line with the truth of the gospel, I said to Cephas in front of them all, "You are a Jew, yet you live like a Gentile and not like a Jew. How is it, then, that you force Gentiles to follow Jewish customs? (Gal 2:11-14)

Reflection questions
a) What did Peter do that made Paul confront him publicly?
b) What impact did Peter's behavior have on the other Jewish believers including Barnabas?
c) What reason did Paul give for opposing him?
d) Do you know leaders who like Peter compromise their ideals due to fear of public opinion? How does this affect their leadership effectiveness?

As Douglas MacArthur pointed out, "A true leader has the confidence to stand alone, the courage to make tough decisions, and the compassion to listen to the needs of others. He does not set out to be a leader, but becomes one by the equality of his actions and the integrity of his intent."[22]

Leaders who stand up for what they believe in attract the attention of their people. Occasionally they may suffer for it, but more often than not, they gain more respect. When people respect their leaders, they follow them.

2. Character produces integrity

Dave Anderson defines integrity as a "Steadfast adherence to a strict moral or ethical code."[23] Integrity is a key building block of character to the extent that the two terms are used interchangeably at times. Integrity is an outcome of a sound character and character manifests through integrity or lack of it.

A person of integrity does what is right in spite of the consequences. She speaks the truth consistently, keeps her promises, lives up to her commitments and does what she says she will do.

Consistency is the essence of integrity. "Solid character will reflect itself inconsistent behavior, while a poor character will seek to hide behind deceptive words and actions."[24]

Lack of integrity is the first indicator of a leader's character deficiency. People do not easily trust a leader who lacks integrity. This lack of trust undermines the leader's ability to influence the people. In case of elective leadership positions, the people will get rid of the leader by voting him or her out at the earliest convenient time. Where it is not possible to remove the leader, the people will rarely support the leaders' efforts to pursue common goals.

2. Leaders' character shapes the organizational culture
The leader's values, preferences, and habits influence how the members behave. It encourages certain attitudes and behaviors and discourages others. Consciously or otherwise, the leader's character will attract or drive people away from the organization depending on how long the leader holds on to the key position.

Leaders of strong character build healthy organizations characterized by a strong work ethic, productivity and healthy relationships where employees are proud to be members of the organization. On the contrary, leaders who lack leadership character create toxic organizations with high staff turnover where members stay only as long as they have nowhere else to go. Like any long-term process, it is fraught with pain and exhilaration.

Conclusion
The leader's character is a complex combination of moral, mental and emotional qualities that influence everything you do. It is the most effective means of persuasion. Your character is the key determinant that draws people to you or drives them away. It is either your greatest asset or your greatest liability. Your character affects your ability to lead directly and indirectly. Your character will either reinforce or weaken your influence with people.

References
1. Schwarzkopf, N. & Petre, P. (1992). It Doesn't Take a Hero: The Autobiography of General H. Norman Schwarzkopf. Bantana Books

2. Bourque, S. A. (2003). Jayhawk: The VII Corps in the Persian Gulf War. Darby, Pennsylvania: Diane Publishing Company.

3. From a sermon given by Frederick Lewis Donaldson in Westminster Abbey, London, on March 20, 1925."

4. Aeterna Press (2015). Aristotle Rhetoric. London, UK

5. Collins English Dictionary - Complete & Unabridged 2012 Digital Edition, William Collins Sons & Co. Ltd.

6. Hall, M. F. & Wagie, D. A. (1996). The US Air Force Academy's Cutting-Edge Character Development Program. Airpower Journal.

7. Allen, J. (1903). As a Man Thinketh. New York

8. Trumbull, H. C. (1889). Character-shaping and character-showing. Philadelphia, J. D. Wattles,

9. LaHaye, T. (1993). Spirit-Controlled Temperament. Wheaton, Illinois: Tyandale House Publishers Inc.

10. John S. Scripture's heart: an empirical study of the word 'heart' in the Bible. <http://www.john-uebersax.com/heart1.htm> 2012.

11. Seijts, G. Crossan, M. & Gandz, J. (2008). The Cross-Enterprise Leader. Ivey Business Journal.

12. Bernard Law Montgomery, L. (2009). The Art of Leadership. Pen & Sword Military.

13. Maxwell, J. C. (2007). The 21 Irrefutable laws of leadership: Follow them and people will follow you. Revised and updated version. Nashville, Tennessee. Thomas Nelson.

14. Crossan, M., Gandz, J., Seijts, G. (2012). Developing Leadership Character. Ivey Business Journal.

15. Maxwell, J. C. (2011). The Five Levels of Leadership: Proven Steps to Maximize Your Potential. Nashville, Tennessee. Thomas Nelson Inc.

16. Mull, B. (2009). Fablehaven: Secrets of the Dragon Sanctuary. New York. Simon & Schuster Children Publishing Division.

17. Sarros, J. C., Cooper, B. K. & Hartican, A. M. (2006). Leadership and character. Leadership & Organization Development Journal Vol. 27 No. 8, 2006 pp. 682-699

18. Thomas Babington Macaulay (1800-1859). British writer and politician

19. Tugaleva, V. (2013). The Love Mindset: An Unconventional to Healing and Happiness. Soulux Press

20. Attributed to Charles Spurgeon in Barber, J. (2010). My Almost for His Highest. Wipf and Stock Publishers. Eu-gene, Oregon.
21. Ralph Waldo Emerson quoted in Parsley, J. (2014). Tapestry of Faith: Discovering God's Beautiful Design in the Laughter, Tears, and Struggles of Life. Lake Mary, Florida. Charisma House.
22. Anderson, D. (2010, September). The vital difference between character and integrity. Dave Anderson's Learn to Lead Blog, http://blog.learntolead.com/archives/tag/the-vital-difference-between-character-and-integrity/
23. MacArthur, D. (2009). Revitalizing a Nation: A Statement of Beliefs, Opinions, and Policies Embodied in the Public Pronouncements. Kessinger Publishing, LLC. The Nonesuch Edition
24. Munroe, M. (2004). Waiting and Dating. Destiny Image

Chapter Three

Developing Your Character

Introduction

Character building is a lifelong process that begins in our infancy and continues until death. Many factors work together at different stages in your life to shape your character. The most important of these include our temperament, early childhood experiences, training and religious faith. Below is a detailed description of each:

Temperament

Temperament refers to the inborn traits passed on by our genes at birth. It is the combination of mental, physical and emotional traits of a person. Temperament provides the template on which character forms.

At birth, we inherit character traits that differentiate us from others. We have unique tastes, preferences, and strengths that combine to give us special ability to be and do certain things with ease. Similarly, we have natural dislikes, disabilities, and weaknesses that hinder us from functioning effectively in certain areas of our lives.

Your temperament has a great impact on your character. Multiple studies including research by Stogdill[1] and Bentz[2] found a relationship between leadership effectiveness and the big five personality traits. Below is a detailed discussion on the influence of temperament on a person's character.

Your natural temperament comprises inborn traits that subconsciously affect your behavior. Your temperament functions like the manufacturer's default settings and determines why you act the way you do.

Your temperament provides you with a working template, which serves as a starting point for understanding and shaping your character. The purpose of character development is to modify your temperament to maximize on your temperamental strengths while minimizing the limitations placed on your potential by your weaknesses. The outcome of character development is a "civilized" temperament.

Human temperaments fall into the two broad categories namely; the introverts and the extroverts. The extroverted temperaments include the Sanguine and Choleric, which are more outgoing, sociable, and people friendly. They function best in crowds and so prefer working with other people.

The introverted temperaments include the Phlegmatic and the melancholy personalities, who are shy and "reserved". They function best alone and feel anxious in crowded contexts, especially at being singled-out.

In real life, it is rare to find a person with only one temperament. Every person has a blend of at least two temperaments; the primary dominant one, and, a secondary less pronounced temperament. In this book, we only focus on the four primary temperaments to illustrate how inborn traits affect one's character.

Each temperament type brings with it inborn character strengths and weaknesses which determine how they relate to other people. Below, is a summary of the character strengths and weaknesses of each temperament.

1. The Sanguine Temperament

People with the Sanguine temperament are carefree, full of energy and hope individuals who live in the present.[4] They pay attention to what is happening now, which they forget about as soon as they move to the next event, activity or environment. Their stimulating and friendly nature makes it easy for them to attract people easily, unfortunately, their lack of discipline and inconsistency makes it hard for them to retain the same friends for long.

Sanguine Character Strengths and weaknesses

The Sanguine is a super extrovert who displays a hearty optimistic disposition.[5] She has a way of making people relax and feel comfortable in whatever situation she finds herself in. The Sanguine has strong people skills and will fit anywhere provided she is the one doing the talking.

The Bible characters that seem to fit the characteristics of a Sanguine are King David and Apostle Peter.

Table 3.1 below shows more of the Sanguine character strengths and weaknesses:

Table 3.1. The Sanguine strengths and weaknesses

Strengths	Weaknesses
Buoyant,	Compulsive talker,
Compassionate,	Disorganized,
Emotional,	Emotional fluctuations
Enthusiastic,	Exaggerates,
Fun loving,	Forgets quickly,
Friendly,	Inconsistent,
Optimistic,	Undisciplined,
Stimulating,	Restless,
Warm.	Weak-willed.

Case Study 3.1: Apostle Peter the Sanguine

The Apostle Peter was a super Sanguine. Every time we meet him in the Gospels, he is talking. His spontaneous and impulsive behavior is evident in the sinful betrayal and easy repentance *"with tears"*. Below is a list of scripture from the gospel according to Matthew where he always appears in action:

a. Impulsive

"Lord, if it's you," Peter replied, "tell me to come to you on the water." "Come," he said. Then Peter got down out of the boat, walked on the water and came towards Jesus. But when he saw the wind, he was afraid and, beginning to sink, cried out, "Lord, save me!" (Mat 14:28-30).

b. Outspoken

Peter said, "Explain the parable to us (Matt. 15:15).
Simon Peter answered, "You are the Messiah, the Son of the living God (Matt. 16:16)." Peter took him aside and began to rebuke him. "Never, Lord!" he said. "This shall never happen to you!" Peter said to Jesus, "Lord, it is good for us to be here. If you wish, I will put up three shelters—one for you, one for Moses and one for Elijah."

c. Egotistical

Then Peter came to Jesus and asked, "Lord, how many times shall I forgive my brother or sister who sins against me? Up to seven times?" (Matt. 16:22).

d. Self-seeking

Peter answered him, "We have left everything to follow you! What then will there be for us?" (Matt. 19:27).

e. The braggart

Peter replied, "Even if all fall away on account of you, I never will." But Peter declared, "Even if I have to die with you, I will never disown you." And all the other disciples said the same, (Matt. 26:33, 35).

f. Weak-willed

Now Peter was sitting out in the courtyard, and a servant girl came to him. "You also were with Jesus of Galilee," she said. But he denied it before them all. "I don't know what you're talking about," he said. Then he went out to the gateway, where another servant girl saw him and said to the people there, "This fellow was with Jesus of Nazareth." He denied it again, with an oath: "I don't know the man!" After a little while, those standing there went up to Peter and said, "Surely you are one of them; your accent gives you away." Then he began to call down curses, and he swore to them, "I don't know the man!" Immediately a rooster crowed. Then Peter remembered the word Jesus had spoken: "Before the rooster crows, you will disown me three times." And he went outside and wept bitterly (Matt. 26:69-75).

Reflection question

- How many other positive character traits associated with the Sanguine temperament can you pick from the life of Peter?

Despite his temperamental weaknesses, Peter became the strong, resolute leader of the Early Church. In the Acts of the Apostles, everything he said was right – because he was spirit-filled.

Impact of Sanguine character weaknesses

How do the Sanguine weaknesses limit her ability to influence people? Although the Sanguine pleasant personality may attract people in the short run, her lack of discipline and endless chatter soon disappoints her followers. The Sanguine finds it hard to sustain trust in relationships due to her inconsistency and tendency to exaggerate which often borders on lying. Sanguine leaders are most vulnerable to lack of integrity, which erodes the trust people have in their leadership.

Sanguine character deficiency
a. Integrity

Jensen defines integrity as "A state or condition of being whole, complete, unbroken, unimpaired, sound, in perfect condition."[6] People with the Sanguine temperament suffer from lack of integrity, which is crucial to earn and sustain trust. Lack of integrity, in turn, limits their ability to inspire others to collaborate.[7] The Sanguine can develop integrity by practicing being thorough, refusing to cut corners, committing to accept responsibility for own actions and most of all, defining ethical no-compromise zones."[8] Cultivating these attributes will help the Sanguine leader to:

- Differentiate between what is right and wrong and, to live it inwardly and outwardly.
- Consistently do what is right even when under pressure to do otherwise.[9]
- Demonstrate honesty consistently.[10]
- Follow through commitments.

b. Conscientiousness

Conscientiousness is another trait the Sanguine needs to cultivate. Conscientiousness makes one inclined to do what is right, especially to do one's work or duty well and thoroughly.[11] Conscientiousness people are organized, systematic punctual, achievement-oriented and dependable. Conscientious leaders are high achievers, who attract more followers to them.[12]

c. Accountability

The Sanguine is prone to taking her shortcomings and failures lightly, which explains her failure to take responsibility for her actions. Sanguine leaders can improve their leadership ability by developing the willingness to accept responsibility and being accountable for their actions. Accountable leaders own and commit to decisions they make, which encourages others to do the same.

If you are endowed with the Sanguine temperament, you can further develop accountability by submitting to a trusted friend or accountability partner to hold you to account whenever you fail the accountability test. If married, your spouse is the best accountability partner you can get since he or she knows you well, means well for you, and is more interested in helping than impressing you.

In the workplace, get a mature and close confidant whom you can submit to and allow him or her to alert you when you are at risk of failing the accountability test. Workmates and even your boss could provide a support system for your improvement if you ask them.

d. Credibility

Sanguine leaders suffer from an inability to sustain trust due to their tendency to exaggerate and failure to keep their word. Credibility is important because it makes the leader worthy of trust. That makes it easy for the leader to influence the thoughts, behaviors, and attitudes of other people. A leader who is not credible will not inspire others to commit to organizational goals.

To be persuasive leaders must be believable; to be believable they must be credible; to be credible, they must be truthful.[13] Sanguine leaders can build trust by cultivating the credibility attribute. Credibility is the ability to lead by example and be a role model for others.[14]

Tim LaHaye, a noted authority in the field of temperaments describes the Choleric temperament in these words:

> Mr. Choleric is a practical activist. All of his life is a utilitarian to him. He is strong-willed, a natural leader and very optimistic. His brain is filled with ideas, projects or objectives, and he usually sees them through.[15]

1. The Choleric Temperament

The Choleric is another extroverted temperament though not as extreme as the sanguine. The Choleric personality shares many of the positive characteristics of the Sanguine since they are both extroverted. Besides, the Choleric has an active, quick, practical and an ambitious personality that makes him a natural candidate for the leadership role.[16] Table 3.2 below shows the Choleric character strengths and weaknesses

Table 3. 2 Choleric character strengths and weaknesses

Strengths	Weaknesses
Action-oriented	Bossy,
Confident,	Cruel,

Decisive,
Determined
Independent,
Optimistic,
Strong willed,
Takes charge,
Results focused.

Domineering,
Hostile, Sarcastic.
Impatient,
Intolerant,
Quick-tempered
Rash decision
Self-reliant.

Choleric character strengths and weaknesses

The Choleric temperament demonstrates many strengths and weaknesses at the same time. Action-oriented, confident, decisive and a risk taker, the Choleric has a greater chance of being a natural leader than any other temperament. Unfortunately, his weaknesses such as anger, intolerance, and hostility often undermine that potential unless he learns to control his negative emotions.

Impact of Choleric Character weaknesses

How do the choleric character weaknesses limit his or her ability to lead people? First, the Choleric is prone to outburst of anger, intolerance, and impatience, which provokes fear, resentment, and hatred in their followers. Their demeanor often leaves their followers feeling bullied, intimidated and scared. Second, due to their unsympathetic nature and dislike for tears and emotions, choleric leaders find it hard to empathize with their followers. The outcome is their inability to sustain a close relationship with followers for long. They attract followers who keep coming and going.

The Bible characters that best fit the characteristics of a Choleric are the apostle Paul, James, Martha, and Titus. In our case study below we look at the traces of Apostle Paul's Choleric character in the scriptures.

Case Study 3. 2: Meet Apostle Paul the Choleric

When the Bible talks about Paul, it paints a picture of a man who was decisive, courageous and determined, traits which explain his natural leadership orientation. But on the other hand, he was cruel, bossy, and confrontational as they come, especially before his conversion. Space does not allow us to exhaust Paul's Choleric character traits, but here we highlight only five of them.

    a. **Paul, the practical activist**

The first time we meet Saul who later became Apostle Paul, he is guarding the clothes of the members of the Sanhedrin as they stone Stephen for presumed blasphemy (Acts 7:58). Like the Choleric he was, Saul stood there, approving of their killing him (Acts 8:1). Perhaps cheering and supervising the event.

b. Paul the cruel, unforgiving crusader

Meanwhile, Saul was still breathing out murderous threats against the Lord's disciples. He went to the high priest and asked him for letters to the synagogues in Damascus, so that if he found any there who belonged to the way, whether men or women, he might take them as prisoners to Jerusalem (Acts 9:1-2).

c. Paul the determined achiever

Once Paul settled on a goal, no amount of persuasion would change his mind. What happened on his last missionary journey serves as a good illustration here. While they camped at Caesarea in Philip the Evangelist's house, a prophet came over to them, took Paul's belt, tied his own hands and feet with it and said:

> "The Holy Spirit says, 'In this way, the Jewish leaders in Jerusalem will bind the owner of this belt and will hand him over to the Gentiles" (Acts 21:11).' When his companions heard this, they pleaded with Paul not to go up to Jerusalem, but Paul would not change his mind. His response below reveals his determination and commitment to his goal:

> Then Paul answered, "Why are you weeping and breaking my heart? I am ready not only to be bound but also to die in Jerusalem for the name of the Lord Jesus." When he would not be dissuaded, we gave up and said, "The Lord's will be done." After this, we started on our way up to Jerusalem (Acts 21:12-15).

d. *Paul the independent, self-sufficient go-getter*

Characteristic of his Choleric temperament, Paul was never deterred by lack of support from other people. When he got converted, the disciples were not sure about his genuineness. Barnabas tried to introduce him to them Paul did not receive enthusiastic reception as he might have expected (Acts 9:26-28). So what did Paul do? He launched out on his own.

Paul was not the type to go begging for acceptance from the apostles or from anyone for that matter. Instead, he reached out to the Gentile world and had a thriving ministry without endorsement from the other apostles. When Mark deserted them on their missionary journey, Paul banned him from joining them on the next trip, which eventually led to split up between Paul and Barnabas (Acts 15:36-41). Of course, we know he did later one tone down and appreciated Mark's contribution as time passed on.

e. Paul the sarcastic, quick-tempered and confrontational

Paul had been arrested and charged before the highest Jewish council. He had just started to make his defense when the high priest Ananias ordered those standing near Paul to strike him on the mouth. Look at Paul's reaction below:

Then Paul said to him, "God will strike you, you whitewashed wall! You sit there to judge me according to the law, yet you violate the law by commanding that I be struck!" Those who were standing near Paul said, "How dare you insult God's high priest!" Paul replied, "Brothers, I did not realize that he was the high priest (Acts 23:2-5).

Reflection question
   a) Can you identify Paul's sarcasm in his response to the Sanhedrin above?
   b) What other Choleric temperament traits can you identify from the Bible? Discuss

The Choleric character attributes to cultivate

For the Choleric, leadership comes naturally. With natural drive, confidence and results focus, the Choleric has all the potential to succeed in any leadership role if it were not for the character weaknesses, which need can be developed as discussed below:

a. Emotional intelligence

Emotional intelligence (EQ) is the capacity to recognize, understand and manage your own emotions to promote healthy relationships.[17] It also involves being aware of your feelings and how they impact the emotions of your followers, more important still, is the ability to respond appropriately to avoid negative reactions from your audience.

The Choleric leader can develop emotional intelligence by pausing often enough to reflect on his own emotions and their impact on other people's feelings. By premeditating on possible outcomes of his reactions to anticipated situations, the Choleric can control his internal motivations, emotions, and his social skills; something ineffective leaders rarely to do well..[18]

Choleric leaders are naturally quick-tempered and do not tolerate being challenged or provoked. Their response is swift and intense without careful attention to the impact of their words and body language on the emotional health of their followers. Such emotionally intelligent deficient leaders leave behind a trail of emotionally wounded workers and followers, who eventually leave the organization with negative memories.

Choleric leaders can significantly increase their leadership effectiveness by cultivating emotional intelligence to moderate their display of anger which drives followers away from them.

b. Agreeableness.
Richard Daft defines agreeableness as "the degree to which a person can get along with others by being good-natured, cooperative, forgiving, compassionate, understanding and trusting."[19]

An agreeable person is polite and trusting, often preferring cooperation to competition. People with this personality trait tend to show kindness and empathize with others, thus increasing their chances of emerging as leaders.

Choleric leaders are naturally courageous, independent-minded and competitive. They do not hesitate to voice their disagreement regardless of their audience. Disagreeableness and sometimes hostility are reflex reactions they display at the slightest provocation. Add this to their strong need to win the argument even when they are wrong, and you have a disaster waiting to happen. That is why they need to develop the attribute of agreeableness.

A choleric leader needs to develop this attribute to counter their natural inclination to bully, intimidate and scare followers away. A little kindness and empathy will go a long way to keep their already scared followers close.

c. Humanity

The terms humanity and compassion are in some cases used interchangeably to mean, "Concern for the suffering or welfare of others."[20] Compassionate leaders are able to suffer with or emotionally identify with others going through difficult circumstances.[21]

Choleric leaders naturally lack the humanity attribute hence, find it hard to relate to others in difficult situations. Consequently, they eventually alienate others.[22] That is why they need to cultivate the humanity attribute to overcome their tendency to be unkind and even cruel, especially when under pressure and stress. Choleric leaders can earn respect and loyalty from their followers by showing concern for suffering members and looking for practical ways to show mercy.

Choleric leaders can cultivate humanity by:

- Intentionally looking for opportunities to show practice kindness
- Being considerate
- Crying with those who are crying and celebrating with those who are celebrating
- Making an effort to understand the needs of their followers and taking steps to address those needs and concerns.[23]

2. The Melancholy Temperament

Melancholy personalities are deliberate individuals who like to analyze issues deeply before making their decisions. They think about every step before they act or speak. On the other side of their strengths, are negative thinking patterns that threaten to plunge them into a pessimistic depression. As such, they tend to see a problem in every solution. Their commitment to high standards and hard work makes them high performers, though the same traits make them hard to work and get along with. Table 3.3 below shows their typical strengths and weaknesses of the melancholy temperament.

Table 3. 3 Melancholy character strengths and weaknesses

Strengths	Weaknesses

Accurate,	Slow to make friends,
Analytical,	Frequently moody,
Compassionate,	Lacks confidence,
Creative,	Overcautious, anxious
Deliberative,	Reserved, Perfectionist,
Detailed, Gifted,	Self- sacrificing and
Hard working, Imaginative,	Self-depreciating,
Modest and unassuming,	Sensitive, easily hurt,
Compliant and yielding,	Indecisive,
High standards.	Lack of initiative

Melancholy character strengths and weaknesses

The Melancholy temperament is the richest, most innovative, creative, and sensitive of the personality types. It is however not an easy temperament to live with. Their tendency to sulk combined with their pessimistic attitude often drives potential supporters away. That is compounded by their perfectionist nature, making them hard to please, and hence most followers give up trying to please them.

Case Study 3. 3. Moses the Melancholy

The Bible is rich with examples of leaders who displayed the Melancholy temperament including Moses, Elijah, Elisha, Jonah, John the Baptist, Apostle John and Thomas. In our case study below, we focus on Moses, perhaps the greatest leader that ever lived.

a. Moses was gifted

The Bible does not reveal much about the life of Moses between the time he was picked from River Nile by Pharaoh's daughter and the killing of the Egyptian for mistreating the Hebrew slave. Nevertheless, even in his early years, "Moses was learned in all the wisdom of the Egyptians and was mighty in words and deeds (Act 7:22). That means, long before he met God in the desert and got his life assignment, he was no ordinary young man. He had some exceptional abilities both in speech and actions.

b. Moses was self-sacrificing

Melancholy leaders find it hard to enjoy a good life and success without a twinge of guilt. To ease that guilt they engage in self-sacrificing commitments to help them feel better.

Moses was no different. Growing up in Egypt surrounded by luxuries of the king's household made him uncomfortable. So, "By faith Moses, when he became of age, refused to be called the son of Pharaoh's daughter, choosing rather to suffer affliction with the people of God than to enjoy the passing pleasures of sin" (Heb 11:24-25).

c. Moses was self-depreciating

Self-deprecation is the act of belittling, undervaluing, or disparaging oneself or being excessively modest, and Moses was good at it. You only need to listen to his conversation with God during their encounter at the burning bush to see how deeply Moses was a captive to this character trait. Here is a paraphrased version of that conversation,

> **God**: Go. I am sending you to Pharaoh to bring my people the Israelites out of Egypt
>
> **Moses**: "Who am I that I should go to Pharaoh and bring the Israelites out of Egypt?
>
> **God**: "I will be with you. And this will be the sign to you that it is I who have sent you: When you have brought the people out of Egypt, you will worship God on this mountain.
>
> **Moses**: "Suppose I go to the Israelites and say to them, 'The God of your fathers has sent me to you,' and they ask me, 'What is his name?' Then what shall I tell them?"
>
> **God**: "If they do not believe you or pay attention to the first sign, they may believe the second. But if they do not believe these two signs or listen to you, take some water from the Nile and pour it on the dry ground. The water you take from the river will become blood on the ground."
>
> **Moses**: "Pardon your servant, Lord. I have never been eloquent, neither in the past nor since you have spoken to your servant. I am slow of speech and tongue" (Ex 3:10-22, Ex 4:8-10)

Melancholy character attributes to cultivate

Because people with Phlegmatic and Melancholy temperaments are introverts, the character traits discussed under the melancholy temperament will also apply to the Phlegmatic leader as well. Leaders with melancholy temperament need to cultivate openness to experiences, initiative, courage and drive.

Character shaping for the melancholy could focus on self-affirmation, resisting negative thoughts and feelings, and spending more time on positive engagements away from self-preoccupation. Besides, melancholy leaders can increase their level of influence by cultivating the following attributes:

a. Inspiration

Inspiration refers to the ability to motivate others to perform at their best. A study carried out by the Harvard Business Review found the quality of being centered key to being an inspirational leader. Centeredness is a state of mind, which enables one to remain calm under stress.

Inspiring leaders empathize, listen deeply, and remain present. Organizations realize real breakthrough when employees are not just engaged but are inspired. Melancholy leaders need to cultivate the inspiration attribute to counter their tendency to be depressed, suspicious, revengeful and self-centered, which undermine their ability to motivate and inspire others.

b. Justice

Justice is the ability to deal with others lawfully and fairly. It involves the equitable distribution of corrections and rewards.[24] Justice produces legitimate decisions that are accepted and reasonable to others, thus soliciting their support. Just leaders deal with their followers in a fair and socially responsible manner.[25]

Due to their pessimistic and hard to please nature, melancholy leaders at times make unreasonable decisions that are considered unacceptable by others. They tend to be too soft to their favorite players and too harsh to those who fall out of favor with them. That is why they need to cultivate the character attribute of justice.

c. Respect

Melancholy leaders are natural perfectionists who set very high standards for themselves and others. They find it hard to understand and accommodate people who do not reach their set standards. They easily get frustrated and irritated by their followers who do not pay attention to details and who do not function decently and in order. There natural reaction to such people is to look down and dismiss them without a second thought. They need to cultivate the character attribute of respect to be able to appreciate the contribution of others even when it does not meet their set standards.

Respect is "holding others in high regard and treating them the way you wish to be treated."[26] Leaders with Melancholy temperament can cultivate respect trait by:

- Being considerate
- Appreciating others' contributions,
- Accepting others as they are
- Appreciating diversity
- Talking respectively about others
- Resolving interpersonal conflicts amicably and
- Not hurting others intentionally.

3. The Phlegmatic temperament

The Phlegmatic personality is relaxed, quiet and warm. Her easygoing nature combined with a clever wit and dry humor make her well-liked by others. Being valued and appreciated means a lot to her. Also, having people around her get along is more important than logic, facts, rules or adventure.[27]

Like the other temperaments, the Phlegmatic temperament comes with some weaknesses, which can become a liability if unaddressed. Chief among these weaknesses is lack of motivation. The Phlegmatic can postpone work indefinitely. Other weaknesses include being stubborn, stingy and indecisive.

Table 3.4 below displays the Phlegmatic character strengths and weaknesses.

Table 3. 4. Phlegmatic strengths and weaknesses

Character strengths	Character weaknesses

Active listener,	Cautious
Adaptable,	Indecisive,
Diplomatic	Lack of drive,
Easy going,	Passive participant,
Efficient,	Procrastinator,
Humble,	Reserved and distant,
Mediator,	Risk-averse,
Reliable	Self-protective,
Stable,	Slow in movement,
Witty,	Resistant to change,
Tactful.	Constant mood

Impact of the Phlegmatic character weaknesses

Individuals with the Phlegmatic temperament have great potential for leadership due to their ability to get along easily with others. However, their lack of personal drive, lack of initiative, resistance to change and the fear to take risks can limit their ability to accept the leadership role and influence others.

Effective Leaders are risk takers who embrace change take the initiative to influence others. For the Phlegmatic to lead change, she must take risks and initiative to do things.

Case Study 3. 4. Abraham the Phlegmatic

The Bible has a good share of personalities who fit the characteristics of a Phlegmatic. Among them, we have Abraham, Joseph, Timothy, and Barnabas. In this case study, we look at the Phlegmatic character traits of Abraham:

a. **Abraham was cautious**

It seems difficult for a Phlegmatic to trust God or other people fully. They tend to be hesitant, indecisive and cautious, and so they take precautionary measures just in case things do not turn out as promised. That is what Abraham did when God instructed him to go from his country, his people and his father's household to the land God would show him (Gen 12:1-9).

> So, Abraham left as God told him, but he took with him Lot his nephew, who was part of his father's household, which he was supposed to leave. He also took his wealth and the people he had acquired at Haran, as security measure just in case God did not come through. That is characteristic of

Phlegmatic personalities. They struggle with doubts, which lead to their indecisiveness and cautious approach to life.

b. Abraham was a peacemaker

Phlegmatic individuals treasure peace and dislike anything that attempts to disrupt harmony in their lives. Abraham displayed this trait when a quarrel broke up between his workers and those of Lot his nephew, whom he should have left behind in the first place.

So Abraham said to Lot, "Let's not have any quarreling between you and me, or between your herders and mine, for we are close relatives. Is not the whole land before you? Let's part company. If you go to the left, I'll go to the right; if you go to the right, I'll go to the left (Gen 13:8-9).

Phlegmatic leaders value peace so much that they will sacrifice relationships for the sake of maintaining their peace, and that is what Abraham did.

c. Abraham was reliable

You can trust the Phlegmatic come through for you in time of need. That is what Abraham did when his separated Lot got into trouble.

Lot happened to be caught up in a battle between two warring alliances of kings where the winning side seized all the goods of Sodom and Gomorrah and all their food; then they went away. They also carried off Abraham's nephew Lot and his possessions, since he was living in Sodom.

When Abraham heard that his relative had been taken captive, he called out the 318-trained men born in his household and went in pursuit as far as Dan. Abraham recovered all the goods and brought back his relative Lot and his possessions, together with the women and the other people (Gen 14:1-16).

Considering their previous quarrel and eventual breakup, Abraham could have said, 'serves him right' after all Lot had taken the best pastureland. However, not Abraham the Phlegmatic, he was dependable at Lot's hour of need.

d. Abraham was passive

Due to their lack of drive, initiative, and courage to take risks,

Phlegmatic leaders tend to be passive, which creates room for the leader's close associates to run the show. The passive trait influences the leader to adopt a hands-off leadership style where the leader does not get involved in what is happening in the organization until things get out of hand.

In Abraham's case, this trait is exposed by the conflict between his wife Sarah and her maid Hagar. The conflict begins with Sarah asking Abraham her husband to sleep with her slave and raise an heir family through her since they did not have a child and God was not keen on fulfilling his promise. Abraham as the Phlegmatic he passively agrees with Sarah's idea sleeps with Hagar and Ishmael is conceived.

As soon as Hagar knows she is pregnant, she begins to despise her mistress. So, Sarah says to Abraham, "You are responsible for the wrong I am suffering. I put my maid in your arms, and now that she knows she is pregnant, she despises me. May the Lord judge between you and me." Again, typical of his passiveness Abraham replies "Your slave is in your hands, "Do with her whatever you think best." Then Sarah mistreats Hagar; so she flees from her (Gen 16:1-6).

Abraham's passive character trait is evident in many other situations including the lying incidences where he persuades his wife to identify herself as his sister.

Phlegmatic character attributes to cultivate
a. Courage
Courage is the ability to do something difficult, dangerous or risky despite the knowledge of possible negative consequences. Courageous leaders make difficult choices and confront the decisions and actions of others when necessary.

Phlegmatic leaders need the courage to make prompt decisions and take action once they have made a decision. This attribute will boost their ability to take the initiative, overcome procrastination and take necessary risks. They need the courage to confront difficult situations head-on and provide direction when needed.

b. Openness to experience
Openness to experience is defined as the personal capacity to entertain different ideas, embrace new experiences and to change

one's behavior accordingly (Business Dictionary). People who are open to experience portray intellectual curiosity, imagination, creativity and, are open to new experiences. They are sensitive to other people's inner feelings even as they seek variety.

Phlegmatic leaders are known for their resistance to change. They prefer operating in the familiar ground where they feel safe and confident. That is why they need to cultivate the openness attribute.

Openness to experience will enhance the Phlegmatic leadership ability by creating a safe environment that allows others to participate in decision-making, accommodate dissent, loyal criticism, and encourage information sharing.

c. Extroversion

Phlegmatic type personalities are natural introverts. They enjoy their own company and prefer to work alone as a way of protecting their personal space. By cultivating the extroversion attribute, they stand a better chance of emerging as leaders and enhancing their leadership effectiveness.[29]

People with this character attribute are outgoing, talkative, sociable and enjoy social occasions. Because of their social dominance, and energy, they inspire confidence which makes people want to follow them. By practicing these behaviors, the Phlegmatic person can become an extrovert by learning.

d. Drive

In some studies,[30] this attribute is called passion and, it describes a strong feeling of enthusiasm or excitement for something or about doing something. Drive is the urge to satisfy a need or to set, pursue and achieve goals.

Followers are more likely to follow a leader with drive and one who shows more excitement and enthusiasm than one who is indifferent. A passionate leader is more persuasive and convincing. Phlegmatic leaders need to cultivate their drive trait to overcome their lack of initiative and the tendency to be passive and unmotivated.[31]

Childhood Experiences

The second most powerful influence on your character after your temperament is your childhood experiences. Such influences center on family life, environment, and adversity. Family-related experiences include early childhood upbringing, the social economic environment in which one grew and other childhood experiences. Below we look at specific factors that impact one's character as a child.

a. Family Background

Early childhood family background has a great impact on the formation of a leader's character. Evidence from research indicates, "The type of emotional support that a child receives during the first three and a half years affects education, social life, and romantic relationships even 20 or 30 years later.[32] Other factors related to family background include:

- Death of parents
  Early childhood bereavement leaves children at higher risk of criminal behavior [33]
- Parents' Divorce
- Trauma, e.g. being abandoned
- Unhappy homes
- Verbal, Physical and sexual abuse among others.

Scientific research has confirmed beyond doubt the impact of early childhood experiences on one's character. According to studies dated as early as the 1930s on the impact of early childhood experiences and personality development, "Inadequate maternal care in childhood and separation of children from those they know and love hurt personality development."[34]

a. Environment

The natural surroundings of the child's home during the formative years play a major role in shaping a person's character. A person growing up in the village will have a different set of values, perceptions, and assumptions about life from the one who grew up in a modern city surrounded by all the luxuries that life can offer.

Village dwellers easily notice people from the city by the way they walk, talk and behave. The same for people from the village when they visit the city, they are easily noticeable in the way they carry themselves.

Case Study 3. 5. The impact the Environment on character
Two great leaders in the New Testament help illustrate the impact

of the environment on character formation. The first one is Saul, who later became the Apostle Paul, and the second one is the Apostle Peter.

Paul grew up in the city, exposed to the best teachers of his time Acts 22:3. He later socialized with the elite Pharisee class of religious leaders. He grew up to be a man of great convictions, courage, and determination. This man could stand before the Greek philosophers of his time and hold their attention without wavering.

> At one time,
> A group of Epicurean and Stoic philosophers began to debate with him. Some of them asked, "What is this babbler trying to say?" Others remarked, "He seems to be advocating foreign gods." They said this because Paul was preaching the good news about Jesus and the resurrection. Then they took him and brought him to a meeting of the Areopagus, where they said to him, "May we know what this new teaching is that you are presenting? You are bringing some strange ideas to our ears, and we would like to know what they mean (Acts 17:18-20)."
> Apostle Peter, on the other hand, grew up in the village of Bethsaida in the province of Galilee with limited exposure. Peter had no formal education, which explains his limited worldview. Later in life, he had difficulty accepting that the Gentiles could be partakers of the gospel with the Jews. His view of the kingdom of God was limited to the Jews.
> At one time Paul had to rebuke him openly for acting hypocritically. "For before certain men came from James, he would eat with the Gentiles; but when they came, he withdrew and separated himself, fearing those who were of the circumcision. And the rest of the Jews also played the hypocrite with him, so that even Barnabas was carried away with their hypocrisy" (Gal 2: 12-13).

Reflection question
a. Does the environment have any impact on a leader's character formation? Discuss giving examples where applicable.
b. Think of someone you know from a different ethnic background. How has his or her environment affected his or her character? (Hint: beliefs, values, practices).

c. Adversity

Misfortunes such as a night of terror, a terrible accident or the treacherous betrayal by a friend can greatly affect a person's Character. A sudden change in the early childhood circumstances forces the child to summon new strength and power to cope with the uncomfortable circumstances. It often alters the elements that constitute character such as attitudes, values and basic beliefs.

A good example is a young girl who grew up to witness periodical physical abuse of her mother and siblings by her biological father. Such betrayal left her deeply hurt to the extent that she developed deep bitterness towards all men. As she grew up in this environment, she swore that she would never get married because according to her, all men were dogs who could not be trusted.

Training

Instructions from parents, teachers, and peers in the formative years play a major role in shaping one's character. Based on that understanding, the writer of the book of Proverbs in the Bible authoritatively said, "Train up a child in the way he should go, and when he is old, he will not depart from it" (Prov 22:6).

Leadership training can have a great impact on a leader's character. It helps leaders understand the importance of character, the desirable values associated with leadership character and the qualities that can be developed to enhance the leader's character. As leaders become aware of their character deficiencies and take the initiative to reflect and practice new habits, their character changes to reflect their new beliefs and practices.

Many leaders either overlook or ignore their need for leadership training because they are not aware of what they do not know. By so doing they end up sabotaging their leadership potential. Since they do not know what they do not know, they assume they are doing well. It eventually costs them their leadership role as their influence wanes instead of growing over time.

Case Study 3. 6. The impact of training on leaders Character

The 12 disciples present a good illustration of the impact of training on the leader's character. The book of Acts presents them as saints who sacrificed their lives to preach the kingdom and change the world. But, were they always that kind, loving and caring? Not really. The disciples presented in the four Gospels were of weak character and unpleasant to live with.

In the initial stages of their association with Jesus, they portrayed a wide range of character flaws that would undermine their ability to influence other people. Besides their individual character weaknesses, here are three examples of their initial character weaknesses that were later transformed through the three years of training they had with Jesus:

a. The disciples lacked courage

The disciples lacked the courage to face opposition and stand up for what they believed in. When Jesus was arrested they all ran and disserted him (Mark 14:50). Peter denied Jesus three times and even swore before a maid that he did not know Jesus, (Matt. 26:69-75). Later on, after Jesus was crucified, the disciples went and hid in fear of the Jews.

This great cowardice would later turn in to courage as they received the baptism of the Holy Spirit and as they reflected on the teachings of Jesus. The disciples became so courageous that even the authorities were amazed. Luke reports in Acts 4:13, that, "Now when they saw the boldness of Peter and John and perceived that they were uneducated and untrained men, they marveled. And they realized that they had been with Jesus."

b. The disciples were driven by selfish ambition

The disciples followed Jesus with mixed motives. They were more interested in their personal agenda than the kingdom of God which Jesus was advancing. They were interested in power and positions for selfish reasons. At one time they had a fierce argument about which one of them was the greatest. Luke 9:46-48 reports that;

> Then a dispute arose among them as to which of them would be greatest. And Jesus, perceiving the thought of their heart, took a little child and set him by Him, and said to them, "Whoever receives this little child in my name receives me, and whoever receives me receives Him who sent me. For he who is least among you all will be great.

In their efforts to outdo each other in gaining a position of prominence, two of them, John and James lobbied for the senior most position in Christ's Kingdom. They even send their mother to influence their master's decision (Mar 10:35-37). Later these same disciples become selfless leaders who changed character was demonstrated by their sacrifice and commitment to live for their master.

c. The disciples were prejudiced

Initially, the disciples were not only intolerant, they were prejudiced and discriminatory. They considered themselves the chosen ones from the favored nation. Like the other Jews, they looked down upon others who were not part of their privileged group. At one time they found another group preaching Jesus and they forbade them (Mark 9:38-39). Peter declined to visit the Gentiles at the invitation of Cornelius until God intervened and sent him a vision to convince him that the Gentiles were part of God's kingdom (Act 10).

Besides these three examples given here, the disciples struggled with many other character weaknesses like all of us do. Three years of training with Jesus and many more years of reflection, practice and teaching the same principles they learned from Jesus transformed them into men of character whose influence continues to be felt in the world up today.

Religious Faith and Character Development

Faith in any religion is a powerful tool for changing a leader's character. You may not always do what you preach, but you will always behave in accordance with what you believe in. Faith operates at the deepest level of the human beings. It influences our basic assumptions, believes and ultimately our practices. Faith is a heart issue and so is a person's character. Faith has the power to transform a human being from the inside out.

There is a big difference between the Christian faith and other religious faiths. While other faiths stop at human reasoning and recorded beliefs, Christian faith goes beyond that; it involves the transfer of life from the Godhead to the believer. The Christian believer who comes to God through faith in Christ receives the life of God. That transfer gives the believer the power to instantly and progressively partake the character of God. The Bible compares this transaction to a new birth according to John 1:12-13 which says:

> But as many as received Him, to them He gave the right to

become children of God, to those who believe in His name: who were born, not of blood, nor of the will of the flesh, nor of the will of man, but of God.

The human spirit gets regenerated at the point of the new birth and a new life principle is introduced in the believer's heart where character resides. Jesus refers to this new life in these words: "That which is born of the flesh is flesh, and that which is born of the Spirit is spirit," (Jn 3:6). The flesh here refers to man's natural inborn character and the spirit refers to the new nature, which Paul refers to in 2 Corinthians 5:17, where he says, "Therefore if anyone is in Christ, he is a new creation. The old has passed away; behold, the new has come."

While character transformation for the Christian believer is not automatic, it is provided for by faith. By faith the Christian:

- Is saved (Eph. 2:8).
- Has his heart cleansed, (Acts 15:9).
- Walks by faith, meaning, he draws life on the spirit of God within to do what is right rather than following the natural bodily senses (2 Cor. 5:7; Gal. 2:20), and
- Lives by faith (Heb. 10:38).

By believing and acting on the promises of God, the believer participates in the very character of God, as Peter points out in 2 Pet. 1:3-4 below:

> His divine power has granted to us all things that pertain to life and godliness, through the knowledge of him who called us to his own glory and excellence, by which he has granted to us his precious and very great promises, so that through them you may become partakers of the divine nature, having escaped from the corruption that is in the world because of sinful desire.

The question then remains, if our old nature, it can be modified by acquiring a new nature, then why do we have so many believers struggling with anger, lying, and bitterness among other many temperamental sins? Where do they miss it?

. According to Tim LaHaye, "Only one source of power can significantly modify our behavior that will appear to change our temperament,"[35] and that power is the Holy Spirit. Character transformation for a Christian is a process, and, becoming a

Christian is just the starting point. The Christian believer must learn to walk by faith to experience the transformational power of the new birth.

Here are four steps through which the Holy Spirit modifies the believer's temperament also called the old nature, the flesh, the old man and the natural man in the scriptures:

1. Receive Jesus Christ in your life.

The power to change from our old nature to the new nature comes from Christ because, "...as many as received Him, to them He gave the right to become children of God, to those who believe in His name." Trying to change your temperament without Christ's power is like trying to lift yourself from the ground using your shoestrings. Try it, and you will realize it does not work.

2. Be filled with the Holy Spirit

The Bible compares being filled with the Holy Spirit to being drunk with wine. In Ephesians 5:18 (ASV) we read, "And be not drunken with wine, wherein is riot, but be filled with the Spirit". Wine has one great impact on human behavior. It modifies human behavior significantly. My brother who is usually very quiet becomes talkative when under the influence of alcohol.

The Holy Spirit in control of the life of a believer has a similar effect. It diminishes the temperamental weaknesses by releasing more grace in the life of the believer. The Holy Spirit transforms the cruel Choleric to a gentle and gracious person; the moody melancholy manifests unusual joy, the attention seeking Sanguine forgets about himself and focuses on others while the polite Phlegmatic person becomes an outgoing person.

3. Meditate on the Word of God

The purpose of meditating on the Word of God is to saturate your mind with the word. Since a man is as he thinks, the idea is to reprogram our mind so that your thoughts are in line with God's instructions for you. For every temperamental weakness in your life, there is a scripture addressing it. A lifestyle of deliberate and focused meditation will shape your thinking pattern to match a godly character. Soon your changed thinking will show in your character.

4. Submit to the Holy Spirit

Paul uses the terms 'works of the flesh' the 'fruit of the Spirit' to compare the two opposing natures that reside in man. Both natures differ by the kind of manifestations they produce. On the one hand, the works of the flesh are adultery, fornication, uncleanness, lewdness, idolatry, sorcery, hatred, contentions, jealousies, outbursts of wrath, selfish ambitions, dissensions, heresies, envy, murders, drunkenness, revelries, and the like." On the other hand, the fruit of the Spirit is love, joy, peace, longsuffering, kindness, goodness, faithfulness, gentleness, self-control (Galatians 5:22-23).

The key determinant of whether you manifest the works of the flesh or the fruit of the Spirit is the life source you depend on. If your source is the flesh which stands for self then you know what to expect – the works of the flesh. If your source is the Holy Spirit who lives in you, then you will manifest the fruit of the spirit.

Jesus said, "Whoever believes in me, as scripture has said, rivers of living water will flow from within them." By this, he meant the Spirit, whom those who believed in him were later to receive" (Jn 7:38).

5. Spend time in God's presence

An encounter with God can have a lasting impact on your character. The Bible and history provide many examples of leaders whose character was transformed after encountering God.

Jacob had deep character flaws before his encounter with God.[36] To him, swindling people came as naturally as breathing in and out. First, he swindled his brother Esau of his birthright. He then deceived his father to give him the birthright blessing. Later on, he used dubious means to swindle his uncle Laban of his livestock (Gen 30: 25-43). Jacob was a conman. That was his character.

When Jacob met with the angel of the Lord (Gen 32: 22- 32) on his way to meet his brother Esau, that experience changed his character from that of a conman to that of a prince. The change in his name from Jacob to Israel reflected a deep-rooted character transformation that lasted for the rest of his life. From that moment, he never deceived anyone else.

Saul of Tarsus is another example of a person with deep character weaknesses. Before his encounter with the Lord Jesus Christ (Act

9:1- 30). Saul was a cruel, intolerant murderer who persecuted the Church of Jesus Christ like no other. Luke in Acts 1:1-2 describes him in these words:

> Then Saul, still breathing threats and murder against the disciples of the Lord, went to the high priest and asked letters from him to the synagogues of Damascus, so that if he found any who were of the Way, whether men or women, he might bring them bound to Jerusalem.

His encounter with Christ led to the change in his name from Saul to Paul. The change in his name reflected a dramatic transformation in his character, which we see in his New Testament letters to the Church. The rough, quick-tempered, cruel and impatient Saul became the gentle Apostle Paul who raised many leaders and laid the theological foundations of the New Testament church.

Although many of us may never have the privilege of a dramatic encounter with God as Jacob and Saul had, we all have the opportunity to experience God on a day-to-day basis with the same results.

You can shape your character by spending intimate time in the presence of God on a daily basis. Apostle Paul points out a direct relationship between character transformation and time spend with God in these words:

> I beseech you, therefore, brethren, by the mercies of God, that you present your bodies a living sacrifice, holy, acceptable to God, which is your reasonable service. And do not be conformed to this world, but be transformed by the renewing of your mind, that you may prove what is that good and acceptable and perfect will of God (Rom. 12:1-2).

Spending time with God reveals hidden character flaws through the conviction of the Holy Spirit, and provides the spiritual resources needed to deal with it through the grace of his son, Jesus Christ. Every serious leader should develop this habit for his or her benefit.

6. Guard your heart

There is a direct relationship between what goes in and what comes out of your heart. What goes into your heart determines what comes out. King Solomon in his wisdom pointed out the relationship between the heart and character in these words: "Above all else, guard your heart, for everything you do flows from it, (Prov 4:23, NIV). Jesus pointed out the centrality of heart to character development in these words:

> "A good man out of the good treasure of his heart brings forth good things, and an evil man out of the evil treasure brings forth evil things (Mat 12:35), and "… out of the heart proceed evil thoughts, murders, adulteries, fornications, thefts, false witness, blasphemies. These are the things which defile a man, but to eat with unwashed hands does not defile a man" (Mat 15:18-20).

Guarding your heart means watching what gets into and out of your heart. The key influencers of what enters your heart include:
- What you watch,
- What you listen to,
- What you read and,
- Whom you associate with.

Here are some measures you can take to guard your heart:

a. Watch what you see

Your eyes are openings to your heart. Whatever you allow your eyes to dwell on will affect the way you think, feel and eventually what you do. That is why Job said: "I made a covenant with my eyes not to look lustfully at a young woman", (Job 31:1, NIV).

What you watch affects either positively or negatively. For instance, watching pornography can lead to porn addiction and sexual perversion.[37] Watching violent movies is likely to produce aggressive behavior. Similarly, exposing yourself to violent media may cause violent behavior or lead to a favorable attitude towards violence."[38]

Many soap operas showing at homes in Television sets may appear innocent, but eventually, they stir lustful thoughts, which in turn fuel sexual desires beyond the control of those watching them. The outcome is a defiled conscience and clouded judgment about what is right, and what is wrong.

Similarly, watching negative media has a negative impact on the viewers' character, which soon shows in their behavior. For instance, research findings indicate, children who watch aggressive cartoon subsequently become more physically active, breaking toys, getting into fights and playing roughly.[39]

Research has also pointed to the negative impact of pornography on marriage. One study found that people who watched porn were more likely to engage in flirting outside their relationships and more likely to cheat in their marriages.[40]

Guarding your heart involves choosing what to watch and what not to. The pictures, movies, and the cartoons you watch never leave you the same. Watching persons of the opposite gender scarcely dressed has an even greater impact. Wise leaders avoid exposing their eyes to negative media to safeguard hearts from the addiction that comes with such exposure.

On the other hand, watching the right media can inspire and improve your leadership character especially if viewed with a leadership bias. Here is a list of eight Movies with valuable leadership lessons in no particular order:

- The Jesus film (1979),
- Apollo 13 (1995),
- Mandela: Long Walk to Freedom (2013),
- The Ten Commandments (1956),
- The Passion of the Christ (2004),
- Cry Freedom (1957),
- Gandhi (1982),
- Lincoln (2012)

The list is not exhaustive, but it serves as a good starting point. As you watch any of the movies, try to identify the leadership values and character traits that made the lead actor role stand out. After you have watched the movie, reflect on the key leadership lessons depicted in the movies.

b. Watch your thoughts

At the core of your character are thought patterns that produce behavioral patterns of actions and reactions. Your thoughts produce feelings that in turn produce actions. When you change your thinking, you change your feelings and your behavior.[41]

Frank Outlaw, Late President of the Bi-Lo Stores summed up the relationship between thoughts, feelings, and actions in this words:

Watch your thoughts; they become words. Watch your words; they become actions. Watch your actions; they become habits. Watch your habits; they become character. Watch your character; it becomes your destiny.

Guarding your heart involves self-awareness. It takes being conscious of your thoughts and deliberately choosing positive over negative thoughts. Apostle Paul understood the power of positive thinking and encouraged the Philippian believers with these words:

> Finally, brothers and sisters, whatever is true, whatever is noble, whatever is right, whatever is pure, whatever is lovely, whatever is admirable—if anything is excellent or praiseworthy—think about such things (Philippians 4:8).

Character transformation begins by focusing your thoughts on the character attribute you wish to develop. It involves meditating on the desirable qualities, and, considering how displaying the desired character traits would add value to your life as a leader.

c. Watch your company

The people you associate with influence you in different ways. These include your friends, colleagues, mentors and business associates. Your associates say and do things that leave a mark in your life. Associating with unethical will corrupt your character while associating with ethical people will leave you a better person.

The life of Jesus and His disciples provide a good illustration of the power of association. When Jesus called the 12 men to follow him, they were just ordinary men. For three years, the disciples walked, dined and listened to Jesus as he taught them about the life principles of his kingdom. When Jesus left them, they were different people. Even their worst critics could not deny that the changed in their lives. "Now when they saw the boldness of Peter and John and perceived that they were uneducated, common men, they were astonished. And they recognized that they had been with Jesus" (Acts 4:13, ESV). Yes, they took note that they had been with Jesus.

Even casual acquaintances can make exceptional impressions on your character, especially in the early years of our lives. Wise leaders under the power of association and choose their friends carefully. They look for mentors and role models who inspire them to greatness while avoiding the company of people who drag them to a life of mediocrity.

d. Watch what you read

There is power in the written word. Reading has a similar effect on a person's character as watching value loaded movies. It has the power to change lives positively or negatively based on what you read. For instance, "Reading aggression in literature can influence subsequent aggressive behavior, which tends to be specific to the type of aggression contained in the story."[42] Similarly, people who read a fictional description of physical violence were more likely to punish an irritating stranger by making him or her physically uncomfortable.

Conclusion

Character building is a lifelong process that begins in our infancy and continues until death. Many factors work together to shape your character including; your temperament, early childhood experiences, training, and, religious faith. The first step in character development is identifying specific character deficiencies and then develop an action plan for growth.

Wise leaders understand the power of association and choose their friends carefully. They look for mentors and role models to inspire them to greatness while avoiding the company of people who drag them to a life of mediocrity. They understand the power of the written word and develop the habit of reading carefully selected books.

References

1. Stogdill, R.M. (1974). Handbook of Leadership: A Survey of Theory and Research. The University of California, Free Press
2. Bentz, V.J. (1985, August). A view from the top: A thirty year perspective of research devoted to the discovery, description, and prediction of executive behavior. American Psychological Association, Los Angeles.
3. Lahaye, T. (1988). Why you act the way you do. Tyndale House Publishers
4. LaHaye, T. (1971). The Transformed Temperament. Wheaton, Illinois: Living Books, Tyndale Publishers, Inc.
5. LaHaye, T. (1984). Why you act the way you do. Carol Stream, Illinois: Tyndale Publishers, Inc.

6. Jensen, M. C. (Fall, 2009). Integrity: Without it Nothing Works. Rotman Magazine 2009. http://ssrn.com/abstract=1511274
7. Crossan, M., Gandz, J., Seijts, G. (January / February 2012). Developing Leadership Character. Ivey Business Journal.
8. Griffin, J. (How to Say it for the first-time managers: Winning Words and Strategies for Earning Your Team's Confidence. New York: Prentice Hall Press
9. Sarros, J. C., Cooper, B.K. & Hartican, A. M. (2006). Leadership and Character. Leadership & Organization Development Journal, Vol. 27 No. 8, pp. 682-699
10. Reave, L. (2005). Spiritual values and practices related to leadership effectiveness. Leadership Quarterly, 16, 655–687.
11. McCall, M., Spreitzer, G. & Maloney, J. (1994). Reprise: Identifying future international executives. Society of Industrial and Organizational Psychologists. National Conference, April 1994, Nashville, TN.
12. Dean, P. (2014). The 5 Fundamentals of Leadership personality. Wharton Magazine. http://whartonmagazine.com/
13. Quoted in McPhail. T. L. (2010). Global Communication: Theories, Stakeholders, and Trends. Malden, MA: Wiley-Blackwell Publishing.
14. Stamoulis, C. (2010). Critical Leadership Attributes: A Review of Leadership Attributes and Skills for the Retail Industry 2010 and Beyond. White paper. Leadership Learning Dynamics & Service Skills SA. http://www.retailexecutive.com.au/
15. Lahaye, T. (1971). The Transformed Temperament: A fresh look at how God changed Peter, Moses, Paul, and Abraham and how he can transform you. Wheaton. Illinois: Living Books, Tyndale Publishing House Inc.
16. Ricketts, C. & Ricketts, J. C. (2011). Leadership: Personal Development Career Success, Third Edition. United Kingdom, Delmar, Cengage Learning.
17. Salovey, P. &Mayer, J. D. (1990). Emotional Intelligence: Imagination, Cognition, and Personality. Vol. 9, pp. 185-211.
18. Goleman, D. (2004, January). What makes a leader? Harvard Business Review, 82(1), 82–91.

19. Daft, R. (2008). The Leadership Experience. Mason, OH. Thomas Learning Inc.
20. Sarros, J. C., Cooper, B. K. & Hartican, A. M. (2006). Leadership and character. Leadership & Organization Development Journal Vol. 27 No. 8, 2006 pp. 682-699
21. Sarros, J. C., Cooper, B. K. & Hartican, A. M. (2006). Leadership and character. Leadership & Organization Development Journal Vol. 27 No. 8, 2006 pp. 682-699
22. Crossan, M., Gandz, J., Seijts, G.(January / February 2012). Developing Leadership Character. Ivey Business Journal.
23. Cooper, B. K., Sarros, J. C. & Santora, J. C. (May/June 2007). The Character of Leadership. Ivy Business Journal. Issue.
24. IEP. (n.d.). Western Theories of Justice. A peer-reviewed resource. http://www.iep.utm.edu/justwest/
25. Crossan, M., Gandz, J., Seijts, G.(2016). Developing Leadership Character. New York, NY. Routledge, Taylor & Francis.
26. Lumpkin, A. (2009). Modern Sports Ethics: A Reference Handbook. Santa Barbra, CA: ABC CLIO.
27. Littauer, F. (2011). Personality plus for couples: Understanding yourself and the one you love. Grand Rapids, MI: Fleming H. Revell.
28. Costa, P. T. & McCrae, R. R. (1992). NEO personality Inventory professional manual. Odessa, FL: Psychological Assessment Resources.
29. Goldberg, L. R. (1990). An alternative "description of personality": The big-five factor structure. Journal of Personality & Social Psychology, 59, 1216–1229.
30. Barker, C. and Coy, R. (2003). The 7 Heavenly Virtues of Leadership, Management Today Series, McGraw-Hill, Sydney.
31. Kirkpatrick, S.A. and Locke, E.A. (1991), "Leadership: do traits matter?", Academy of Management Executive, Vol. 5 No. 2, pp. 48-60.
32. Raby, K. L., Fraley, R.C., Roisman, G. I. & Simpson, J. A. (2015, May/June). The Enduring Predictive Significance of Early Maternal Sensitivity: Social and Academic Competence through Age 32 Years. Child development. Vol. 86. No. 36. Pp. 695- 708.

33. Mack, K.Y. (2001, Jul-Aug). Childhood family disruptions and adult well-being: the differential effects of divorce and parental death. Death Stud.; 25(5):419-43.
34. Castillo, H. (2003). Personality Disorder: Temperament or Trauma. London. Jessica Kingsley Publishers.
35. LaHaye, T. (1991). I Love You, But Why Are So Different? Making the Most of Your Personality Differences in Marriage. Eugene, Oregon: Harvest House Publishers.
36. Wilson, R. F. (2018). Jacob the Deceiver: Discipleship Lessons from the Life of Jacob. Jesus Walk Bible Study Series.
37. Lousada, M. & Mazanti, L. (2017). Real Sex: Why Everything You Learnt About Sex Is Wrong. Hay House Inc.
38. Nicholas, L. (Ed). Introduction to Psychology, 2nd Edition. Cape Town, UTC Press.
39. Heffner, C. L. & Tompkins, A. (2003). The Psychological Effects of Violent Media on Children. AllPsych Journal.
40. Lambert, N, M., Negash, S., Tyler F.S., Spencer B. O.; Fincham, F. M. (2012) "A Love That Doesn't Last: Pornography Consumption and Weakened Commitment to One's Romantic Partner," Journal of Social and Clinical Psychology, vol.31, no.4, 410-438.
41. Borek, J., Lovett, D. & Towns, E. (2005, p.130). The Good Book on Leadership: Case studies from the Bible. Nashville, Tennessee. Broadman & Holman Publishers.
42. Coyne, S. M., Ridge, R., Stevens, M., Callister, M.; Stockdale L. (2011). Backbiting and bloodshed in books: British Journal of Social Psychology, Volume 51, Issue 1 March 2012 Pages 188–196

Chapter Four

Clarifying Your Vision

Introduction

Many books on leadership and management discuss vision as something a person crafts based on his intellectual ability and logical analysis. The challenge with that approach is the assumption that the creature can actually discover it purpose without reference to its maker. This book takes a different approach to vision development based on the following two assumptions:

a. God made everything that exists

Everything in this universe has a beginning. Someone made it for a purpose. That includes you, everything and everyone else that has ever existed. The Bible attributes the existence of everything to God's creation. Accordingly, "God made everything with a place and purpose; even the wicked are included - but for judgment" (Prov. 16:4, MSG).

b. God made everything for a purpose

Since God made everything in the universe, He has a unique purpose for every generation and every person that has ever lived in this world. That includes you and me. Therefore, "Your purpose in life is to find your purpose and give your whole heart and soul to it."[1] The key to your greatness is serving God's purpose for your life. Greatness and glory are not found in titles, positions or wealth. That is why the best thing you can do for yourself and the world is to find God's purpose and serve it.

Identifying Your Life Purpose

Purpose defines the function, and function leads to vision. In other words, your vision is an educated guess of how life will look like after you have lived your purpose. Trying to develop your vision before clarifying God's purpose for your life is like putting the plow ahead of the ox. It does not work.

Your life purpose on earth can be discovered. It defines who you are and the function you were born to serve.[2] It is an enduring conviction and longing in your life that never gets extinguished. As long as it is undiscovered, it keeps beckoning and nagging you on.

A clear sense of purpose gives meaning to your life. It generates passion and the energy to strive to make a difference. Without a clear purpose, you meander through life aimlessly in search for meaning. It is boring, meaningless and unfulfilling. Its end if filled with regrets, and despair especially towards the end of your days on earth.

The following 3 steps will get you closer to pinpointing God's purpose for your life. Reflect on each step and prayerfully listen to your maker's voice as you read through:

1. **Read your user manual.**
The first step in discovering the purpose for anything involves understanding the creator's mind. The creator explains the purpose and functions of his creation in the user manual. The user manual describes the maker's purpose for inventing items made, cautions against the wrong use and provides the user with systematic procedures for access and maximum use.

God, the creator of the universe, has given mankind the Bible to reveal his purposes for the creation. The surest way to find out your purpose, therefore, is to read your creator's user manual. From the Bible we discover the following broad purposes for man:

a. To be God's delegated authority
God created man to act as his delegated authority on earth. The Bible, which is God's user manual for man explains the purpose of man in these words,

> Then God said, "Let us make mankind in our image, in our likeness, so that they may rule over the fish in the sea and the birds in the sky, over the livestock and all the wild animals, and over all the creatures that move along the ground (Gen 1:26-27).

Authority means the right to act in a specified way, delegated from one person or organization to another. It includes the power or right to give orders, make decisions, and enforce obedience (Oxford English Dictionary. The man was made to have the authority and to rule over God's creation on behalf of God. That is his purpose, to exercise delegated authority.

b. To bring God glory
God created every person to bring glory to him. Isaiah says

"...Bring my sons from afar, and my daughters from the ends of the earth—everyone who is called by my name, whom I have created for my glory; I have formed him, yes, I have made him" (Isa 43:6-7).

But what does it mean to bring glory to God? It means to bring honor to Him through what we say, what we do, and how we think. Apostle Paul writing to the Corinthian believers encourages, "So whether you eat or drink or whatever you do, do it all for the glory of God" (1 Cor 10:31). The idea is to draw attention to God's goodness and greatness. Jesus urged his disciples to bear much fruit because by so doing they would bring glory to God (Jn 15:8). Bearing fruit means living in a way that draws attention to God's character and works.

c. To do good works

The function determines the form and shape of creation. The auto manufacturer has travel and transport in mind before he makes the automobile. God created every man to perform a specific function in a specific place at a given time. God describes the man as "... God's handiwork, created in Christ Jesus to do good works, which God prepared in advance for us to do" (Eph. 2:10).

It is not enough to understand God's broad purpose for man. Knowing man's general purpose is the beginning. It lays the foundation for discovering our specific purpose. From there, each one of us must discover his or her specific works prepared in advance for him or her. Your divine authority functions best with that function. It is the specific way to bring glory to God and live a fulfilling life.

Only those who have discovered God's specific purpose for their lives can say like Paul at the end of life. "I have fought the good fight, I have finished the race, I have kept the faith."

2. Ask your maker

Step two in discovering God's purpose for your life is to ask God, your maker. Leading companies provide user manuals and maintain vigorous customer service department to address customer concerns. The purpose of the customer service department is to satisfy specific customer concerns that the user manual does not address. Best practice customer service requires 24-hour communication channel that serves customers as they call.

God has provided man with unlimited access to his presence to ask for anything that matters to him. That is possible through prayer. God has pledged to answer and reveal great and unsearchable things to a man in response to prayer (Jer 33:3). He is able and willing to reveal his specific purpose for your life because he is the author of that purpose.

The Bible records many incidences when God revealed his purpose for particular individuals. For instance:

- God created Pharaoh to show his power in him, and that God's name may be declared in all the earth (Ex. 9:16).
- Jesus was born to be a king and to bear witness to the truth (Jn 18:37) and to destroy the works of the devil (1 Jn 3:8).
- Jeremiah was born to be a prophet (Jer 1:5), and
- Paul was born to be an apostle of Jesus Christ and to take the gospel to the Gentiles (Act 9:15).

3. Examine your functional abilities

Every product is designed to fulfill its purpose. You are no exception. You can learn a lot about your purpose by exploring your special abilities. As you look within yourself, you will find clues, to guide you in your search for your life purpose. These include your passion, talents, natural strengths and your spiritual gifts. Other not so obvious abilities include the ability to get along well with other people, sense of humor, attention to details, and so on. All these special abilities have a role to play in God's purpose for your life.

The following are some questions to consider as you look within for clues to your life purpose:

a. What are you passionate about?

Your passion is your source of motivation. It reveals what inspires you and stirs the fire within you. Passion releases creative energy within you. Identify activities you engage in that leave you feeling strong and fired for more action. There lies your most obvious pointer to your life purpose.

b. What do you do best?

You perform your best when your efforts are aligned with your

life purpose. That is where you produce maximum output with

minimum effort. If you do not know what you do best, ask your friends and associates. They know what you do best. That is where people comment on your performance. What you do best is something people want you to do over and over again because they enjoy your performance.

c. What gives you maximum satisfaction?

To answer this question, you need to focus on what you do for pleasure. Consider your hobbies. What do you do to pass time? What is that one thing you like to do whenever you have a free moment? Within your life purpose, you not only enrich others but also get fulfillment. The key to living a fulfilled life is discovering and living your purpose.

d. What bothers you?

In life, there are things you do not notice, and if you do, they do not bother you. Such things lie beyond the scope of your purpose. Matters related to your purpose attract your attention. You notice when they are happening and when they are not. You also notice when certain things are not done well. What you notice and what bothers you are closely related to your life purpose.

Once you identify what attracts your attention, what makes you angry and what burdens your heart with concern, you will be within the range of your life purpose. Your answer to these four questions will point to the same direction. As you consider the answers to the questions prayerfully, God will confirm his purpose for you. "Identify your life's purpose, and you'll have the unique compass that will lead you to your true north every time."[3]

Case Study 4. 1: David served God's purpose

The Bible in the New Testament sums up David's life in these simple words; For David, after he had served the purpose of God in his own generation, fell asleep, …(Act 13:36, NASB). That is the best compliment anyone can ever get at the end of his or her life! He accomplished his life's assignment.

Of course, David accomplished much in his lifetime. He was a man after God's own heart; he killed Goliath, he was a mighty warrior, the greatest king Israel ever had, a worshiper, and so on! All that and much more is summed up in this statement - he served God's purpose in his generation.

But who is this David and how did he serve God's purpose in his own generation? David was the last born in Jesse's family of eight sons. After God rejected Saul as king over Israel, He instructed Prophet Samuel to go to Jesse's house to anoint Saul's replacement. Unfortunately, God did not specify which one of Jesse's son's he had chosen. So Samuel visited Jesse's house to anoint a king over Israel (1 Sam 16:1-13).

Jesse paraded his seven sons before the prophet, but none of them qualified to be God's anointed. So Samuel asked: "Are all the young men here?" Then he [Jesse] said, "There remains yet the youngest, and there he is, keeping the sheep." And Samuel said to Jesse, "Send and bring him. For we will not sit down till he comes here," (1 Sam 16:11).

That was David, a boy so insignificant that even his father did not invite him to such a great occasion where a king was being anointed from his own family. That is the same man the New Testament testifies that he served God's purpose in his generation. All his life was marked by service to God and his fellow men. Below are a few cases of his service to God through his fellow men:

a. David served His family

David faithfully served his family without complaining. In 1 Sam 16:11 he is out in the fields taking care of his father's livestock while the rest of the family is having a great ceremony. Besides, he was also the family's errand boy. In 1 Samuel 17:20-22, we see him taking supplies to his brothers as they served in King Saul's army. He did this without complaining.

b. David served His flock

David did not just take care of his father's flock, he risked his life to protect his herd from world animals. In 1 Samuel 17:34-35 David narrates his commitment to his flock in these words:

> Your servant used to keep his father's sheep, and when a lion or a bear came and took a lamb out of the flock, I went out after it and struck it, and delivered the lamb from its mouth; and when it arose against me, I caught it by its beard, and struck and killed it.

c. David served the King

David served God's purpose in his generation by serving King

Saul. 1 Sam 16:21 and 23 records;

> So David came to Saul and stood before him. And he loved him greatly, and he became his Armorbearer. And so it was, whenever the spirit from God was upon Saul, that David would take a harp and play it with his hand. Then Saul would become refreshed and well, and the distressing spirit would depart from him.

David did more than play music for the king. He fought the king's battles. He killed Goliath and fought the Philistines on behalf of the king. David served the king's best interest until the day King Saul died.

d. David served the disadvantaged

David not only served the great and the famous, he also served the disadvantaged and the vulnerable. Among this group were a group of misfits who followed him to the caves of Adullam when he ran away from King Saul's threats. 1 Samuel 22:2 describes them in these words: "And everyone who was in distress, everyone who was in debt, and everyone who was discontented gathered to him. So he became captain over them. And there were about four hundred men with him."

This may look normal under normal circumstance but not for a person in David's situation. He already had enough trouble with his master the king who was trying to kill him. What value would men in distress, in debt and discontented lot add to him anyway? The last thing he needed was more trouble from social misfits like these men. But David accepted them and became a captain over them. And guess what, in a few years, he turned them into the mighty men of David (2 Sam 23:8-17).

Besides the discontented and the distressed, David served the vulnerable. A good example of David's concern for the disadvantaged and the vulnerable is illustrated in 2 Samuel 9:6-7 which states the following;

> Now when Mephibosheth the son of Jonathan, the son of Saul, had come to David, he fell on his face and prostrated himself. Then David said, "Mephibosheth?" And he answered, "Here is your servant!" So David said to him, "Do not fear, for I will surely show you kindness for Jonathan your father's sake, and will restore to you all the land of Saul your grandfather; and you

shall eat bread at my table continually." Mephibosheth was a cripple who could never repay David's kindness in any way. Yet David reached out to him and restored his father's property to him. He also provided housing and food for Mephibosheth in his entire life. As if that was not enough, he elevated his status to the status of the ruling class.

Mephibosheth dined with the king continually. Few people in David's position are willing to take someone without a possible way of repaying them and treat them the way he treated Mephibosheth

e. **David served his nation - 1 Sam 17:32 1 Sam 23:1ff,**
David's life purpose was to serve as the king of Israel. God revealed that purpose to David through Prophet Samuel while was still a teenager. In 1 Samuel 16:1 God told Samuel; "Fill your horn with oil, and go; I am sending you to Jesse the Bethlehemite. For I have provided myself with a king among his sons."

David's contribution to God's purpose in his generation is extensive, but for our purpose let's look at a few examples:

- David defended God's people against the oppression by Philistines (1 Sam, 17)
- David revealed God's power by killing Goliath for humiliating God's people
- David contributed to true worship in the nation of Israel by composing many psalms. The Davidic worship is the foundation of today's worship style in the church
- David revealed much about the nature of God, his love, mercy and his faithfulness to his people
- David expanded the Physical kingdom of Israel
- David laid the foundation for building a temple for God

Reflections questions

- What lessons do we learn from David's life about finding and serving God's purpose in our generation?

From Your Purpose to Your Mission
After discovering your life purpose, your next step is to write down your mission statement, which is a written expression of what you do to fulfill your purpose. Ideally, your purpose should determine

your mission and should be developed before your organizational mission statement.

Personal purpose and mission are best actualized through the organizational setup. People with a purpose start organizations as a vehicle through which to pursue their purpose and mission. Those who cannot start their organizations look for organizations, which resonate with their mission and join them to work towards the fulfillment of their mission.

If you decide to start an organization join one as the chief executive, developing the organizational mission statement is the place to start your corporate leadership journey. An organizational mission statement describes the organization's purpose and, whom it serves and what it does for them.[4] It is a concise summary of the organization's reason for existence and what it does to fulfill the owners' purpose. It is stated in a simple, clear and easy manner that everyone can understand and remember.

Benefits of a Clear Mission Statement

Activities and events play an important role in the life of an organization. However, without a clear sense of mission, activities, and meetings can easily become an end in themselves, instead of serving as a means to fulfilling the God-given mission.

On the other hand, a clear, well-written mission statement delivers the organization from the risk of going through meaningless routines that do not contribute to the mission and vision of the organization. Below are four benefits of a well-written mission statement.

Having a clear written mission statement will help you and your organization in the following ways:

   a.   **It clarifies your direction**

A clear mission statement declares the purpose of existence for the organization and all those who interact with it.[5] It helps you to focus your efforts on what you want to accomplish. It helps you decide where to invest precious time and resources and why. It safeguards you from sideshows and other distractions that may keep you from doing what matters most. A clear direction frees you up to fulfill your purpose. It also helps rally your members around that one thing for which the organization exists to do.

A well-written mission statement can be a powerful tool for understanding, developing, and communicating important organizational objectives.

b. It defines expectations.

People join organizations for many reasons. Many employees join for the paycheck. At the point of entry, many do not understand the mission of the organization, and some do not even care. In volunteer organizations like the church, members come with various expectations and experiences from their previous organizations. A well-defined mission statement helps them to adjust and appreciate to see what is expected.

c. It informs the public.

A mission statement tells members the organization's main business. It also informs outsiders about what to expect. A clear mission statement serves as an announcement as to where the organization is headed so those going the same direction can get on board.

d. It serves as a decision-making criteria

Every organization faces many options on what to do and how to utilize its scarce resources. There are lots of needs and good things to do out there, that no one particular organization can fulfill in its entire lifetime. Faced with so many open doors, opportunities, demands and needs, a clear mission statement gives the organization a standard by which to weigh the options and decide whether the new ventures are taking it to where it wants to go.[6] It helps to decide when to say 'No' to opportunities and when to invest in new opportunities

Besides, a clear mission statement could serve as:

- The basis for aligning new members with the organizational direction
- Means to determine the positive change
- Guide in planning

Writing a clear mission statement

A Mission Statement is a one-sentence statement describing the reason a person, an organization or program exists. It is used to help guide decisions about priorities, actions, and responsibilities.[7] The best mission statements do not exceed one or two paragraphs and should be:

- **Concise.** It should be clear, and memorable. It should accurately explain why your organization exists and what it hopes to achieve in the future,[8]
- **Simple.** It should be expressed in a layman's language as opposed to technical terms or jargon,
- **Brief.** It should be short enough so that anyone connected to the organization can easily repeat it,
- **Inspiring.** It should express the purpose of your organization in a way that inspires support and ongoing commitment from members, it should motivate others to engage in pursuing key objectives actively,
- **Convincing.** It should be stated in a way that is persuasive and easy to grasp.

Examples of mission statements

The following are mission statements sampled from a wide range of organizations.

- To refresh the world in mind, body, and spirit. To inspire moments of optimism and happiness through our brands and actions- Coca-Cola Company.
- To revive believers, reach friends, and renew culture. Prism Volunteer organization[9]
- To follow our Lord and Savior, Jesus Christ, in working with the poor and oppressed to promote human transformation, seek justice and bear witness to the good news of the Kingdom of God - World Vision Kenya.

A vision statement is a future-oriented declaration of the organization's purpose and aspirations.[10] The purpose of a vision statement is to motivate, inspire and energize the members of your organization to rise and work towards the realization of the organization's desired future.

Vision is a vivid mental picture of a possible and desirable future, But that is not all, "A vision is not just a picture of what could be; it is an appeal to our better selves, a call to become something more."[11] It is an expression of how the organization will be when your mission is accomplished.

Clarifying Your Vision

By this time you have identified your life purpose and have a mission statement. It is now time to think about your vision. The word vision conjures different ideas in people's minds. To some, it is a mystical concept that is hard to grasp. To others, a vision is a literal dream received from the gods at night as one sleeps. To others still, is any goal that one want's to achieve.

For our purpose in this text, we treat vision as the future outcome of fulfilling your purpose and mission. It is a vivid mental picture of the future as it will appear after you have accomplished your life purpose and mission. It describes your life and your world after you have made your contribution to God's greater purpose for the universe. Your vision is a picture of the world after you have completed God's assignment for you on earth.

Ultimately then, vision is foresight, or forecast or, insight into the future. It is the picture of your destiny or accomplishment, or simply what you are meant to do or become.[12] According to Gray, vision is "the God-inspired ability to see a future that does not yet exist but should. This future is so Messiah-exalting and life-giving that people run into the future and drag back to the present."

Vision, how and where to get one
Leadership begins with a vision, and every leader should have a one. Maxwell calls it the "indispensable quality of leadership".[13] Vision is the quality that separates leaders from followers. A clear vision is necessary to provide direction and mobilize people to pursue the vision.

To be a leader without a vision is a contradiction of sorts because "The very essence of leadership is that you have to have a vision. It's got to be a vision you articulate clearly and forcefully on every occasion."[14] Without it, you may be a manager, a foreman, supervisor, director or whatever other title people may give you, but you are not a leader.

Developing a clear vision can be a challenging task for many leaders. That explains why there are so many leaders without a clear direction of where they are taking their people. Even those who have a vision, many cannot articulate that vision clearly.

Some people develop a clear vision at an early stage in their leadership journey without much struggle. But, for many, developing a clear vision is a slow, frustrating and a discouraging task. So, how does a leader develop a lifelong vision? What factors inspire leaders to develop a vision for their people? What follows is our attempt to identify inner motivations that trigger the formation of a vision in a leader's life.

1. **The drive to overcome challenges**

The desire to overcome an existing challenge is a strong vision trigger for some leaders. Some people love challenges. It provides an opportunity for some leaders to develop great dreams. A good example is David.

Case Study 4. 2: *David thrived on challenges*

David thrived on challenges. One day, young David was sent by his father to deliver supplies to his brothers who were soldiers in King Saul's army. As David arrived,

A champion named Goliath, who was from Gath, came out of the Philistine camp. His height was six cubits and a span. He had a bronze helmet on his head and wore a coat of scale armor of bronze weighing five thousand shekels; on his legs, he wore bronze greaves, and a bronze javelin was slung on his back. His spear shaft was like a weaver's rod, and its iron point weighed six hundred shekels. His shield bearer went ahead of him. Goliath stood and shouted to the ranks of Israel, "Why do you come out and line up for battle? Am I not a Philistine, and are you not the servants of Saul? Choose a man and have him come down to me. If he can fight and kill me, we will become your subjects; but if I overcome him and kill him, you will become our subjects and serve us." Then the Philistine said, "This day I defy the armies of Israel! Give me a man and let us fight each other. " On hearing the Philistine's words, Saul and all the Israelites were dismayed and terrified (1 Sam 17: 4-11).

Goliath may have terrified Saul and his soldiers but not David. On the contrary, the challenge stirred David to fight the giant. Not only that, this was not the first time for David to face a challenge head-on, he had killed a lion and a bear that had threatened to take away his flock. Goliath presented a challenge to David that he could not resist. His vision for the safety of his flock and that of his nation was motivated by his drive to confront and overcome challenges.

Reflection questions
a. What challenge did Goliath present to Saul and his army?
b. How did Saul and his soldiers react to Goliath's challenge?
c. How did David react to Goliath's challenge?
d. Do you know a leader who loves to tackle challenges? Explain

2. Self-interest

The fulfillment of a great vision brings with it many benefits to the leader. It promises power, fame, respect and financial gain and security. Some leaders are driven by self-interest and desire for a reward to develop and pursue great visions.

Case Study 4. 3: David, the giant slayer

David as a teenager was motivated by self-interest to face Goliath in a battle that appeared impossible. Besides other factors, the rewards promised to the would be the slayer of Goliath provided enough motivation for David to take the risk.

When David arrived at the battlefront, the battle lines were already drawn, and Israel soldiers were already intimidated. But before David could make a move, he overheard the soldiers talking about the rewards that would be given to whoever would slay the giant. So he asked:

What shall be done for the man who kills this Philistine and takes away the reproach from Israel?" and the soldiers replied: The man who kills him the king will enrich with great riches, will give him his daughter, and give his father's house exemption from taxes in Israel (1 Sam 17:25).

Reflection questions
a) What rewards did the king offer to whoever would kill Goliath?
b) Why do you think David was asking what was to be done to Goliath's killer?

The thought of the king's daughter for a wife, tax exemption for his family, freedom from forced labor to the state as well as many riches was enough to give him the courage to fight the giant. Likewise, some leaders are inspired by the benefits that come with the realization of a great vision.

3. Dissatisfaction with the status quo

Some visions arise from intolerance to unacceptable conditions. Some leaders unhappy with the status quo develop their visions in their search for a solution to the existing problem. The famous Martin Luther King's vision was born out of frustration with the discrimination and the injustice that he witnessed in his country. That vision expressed in these inspiring words: "I have a dream that my four little children will one day live in a nation where they will not be judged by the color of their skin, but by the content of their character"[15] has lived to inspire hundreds of other leaders today.

Sometimes dissatisfaction with the status quo comes as a deep concern for the people combined with a strong urge to provide a solution. Such was the case of Nehemiah regarding Jerusalem. Read the account as narrated by Nehemiah in the case study below:

Case Study 4. 4: Nehemiah rebuilds the wall of Jerusalem

It happened:

> "…that Hanani one of my brethren came with men from Judah; and I asked them concerning the Jews who had escaped, who had survived the captivity, and concerning Jerusalem. And they said to me, "The survivors who are left from the captivity in the province are there in great distress and reproach. The wall of Jerusalem is also broken down, and its gates are burned with fire." So it was, when I heard these words that I sat down and wept, and mourned for many days; I was fasting and praying before the God of heaven (Neh 1:2-4).
>
> The king said to me, "What is it you want?"
>
> Then I prayed to the God of heaven, and I answered the king, "If it pleases the king and if your servant has found favor in his sight, let him send me to the city in Judah where my ancestors are buried so that I can rebuild it" (Nehemiah 2:4-5).

Reflection questions
a) What report did Hanan give to Nehemiah?
b) How did Nehemiah react to the news about Jerusalem?
c) What step did Nehemiah take to solve the problem at Jerusalem?

Nehemiah's vision to build the wall of Jerusalem developed out of his concern for the people in Jerusalem. The report from one of his brothers Hanani laid a heavy burden on his heart. So heavy was the burden that he sat down, wept, mourned for days, prayed and fasted. Out of this great need was born a mission and vision for Nehemiah. In his vision, Nehemiah saw a safer Jerusalem secured by a wall around it where the inhabitants lived in peace. The vision was a wall around the city of Jerusalem, and the mission was, to build the wall of Jerusalem.

4. Available Resources and opportunities

While resources follow the vision under the normal circumstances, it is not unusual to have a vision sparked by the available resources. For instance, a leader has a piece of land, money, buildings and as a result, he starts to wonder, how can I use these resources constructively? Out of this question, a leader may come up with a vision that goes a long way in meeting a felt need.

The same goes for opportunities that come along your way. When Esther was reluctant to intercede for the nation of Israel as it faced possible extinction from Haman's threat, this is how Mordecai responded:

> Do not think in your heart that you will escape in the king's palace any more than all the other Jews. For if you remain completely silent at this time, relief and deliverance will arise for the Jews from another place, but you and your father's house will perish. Yet who knows whether you have come to the kingdom for such a time as this?" (Est 4:13-14).

Wherever you are, whatever resources you have, God may have arranged your circumstances for such a time as this. Your vision may lie there.

5. Imitating success

Some people get their vision by copying what others are doing. Sometimes it is something that worked for them in the past, and so they try to repeat it over and over again. The logic behind imitation of success is the belief that what worked yesterday will work today or, what worked for the other organization will work for us!

While it is okay to copy those who appear successful, a Christian leader should not rush to imitate the vision of others no matter how successful they have been. It is okay to copy methods and even strategies, but not the vision itself. God-given visions are unique and personal, and the Christian leader should seek assurance that what they are pursuing is God's vision for the people. It is also hard to keep a borrowed vision in the long run.

6. Vain ambition

Selfish ambition refers to the "motivation to elevate oneself or to put one's interests before another's." It is a self-above-others approach. Self-importance, vanity, and egoism can drive a leader to come up with lofty visions to draw other people's attention to their importance.

Leaders who are driven by vain ambition thirst for praise and recognition from other people. That need drives them to come up with impressive visions as a proof of their power and greatness. They imagine how success would make them feel important, how people would bow before them, and how much glory would be theirs as people see what they have accomplished.

Case Study 4. 5: Beware of vain ambition

Vain ambition is not the right motivation of vision for a leader.

God speaking through prophet Jeremiah sounded a warning against leaders who would develop and pursue lofty visions driven by vain ambition. To such leaders, He said, "And do you seek great things for yourself? Seek them not, for behold; I am bringing disaster upon all flesh, declares the Lord. But I will give you your life as a prize of war in all places to which you may go" (Jer 45:5 ESV).

7. Revealed vision

God has an agenda for this world, and He accomplishes that agenda through people whom he reveals His purpose to and empowers them to do as He pleases. The question however is, how does God reveal his vision to his people?

To some, he speaks audibly. To others, he speaks through dreams, visions, and circumstances. God can also use other people to reveal his vision and purpose for you.

As a visionary God, He makes known the end from the beginning and reveals things that are still to come. Through the mouth of Isaiah, he declared, "I make known the end from the beginning, from ancient times, what is still to come. I say, 'my purpose will stand, and I will do all that I please" (Isa 46:10).

Even before God created man, he anticipated that man would fall. So he provided Christ as "... the Lamb who slain from the creation of the world" (Rev 13:8).

God is the author of vision

Having defined vision as foresight, in this section, we examine scriptures that point to God's visionary leadership. The Bible has plenty of illustrations pointing to God's visionary nature. Through the prophet Isaiah, God declared concerning himself, "I make known the end from the beginning, from ancient times, what is still to come. I say, 'my purpose will stand, and I will do all that I please (Isa 46:10).

God's visionary nature is evident in His foresight as he provided Jesus to be "the lamb of God who slain from the creation of the world." This same Jesus "was chosen before the creation of the world but was revealed in these last times for our sake (1 Pet 1:20).

Case Study 4. 6. *Human vision as a matter of conviction*

Unlike God who perfectly knows the past, present and the future, human beings can only see the future partially. Human vision is the ability to see things as they could be. And so by faith, man pursues the vision moved by an inner conviction that it will come to pass. Abraham provides a good case for consideration of this fact.

> Now the Lord had said to Abram:
> "Get out of your country,
> From your family
> And from your father's house
> To a land that I will show you.
> I will make you a great nation;
> I will bless you
> And make your name great;
> And you shall be a blessing.
> I will bless those who bless you,
> And I will curse him who curses you;
> And in you, all the families of the earth shall be blessed." Gen. 12:1-3

By faith Abraham, when he was called to go out into a place which he should after receive for an inheritance, obeyed; and he went out, not knowing whither he went. By faith, he sojourned in the land of promise, as in a strange country, dwelling in tabernacles with Isaac and Jacob, the heirs with him of the same promise: For he looked for a city which hath foundations, whose builder and maker is God (Heb 11:8-10).

Reflection question
a) When God called Abraham to leave his country and people to go to a place that God would show him, did Abraham have a clear picture of where he was going?
b) What made Abraham obey even when it was not sure where he was going?

How leaders get a revelation of God's vision

God uses different ways and means to reveal his vision to people. To some, he gives a vivid mental image, to others it is a dream and to others, he just lays a conviction in their hearts. Below we look at a few examples of men that got a vision from God:

a. To Abraham, God gave a promise and a picture

When God decided to reveal his purpose for Abraham, He gave him a promise and then painted a picture[16] of what he wished wanted him to achieve. That became Abraham's revealed vision The promise was, "You will be the father of many nations" (Gen 17:5). To create a mental picture of the future for Abraham, "He took him outside and said, "Look up at the sky and count the stars--if indeed you can count them." Then he said to him, "So shall your offspring be" (Gen. 15:5)

b. To Moses, God gave commission and a sign

Moses, one of the greatest leaders that ever lived serves as a good illustration of how God reveals His vision to His leaders. God appeared to him in the burning bush (Ex 3 & 4) and commissioned him as the deliverer of the nation of Israel, through a prolonged conversation that convinced Moses beyond doubt what God's purpose for him was.

The commission was, "So now, go. I am sending you to Pharaoh to bring my people the Israelites out of Egypt" (Ex 3:10).

The sign was, "And God said, "I will be with you. And this will be the sign to you that it is I who have sent you: When you have brought the people out of Egypt, you will worship God on this mountain (Ex 3:12).

If you are familiar with, the story of Moses, you will remember his clarion call to Pharaoh was, "Let my people go, so that they may hold a festival to me in the wilderness" (Ex 5:1; 3:18; 7:16; 10:9). That his vision. That is why Moses could not take the Israelites beyond the wilderness. Leaders do not lead beyond their vision.

Like with Moses, God reveals his vision to leaders through a prolonged nagging push to move in a certain direction or to do a certain thing. Eventually, they give in to that push and embark on a journey to fulfill that vision. Like many people, Moses was a very reluctant candidate for God's vision. But since it is God who works in us to will and to do his good purpose, Moses did well in spite of his initial reluctance.

    c.   **To Nehemiah, God gave a burden and an assignment**

God can use an overwhelming burden or concern for people in a given situation to trigger a vision for a leader. In this regard, Nehemiah serves as a good example.

Nehemiah got the revelation of the vision to rebuild the wall of Jerusalem through a simple message delivered by his brother Hanani. The impact of the situation at Jerusalem weighed him down so heavily that he says, "When I heard these things, I sat down and wept. For some days I mourned and fasted and prayed before the God of heaven." Out of this overwhelming concern for the people and their situation in Jerusalem, Nehemiah developed a vision to rebuild the wall.

Reflection questions
a) How else do leaders get a revelation of God's vision for their lives? Discuss
b) Visit a well-known leader who has a great vision, and ask him or her how he or she developed her vision

As Jon Byler points out in his book *The Art of Christian Leadership;* "Every genuine vision comes from God and is birthed in prayer." [17] That is a key observation for any leader who wants to find and pursue God's vision for his or her life. Notice that Nehemiah fasted and prayed for many days.

Principles for Sharing Your Vision

Warren Bennis defines leadership as the capacity to translate vision into reality.[18] Leaders translate vision into reality by sharing their vision with their followers until they buy into and commit to pursuing it.

Kenneth Boa[19] tells a story of a man who was struggling to get his washing machine through the front door of his home as his neighbor was walking past. The neighbor, being a good person, stopped and asked if he could help. The man breathed a sigh of relief and said, "That would be great. I'll get it from the inside, and you get it from the outside. We should be able to handle this quickly."

But after five minutes of continual struggle, they were both exhausted. Wiping the sweat from his brow, the neighbor said, "This thing is bigger than it looks. I don't know if we'll ever be able to get it into your house."

"*Into* my house? I'm trying to get this thing out of my house!"

Why do you think the two men in Boa's story could not get the washing machine out of the house despite exerting all the energy and sweating so much? While the man was trying to get his washing machine out of the house, his neighbor was working hard to get it in! The man had not communicated what he was doing to the neighbor effectively.

That is what happens when leaders fail to communicate their vision. Instead of people directing their energy towards the desired goal, they get into each other's way and finally give up trying after wasting much time and effort in fruitless activity. Thus, having a vision and expressing it in a clear written vision statement is not enough. For it to become a reality, vision must be communicated effectively. "The very essence of leadership is that you have to have a vision. It's got to be a vision you articulate clearly and forcefully on every occasion. You can't blow an uncertain trumpet."[20]

One remarkable difference between great leaders and average leaders is, while they both have a vision, great leaders share their vision with members until it becomes a shared vision while average leaders are unable to share their vision effectively. The ability to inspire a shared vision is one of the things great leaders do well.[21]

Vision casting is the process of persuading reluctant people to contribute their time, energy, money and other resources to achieve a goal the leader considers worthwhile. Vision casting is not as complicated as it may seem. It is something all of us do sometimes unconsciously. For a wife, it may involve convincing your reluctant husband to buy you a beautiful dress when he does not think it is important. For a husband, it may involve convincing your wife to invest your precious family resources in a promising project, which she considers too risky! For a child, it may involve convincing your parents to buy you the latest pair of shoes in fashion while they consider that a luxury.

Since many leaders find it hard to communicate their vision effectively, we are going to learn how to do it well. The following principles will guide you as you share your vision with your team:

Principle # 1: Write down your vision
One of the greatest hindrances to developing an effective vision is the fear that it may not be realizable. But, as Francis Chan points out, "Our greatest fear should not be of failure but of succeeding at things in life that don't matter."[22] To overcome this fear, write down your vision so that it may serve as a lasting reminder in times of uncertainty. That was God's instructions to Habakkuk as he faced a similar frustration of uncertainty. "The Lord answered me: Write down the vision; write it clearly on clay tablets so whoever reads it can run to tell others" (Hab 2:2).

Case Study 4. 7: Write the vision
It is hard to talk about vision without reference to God's command to Habakkuk to write the vision. Read the case below and respond to the questions that follow,

> I will take my stand at my watch post and station myself on the tower, and look out to see what he will say to me, and what I will answer concerning my complaint. The Righteous Shall Live by His Faith. And the Lord answered me: "Write the vision; make it plain on tablets, so he may run who reads it. For still the vision awaits its appointed time; it hastens to the end—it will not lie. If it seems slow, wait for it; it will surely come; it will not delay (Hab 2:1-3, ESV).

Reflection questions
a) What was Habakkuk doing when God told him to write the vision?
b) Why do you think God meant when He told Habakkuk to make it plain?

    c) Why does God instruct Habakkuk to write the vision?
    d) What do you think God means by saying, "the vision awaits its appointed time?"

Notice, what King James Version calls vision is translated as revelation in New International version and other translations. What follows are key observations regarding God-given vision based on Habakkuk 2: 1-3. These observations may not always apply to human-generated visions but are true of God revealed vision:

1. God reveals His vision to those who are ready to listen. It takes time to hear and conceptualize God's purpose.
2. It is easy to lose sight of God's vision, therefore write it down. That will serve as a reminder and inspiration to yours and the future generations
3. God rarely gives the entire picture; therefore make it plain through prayer and meditation.
4. God's vision is for generations, preserve it for future generations by sharing and writing it down,
5. God's vision is for an appointed time, meanwhile, write it down, share it and prepare for it.
6. God's vision is guaranteed to happen, wait and work with assurance with assurance even when it does not make sense or appear possible.

Writing your vision helps you to capture your thoughts as they come. Later you can continue to refine it by selecting the best words that will inspire you and your members to pursue it.

The purpose of writing your vision is to have a brief statement, which articulates your vision in a straightforward manner. A vision statement is a short description of 2-4 sentences describing what you or your organization aspire to become. It provides a broad ambitious image of the future you wish to create. A good vision statement will inspire and motivate you and your members to take the necessary steps to realize your long-term dream.

Characteristics of a good Vision Statement

A poorly articulated vision adds little purpose to the leader's life. It is difficult to communicate and hard for the followers to conceptualize. A good vision statement should be attention-grabbing, easy to identify with, and attractive to those reading it.

You can develop a good vision statement by making sure it is:

a) **Forward-Looking.** A vision is always something we are looking forward to. It should, therefore, be described as what we aspire to be or happen. The best vision statements begin with these words "To be...."

b) **Appealing.** An effective vision statement is one that makes your members want to be part of the future of your organization. It appeals to your members' needs, desires, and aspirations. God's visions are always desirable. For the Israelites in Egypt, the Promised Land was a land flowing with honey and milk (Ex 3 & 4). For the Israelites in captivity, God's vision was to "give you a future and a hope (Jer 29:11). A dry, boring vision will never stir excitement and commitment.

c) **Imaginable.** An effective vision statement paints a picture of an exciting future worth following. It is easy to grasp with the mind and easy to remember. The easier it is to imagine, the more effective it is. Just imagine, a land flowing with milk and honey! That is just what the Israelites in Egypt needed to hear. To make your vision imaginable, use captivating words, illustrations and figures of speech that make your vision memorable.

a. **Big.** A well-written vision statement will create a tension between the present reality and the desired state. The tension comes from the irresistible nature of the future state and the realization that it is almost impossible to make it happen. The appealing aspect of the vision must be greater than the fear of never making it happen. God's vision is too big to realize without him yet; it is also realistic enough to motivate people to want to work for it. If your vision is too small, most likely it is not from God.

b. **Relevant.** A good vision statement resonates with the desires, wants and the needs of the people it seeks to serve. It must raise their hopes for a better future. It should communicate specific benefits others can expect to get by pursuing it.

c. **Brief.** A good vision statement is brief enough to capture the imagination of the listener. The statement should paint a definite picture of how the world will look like when it has been realized. To make your vision clear, use specific words to define your expected future.

Principle # 2: Capture the people's attention

You may have a great vision, but if you do not capture the people's attention, then they will not have a chance of hearing what you are telling them. The first thing you need to do to cast your vision effectively is to get people's attention. That requires you come up with a creative way of arousing and sustaining their curiosity as you share your vision.

Capturing the people's attention involves choosing the right time, the right place and creating a conducive environment where people are attentive and ready to interact with what you have to say.

Principle # 3: Paint a clear picture of the future

After capturing the attention of the people, paint a vivid picture of the future the vision promises. Remember, vision is as a mental picture of a desirable future. Your aim should be to leave your people with a clear mental image of a future that inspires them to get on board and invest in pursuit the vision.

To create a vivid picture of your vision, you can use:

- Pictures and diagrams
- Artifacts or objects that stand for what your vision seeks to achieve or to be
- Poetic language like idioms, word expressions
- Stories and other forms of illustrations

I still remember many years ago when I visited the office of the Lighthouse Church in Nairobi with Rev. John Byler. Placed on the walls were pictures of lighthouses, in every room there was a miniature lighthouse, and on every written material by the Church, there was a logo of a lighthouse. These served as powerful tools for communicating their vision to the members and the world that, the Church wanted to be a lighthouse to the world.

Your aim should be to inspire your audience to own the vision. As John Quincy Adams pointed out, "If your actions inspire others to dream more, learn more, do more and become more, you are a leader".

Principle # 4: Compare the present to the future

Comparing the desirable future with the current state of affairs appeals to the people's need to have a better tomorrow. God did this in Ex 3: 7 – 9 by promising a good and spacious land flowing with honey to the desert and hard conditions in Egypt where the people were squeezed and limited piece of land in Goshen. Housing was inadequate given their fast-growing population. By promising a spacious land flowing with honey and milk, God was contrasting their desert condition in Egypt with the fertile land that awaited them. Now that was appealing.

To communicate your vision effectively, show how pursuing the vision will translate to a better tomorrow for the people. That will motivate them to become part of the vision.

Principle # 5: Identity with the people
A major challenge to vision casting is the perception that it belongs to the leader and the people are mere tools to help him or her to achieve his dreams. This challenge can be overcome by applying the principle of identification.

The principle of identification involves putting yourself in the shoes of your audience. It contributed much towards the success of Nehemiah when building the wall of Jerusalem. When he arrived at Jerusalem from Persia, he found the people in a very demoralized state. Coming from the king's palace, Nehemiah had no reason to be ashamed.

Yet look at the language Nehemiah is using, "You see the distress that we are in, how Jerusalem lies waste, and its gates are burned with fire. Come and let us build the wall of Jerusalem, that we may no longer be a reproach,"(Neh 2:17).

Nehemiah used the word 'we' to indicate that he was one of them. Nehemiah was not in any trouble! He had a secure Job working as a statehouse senior officer who was on good terms with the king. If anything, the people in Jerusalem were the ones in trouble. But he took upon himself the distress of the people.

By using the word 'we', he was communicating his solidarity with the people. He was one of them, and their pain was his pain. He was telling them that he cared.

To cast your vision effectively, identify with the people and let them see that you care and are committed to their well-being. Remember, people do not care how much you know until they know how much you care.

Principle # 6: Enlist the support of key leaders
The law of the inner circle in leadership says, "Those closest to you determine the level of your effectiveness."[23] Effective leaders know how to obtain and make use of the support of key leaders around them. Such include leaders at higher levels of authority, those at your level as well as those below you.

Share your vision first with those closest to you – especially the key leaders who are respected by the people. If you can get them to buy into the vision, then you can get anyone else in. That is how Moses did it as revealed in the case study below:

Case Study 4. 8: Moses Shares his vision with key leaders
So Moses told Aaron all the words of the Lord who had sent him, and all the signs which He had commanded him. Then Moses and Aaron went and gathered together all the elders of the children of Israel. And Aaron spoke all the words which the Lord had spoken to Moses. Then he did the signs in the sight of the people. So the people believed; and when they heard that the Lord had visited the children of Israel and that He had looked on their affliction, then they bowed their heads and worshipped (Ex 4:28-31).

Reflection question
a) Identify the key leaders Moses shared his vision with, in the case above
b) What challenges do you think Moses would have faced if he had gone to share the vision directly with the people

Moses shared the vision with Aaron first, then Moses and Aaron shared the vision with the elders, then Aaron did the signs before the people. The people believed and worshipped.

Before you share your vision with the general audience, you should have your key leaders by your side. In fact, they should be the ones to introduce the subject and give you a chance to clarify the vision and answer any questions that may arise.

Principle # 7: Inspire the People's Confidence
To empower is to make someone feel well able. It is to make a person have the confidence that they can do what seems impossible. The bigger the vision, the more likely it is to make the people feel helpless and powerless.

Good leaders know how to inspire their people to rise above their fears and helplessness. Outstanding leaders go out of their way to boost the self-esteem of their personnel. If people believe in themselves, it's amazing what they can accomplish - Sam Walton.

Just imagine, Moses going back to Egypt and sharing the vision of getting them out of Egypt! That would sound ridiculous and impossible for the people who had been slaves all their lives. Of course, like most of us, Moses felt too inadequate to fulfill such a great task. That is the most common reaction of people when faced with the realities of fulfilling a God-given vision. They feel powerless. That is why they need to be encouraged and inspired.

The following are some steps you can take to inspire the confidence of the people as you share your vision:

a) Tell them who is on your side

People are encouraged to know you have the support of those in authority. Moses inspired the Hebrews in Egypt by narrating to them how the God of Abraham, Jacob and Isaac had appeared to him and promised to give them a spacious and fertile land (Ex. 4:29-30). Nehemiah told of the support he had received from the king (Neh 2:18).

As you share your vision with the people you lead, let them know that you have the blessing and the goodwill of God and the people above.

b) Help them see their potential.

Point out what they have which makes them qualified for the task. Express your belief in your people and, challenge them to rise above their self-imposed limits to become part of what God is doing through the vision you are sharing.

c) Point out what they need to do.

Rather than focus on the entire vision, break it down into small actions that each can easily do with reasonable effort.

Principle # 8: Ask for a commitment

The eighth and the last principle for us to consider on vision casting is about asking for a commitment. That is the final test of whether you succeed or not. Asking for commitment helps people decide whether they are going to be part of the vision or not. Nehemiah asked for a commitment by calling on the people to rise and build the wall. He challenged them, "Come and let us build the wall of Jerusalem, that we may no longer be a reproach" (Neh 2:170). He then assigned each family unit to build a specific and a measurable part of the wall. As each completed his or her small part of the task, the entire wall was completed within fifty-two days.

You can easily tell whether your people have bought into your vision by the kind of response you get when you ask for a commitment. Their facial expressions, the questions they ask, and the emotions they display will be a pointer to how well you have done.

Conclusion

What is your purpose in life? What has God created you to do in this life? Have you translated your purpose into a vision? These questions deserve serious responses on your part. Take time to think, pray, and clarify God's purpose and vision for your life.

Your leadership journey begins when you discover God's purpose for your life. Your mission and vision, are critical factors in your leadership that should flow out of your purpose.

After discovering your life purpose, your next step is to write your mission statement articulating what you do to fulfill your purpose. A well-written mission statement is a powerful tool for understanding, developing, and communicating important organizational objectives.

Once you have a clear mission statement, you are ready to write your vision statement; a future-oriented declaration of the organization's purpose and aspirations. Your vision statement should be articulated to motivate, inspire and energies the members of your organization to rise and pursue the organization's desired future.

References

1. Attributed to Gautama Buddha in Lolekonda, M. (2017). The Purpose Roadmap: Clarify Your Purpose, Define Your Calling, Claim the Fulfilling Life you were meant to have. Victoria, BC: Friesen Press.
2. Vudzijena, A. (2013). Discover your purpose and enjoy personal fulfillment. Bloomington, IN: AuthorHouse.

3. Reynolds, G. J. (2011). The Playful and Powerful Warrior within YOU! How to Reclaim Your Personal Power and Live a Fulfilling Life of True Adventure! Beachlifestyle Publishing
4. Lawson, K. (2009). Leadership Development Basics: A complete guide to guide you. Alexandria, Virginia. ASTD Press; 1 edition
5. Belcher, L. M., & Media, D. (2015). Reasons for Mission Statements in a Company. Houston Chronicle.
6. The Growth Coach. (2015, July 20). 7 Reasons Why Your Company Needs a Clear, Written Mission Statement. TheGrowthCoachHouston.com:
7. Korlaar, C. V. (2013, March 28). 50 Examples of Volunteer organization Mission Statements. Volunteer organization Relevance. http://Volunteer organizationrelevance.com/
8. Radtke, J. M. (1998). How to Write a Mission Statement. Retrieved from http://skylinecollege.edu/
9. Prism Volunteer organization. http://prismVolunteer organiza-tion.com/about/mission/
10. Carpenter, M., Bauer, T., & Erdogan, B. (2010). Principles of Management. Open source: Flat World Knowledge, Inc.
11. Rosabeth Moss Kanter as quoted in Williamson & Blackburn, 2013, p.167
12. Ayivor, I. (2014). The Great Hand Book of Quotes. CreateSpace Independent Publishing Platform
13. Maxwell, J. C. (1993). Developing the Leader within you. Nashville, Tennessee. Thomas Nelson Publishers
14. Theodore M Hesburgh, Quoted in Philip, M. (2008). You can lead effectively. Xulon Press
15. Martin Luther King (1963). I have a dream… A speech given at "The March on Washington." https://www.archives.gov/
16. Blackaby, H. T., & Blackaby, R. (2011). Spiritual Leadership: Moving People to God's Agenda. Nashville, Tennessee: B&H Publishing Group.
17. Byler, J. (2009). The Art of Christian Leadership. Lancaster, PA. Global Disciples.
18. Warren Bennis cited in Dianna Daniels Booher (1991). Executive's portfolio of model speeches for all occasions. p. 34

19. Boa, K. (2005, October 21). Communicating Vision. https://bible.org/seriespage/17-communicating-vision
20. Quoted in Maxwell, J. C. (2010). The Right to Lead: Learning Leadership Through Character and Courage. Nashville, Thomas Nelson, p.26
21. Kouzes, J. M., & Posner, B. Z. (1995). The leadership challenge: how to keep getting extraordinary things done in organizations. San Francisco: Jossey-Bass Publishers.
22. Chan, F. (2013). Crazy Love: Overwhelmed by a Relentless God. Colorado Springs, CO: David C. Cook
23. Maxwell, J. C. (1998). The 21 irrefutable laws of leadership: Follow them and people will follow you. Nashville: Thomas Nelson Publishers.

Chapter Five

Achieving Your Goals

Introduction

Great achievements rarely happen by chance. They are a result of deliberate efforts carefully planned and executed by those who desire to make a difference. That is what effective leaders do. They determine what they want to achieve ahead of time.

Effective leadership begins with a clear sense of purpose, mission, and vision followed by goal setting. Goal setting involves determining the specific actions to take to achieve desired results that move you closer to realizing your vision.

In practice, vision and long-long goals are used interchangeably to identify milestones towards the vision realization. In this text, we use the term 'goals' to mean the long-term strategic goals while the term 'objective' refers to short-term operational goals. Objectives are discussed in more detail in chapter nine.

Setting Your Goals – Why It Matters

Locke and Latham define a goal as "an idea of the future or desired result that a person or a group of people envisions, plans and commits to achieve."[1] People endeavor to reach goals within a limited time by setting deadlines. Goal setting involves action planning designed to motivate and guide a person or group towards a specific goal.[2]

There is a close relationship between setting goals and success in life. Numerous studies[3] indicate that only three to five percent of people in the world have written goals. The same three to five percent achieve success in business and earn considerable wealth.[4] Additional facts about goal setting real the following about goal setting:

- People with written goals are 50% more likely to achieve their goals
- A whopping 92% of New Year's goals fail by January 15th
- Only 3% of adults write down their goals on paper
- Further, 95% of people who set goals achieve them[5]

Setting a goal is the first and crucial step in turning the invisible into the visible. Setting and writing down your goals is important for the following reasons:

a. Goals clarify your purpose

Writing down goals forces you to be clear about what you want to achieve. Written goals serve as a fixed reference point where you can go back and refresh your memory on what exactly you want to do.

b. Goals strengthen your commitment

The goal setting process challenges you to think through what you specifically want to achieve, how and when. Once you have written down your goals, they become leadership tools that strengthen your resolve to pursue your goal until it is attained.

c. Goals help to measure your progress

Once you have determined what you want to accomplish in your life or organization, you can always look back and gauge where you are compared to where you should be. It also helps to assess whether you are progressing at the expected rate.

d. Goals provide a Standard for performance evaluation

Goals serve as a standard or point of reference for measuring your performance. We can therefore report and say you are making good progress when you are reaching our goals on time. Even when you do not reach your goal, you can tell by how much you missed the target.

e. Goals help improve performance.

Research has established a positive relationship between goals and performance under certain circumstances. For instance, goals are like to help improve performance when, the goal is considered important to those involved,[6] and when they participate in the goal-setting process,

Operating below your set goals and standards is an indication that you are underperforming. You can, therefore, identify those areas where improvement is needed and take necessary corrective measures to improve our performance.

According to Daudkhane, setting goals affect performance in four ways:

- **Choice**: Goals narrow attention and direct efforts to goal-relevant activities, thereby steering away from goal-irrelevant actions.

- **Effort**: Goals lead to increased effort when set above the status quo. The realization that extra effort is needed to accomplish the set goal motivates greater commitment to the goal than one would otherwise invest.

- **Persistence**: Someone becomes more likely to work through setbacks if pursuing a goal.

- **Cognition**: Goals can lead individuals to develop and change their behavior.

f. **Goals align attention and effort**

Goals direct attention and effort towards goal-relevant activities. Well-set and prioritized goals serve as an indicator of where you want to channel our efforts. Besides, goals help you to make better decisions. Every time an opportunity shows up, you can always decide whether you want to pursue it by checking whether investing time and resources in it helps you reach your goals or not.

g. **Goals help you manage your accountabilities**

Goals are statements of what you and your people are committed to accomplish within a given time. Leaders use goals to hold themselves and their followers accountable for their performance. When goals are not met on schedule, it is time to ask – what went wrong and what can be done to help meet set goals.

The terms mission, vision, goals, and goals are often used interchangeably in many textbooks. To avoid the confusion that may result from the interchangeable use of the terms, the meaning of each term is described as used in this book:

The mission is a general description of what the organization does to fulfill the purpose for which it was formed to serve.[7] It answers the question, why are we here? What do we exist to do? What do we do

Vision is the desired future state of the organization. Vision explains how the world will look like after accomplishing the organizational vision.

Goals are broad statements indicating the major steps the organization intends to take in pursuit of the organizational vision and mission. Goals are generally abstract, intangible and hard to measure. Goals may are classified into long-term and short-term.

Long-term goals take a long time to achieve. They are broad outcomes the stakeholders seek to achieve to transform the organization from its status to the state described in its vision statement. Long-term goals are also known as strategic goals because they aim at deliberate, incremental changes that lead to the realization of the organizational vision.

Short-term goals deal with routine activities that the organization engages on a day-to-day basis. They are also known as operational goals or goals. Operational goals result from the breakdown of strategic goals into smaller manageable activities that when systematically achieved will culminate in the realization of the long-term goals.

Turning Your Goals into Actions
By this time, you have clarified your purpose, mission, and vision. But, that is not enough. Many leaders with big, hairy, audacious goals get frustrated because they are unable to make their goals materialize.

Turning your goals into concrete actions is the key that turns your planning into reality. You turn your goals into actions by developing action plans. Your next move is to develop plans to implement your goals.

An action plan is an outline of individual and collective actions that need to be taken systematically to ensure sustainable growth. It lists the steps to achieve a specified goal. A good action plan should address the following concerns:[8]

- **What** actions or changes will occur
- **Who** will carry out these changes
- **By when** they will take place, and for how long
- **What resources** (i.e., money, personnel) are needed to carry out these changes
- **Communication** (who should know what?)

Implementing Your Goals and Plans
Goal setting yields the best outcome followed by plans.[9] The following are the steps you need to take during and after the planning process to ensure successful implementation of your goals

and plans:[10]

At the planning stage
1. Communicate.
Keep your key players informed about the planning process from the beginning of the goal setting and planning process. Let them me know the purpose and the expected impact of the goals and plans. Keeping people informed prepares them psychologically for any involvement or contribution required of them at a future date, especially during the implementation stage.

2. Engage.
One of the greatest mistakes you can make in goal setting and planning is failing to involve everyone in the process. When that happens, the final plan becomes difficult to implement because the people supposed to implement it have no clue or, feel offended because their contribution was taken for granted. To avoid this scenario, involve everyone affected by the plans directly or indirectly. Everyone whose input will be needed during the planning and implementation stages should be involved from the initial stages.

For instance, planning for a church should involve all the stakeholders including; leaders at all levels, committee members, team leaders and potential members the Church wishes to reach out to. Engaging and involving people in the planning process sends the message to them that they matter, that you value their contribution and that you care what they think. It is a necessary step to get their good will.

3. Align effort and priorities
To align is to fit in with the bigger picture to avoid the pull and push that comes with conflicting priorities. For instance, departmental goals and plans should be aligned with the organizational goals and plans. The vision and mission of the organization should align with the vision and mission of the regional or global. The purpose of aligning effort and priorities is to the smaller units contribute towards the realization of the mother organization.

At the implementation stage

4. Ensure visible support from the top

Get the top leadership to champion the implementation process. Visible support from the Chief executive office goes a long way to encourage buy-in from members at the lower levels of the organization. The top leadership organs can demonstrate visible support by publicly taking ownership of the planning process and encouraging stakeholders to support the process. Also, they can show support by regularly checking on the progress, asking for possible ways to help and recognizing the simple milestones realized by different departments.

5. Set priorities

Since you cannot accomplish all your goals at the same time, it is important to decide the order in which to implement the goals. Goal related activities should be spread over the entire planning period so that at any given time it is possible to tell what goal the specific department should be working on.

6. Appoint a champion for each major goal initiative

The goal champion should be a person who is well respected and enjoys support from key influences within the organization. The role of the goal champion is to own and be accountable for the goal and for monitoring the progress. He or she provides regular progress reports, coordinates the implementation activities, facilitates resource allocation for the particular goal and keeps the team focused on the goal completion.

7. Clarify expectations

Making expectations clear can be done by allocating responsibilities and accountabilities. Clarify who is responsible for what action and what is expected at any particular time. That helps transfer the ownership of the specific activities to specific people who are empowered to do whatever it takes to get the task done.

8. Evaluate regularly

Frequent evaluation of goals and plans increase the chances of successful implementation significantly. It allows the timely detection of deviations from the plans and allows well-timed corrective measures before much damage can occur.

Evaluation meetings can be scheduled to coincide with deadlines for major goals. For instance, if an action point was due for completion within three months, at or by the expiration of the three months, call a meeting to evaluate whether that action was completed as scheduled.

Regular evaluation events help to keep goal implementation on track. Where an action is overdue, questions regarding why it was not possible to get it done should be addressed.

9. Celebrate accomplishments

Develop an easy way to track and summarize progress and celebrate as often as possible. A celebration even of accomplishments can motivate your people beyond your expectations. Do not wait until the whole goal is accomplished since some goals will take more than a year to accomplish. By then people will have been discouraged and demoralized. Have a way of recognizing even small activities and celebrating them. To keep people motivated, make a habit of regularly celebrating progress.

10. Report the progress regularly

Keep everyone involved in the organization updated on the progress. Let people know where the where they are compared to the set goals. Use different methods to communicate. Include update reports in the organization's bulletins, newsletters, announcements and on the website.

11. Learn and adjust as you move on

The plans and goals are not cast on stone. Sometimes things beyond your control will affect your progress. Some activities will be overtaken by time and events. As you move on, learn from the past, make adjustments but remain focused on the main goal.

Obstacles to Implementing Goals

Many planning and goal setting attempts fail because of poor implementation. Other factors that may keep you from realizing your desired results include:

1. Setting unrealistic goals

At the goal setting stage, it is all right to unleash your imagination and ambition, put your reservations aside. Think and dream as big as you can. But once you have set the goal, make sure that it is realistic, and that you can achieve it in the time frame that you have set for yourself.

Setting unrealistic goals can have a negative impact on your followers and the organizational performance.[11] For instance, in the short-term, unrealistic goals can lead to:

- Missed delivery dates,
- Reduced work quality,
- Increased running costs,
- Increased absenteeism.

In the long-term, consistently setting unrealistic goals may lead to:

- Low morale
- High staff turnover
- Less commitment
- Lost respect – people feel you are setting them up for failure

2. Inadequate resources

The purpose of goal setting and planning is to make you a proactive leader who takes advance action to facilitate desired results. Resources include money, equipment, facilities, ideas and other materials necessary for successful implementation of your goals and plans.

For faith-based organizations, resources may include transportation, Public Address system, learning materials and accommodation for missioners among other things. Many people are willing to volunteer service, but they still need facilitation. When that facilitation is not available, many people may not volunteer to serve, which will limit effective implementation of the goals and plans.

The top leadership should commit necessary resources to facilitate implementation of organizational goals and plans for maximum returns.

3. Inadequate motivation

It takes highly motivated personnel to follow through the entire goal setting and planning process. Effective implementation of goals and plans can be challenging when dealing with people at varying levels of motivation, commitment and dedication.

In the corporate world, money is the main source of motivation. Luckily, for organizations like the Church and other charity organizations, money is not a major consideration for inspiring volunteers to serve. Nevertheless, people still need to be motivated enough if they are going to implement growth strategies effectively.

Basic understanding of what motivates different people will help much. Public recognition motivates some people; others are motivated by appreciation, good titles and position of honor. Still, others prefer to work behind the scenes without much publicity. The leader must be aware of what motivates his or her people and offer that kind of support to them.

4. Inadequate time

It takes time, sometimes a long time to implement strategies for growth. That makes sense considering we the long-term goals. Where enough time and attention is not devoted to the process of implementing the plans, usually the plans will not be successful. The leader must allocate adequate time to implement agreed action plans.

5. Failure to monitor the plans

Many organizations spend good time planning, then apply the plans for a few months and forget about them. They fall back into the same routine activities without much regard for the plans. By the end of the year, they are even ashamed to evaluate their performance because they know they never followed the plans they had made. Effective execution of growth strategies require tenacious commitment and follow up on the plans to ensure each plan is brought to completion.

Case Study 4. 9. The 12 Disciples: A case of conflicting goals

When Jesus called his twelve disciples to follow him, they had high hopes of changing their lives for the better. So, they followed without a second thought when He told them, "Follow me, and I will make you fishers of men" (Mat 4:19).

By the time of their calling, Israel had been waiting for a Messiah to come and overthrow their oppressive Roman masters and reestablish the Jewish kingdom. And Jesus seemed to fit the description of the would-be Messiah. With his miracle-working powers, he would make a great business partner or a great deliverer, whichever way you chose to look at it. So they followed enthusiastically. They left their families, businesses, careers, and everything else to follow him.

As time went by, they made their expectations clear. They wanted to play a key role in government after Jesus restored the Jewish self-rule. The first disciples to lobby for a senior position in the would be government were the sons of Zebedee James and John. At an opportune moment, they came to Jesus and said, "Teacher, we want you to do for us whatever we ask." What do you want me to do for you? Jesus asked. They replied, "Let one of us sit at your right and the other at your left in your glory" (Mar 10:35-37).

Jesus tactfully declined their request, but that was not enough to deter them from pursuing their goal. Soon afterward "the mother of Zebedee's sons came to Jesus with her sons and, kneeling down, asked a favor of him. "What is it you want?" he asked. She said, "Grant that one of these two sons of mine may sit at your right and the other at your left in your kingdom" (Mat 20:20-21).

James and John where not the only disciples who were expecting to be rewarded with posh positions in Jesus earthly kingdom. Two disciples on their way to Emmaus expressed their dashed hopes to Jesus as He joined them and asked them, "What are you discussing together as you walk along?" They stood still, their faces downcast. One of them, named Cleopas, asked him, "Are you the only one visiting Jerusalem who does not know the things that have happened there in these days?" "What things?" he asked. "About Jesus of Nazareth," they replied. "He was a prophet, powerful in word and deed before God and all the people. The chief priests and our rulers handed him over to be sentenced to death, and they crucified him, but we had hoped that he was the one who was going to redeem Israel. And what is more, it is the third day since all this took place (Luk 24:17-21).

Jesus seems to have noted with concern the conflict between his agenda and that of the disciple's. He, therefore, started to talk about the kingdom of heaven. He then began to teach them that the Son of Man must suffer many things and be rejected by the elders, the chief priests and the teachers of the law and that he must be killed and after three days rise again. He spoke plainly about this, and Peter took him aside and began to rebuke him. But when Jesus turned and looked at his disciples, he rebuked Peter. "Get behind me, Satan!" he said. "You do not have in mind the concerns of God, but merely human concerns" (Mar 8:31-33).

Finally, the disciples could not take it any longer; they decided to come out to the open and ask the question that had bothered them all along. On their behalf, Peter said to him, "We have left all we had to follow you!" "Truly I tell you," Jesus said to them, "no one who has left home or wife or brothers or sisters or parents or children for the sake of the kingdom of God will fail to receive many times as much in this age, and in the age to come eternal life (Luk 18:28-30).

Reflection questions

a) What was the conflict between the goal of and that of his disciples?

b) Was the goal of Jesus relevant to the needs of the disciples? explain

c) Did Jesus address the conflict between his goal and that of his disciples adequately?

d) What is the impact of irrelevant goals on organizational performance?

e) What can the leader do to address the conflict between organizational goals and goals of the individual stakeholder?

Conclusion

Great achievements do not happen by chance. They are a result of deliberate efforts carefully planned and executed by those who desire to make a difference. Effective leadership begins with a clear sense of purpose, mission, and vision followed by clear goals.

Many leaders with big, hairy, audacious goals get frustrated because they are unable to make their goals materialize. Effective goals focus more on results than on activity. While activity is necessary for objective achievement, not every activity contributes to the achievement of a given objective.

References
1. Locke, E. A.; Latham, G. P. (1990). A theory of goal setting & task performance. Englewood Cliffs, NJ: Prentice Hall.

2. Daudkhane, Y. S. (2017). Why SMART Goals are not 'Smart' enough? Imperial Journal of Interdisciplinary Research (IJIR). Vol-3, Issue-6. ISSN: 2454-1362,

3. Carson, P., Carson, K. D. & Heady, R. B. (1994). Cecil Alec Mace: The man who discovered goal setting. International Journal of Public Administration 17(9):1679-1708., Kim, J. S. (1984). Effect of Behavior Plus Outcome Goal Setting and Feedback on Employee Satisfaction and Performance. The Academy of Management Journal 27(1):139-149.

4. Brooks, T. (2012, April 30). The power of writing down your goals. The Leadership Training Workshop.

5. Mabika, E. (2013). Success Gravity. Peterborough, England: FastPrint Publishing.

6. Stajkovic, A. D.; Luthans, F. (September 1998). "Self-efficacy and work-related performance: a meta-analysis". Psychological Bulletin. 124 (2): 240–261.

7. Mullins, L. A. (2013). Management & Organizational Behaviour, 12th Edition. Edinburg, UK. Pearson Education

8. Community Tool Box. (2015). Developing an Action Plan. Retrieved from http://ctb.ku.edu/en/table-of-contents/structure/strategic-planning/develop-action-plans/main

9. Byler, J. (2008). The Art of Christian Leadership. Lancaster, PA: Global Disciples.

10. OPIA. (2009, May). Implementing a Strategic Plan. Innovation Insight Series, 21, 1-2. Retrieved from http://www.opia.psu.edu/sites/default/files/insights021.pdf

11. Half, R. (2018, Jan. 16). The hidden risk of unrealistic expectations in the workplace. Employer Articles. Accessed on May 19, 2018: https://www.roberthalf.com.hk/

Chapter Six

Developing Your Emotional Intelligence

Introduction

This chapter focuses on the development of emotional intelligence as the foundation of people skills, which are indispensable for effective leadership. Great leaders understand the law of connection, which states, "Leaders touch a heart before they ask for a hand."[1] Without people skills, the leader is unable to connect emotionally with the people and therefore unable to inspire commitment.

Effective leaders possess four categories of skills, which set them apart from their peers, including conceptual, technical, political, skills, and people skills.[2] Since the focus of this chapter is people skills, we are going to briefly describe conceptual, technical and political skills first and then move on to discuss emotional intelligence as the precursor of people skills.

1. Conceptual skills

Conceptual skills include the ability to analyze, communicate, and think creatively to solve problems. Conceptual skills enable the leader to see the big picture, and to coordinate the organization's interests and activities for maximum results. Without conceptual skills, the leader is unable to make the most out of the people's gifts and the organizational resources. The leader needs conceptual skills to steer the organization to realize its potential

2. Technical skills

Technical skills include the knowledge and abilities needed to perform tasks specific to one's profession. A person has technical skills when he or she can carry out procedures and techniques specific to his or her specialized field effectively.[3] For instance, in the medical profession basic technical skills include the ability to diagnose a patient's illness accurately and prescribe appropriate medication. Technical skills for a manager include the ability to plan, organize, control and direct the affairs of the organization to achieve its objectives.

3. Political skills

Braddy and Campbell defined political skills as "...the ability to maximize and leverage relationships to achieve organizational, team, and individual goals."[4] Leaders with political skills;

- Observe and understand other people's behaviors and motives,
- Influence others through a compelling and charismatic interpersonal style,
- Build networks across and outside of the organization and,
- Relate to others in a forthright, open, honest, and genuine manner.

4. **People skills**

People skills are relational abilities that enable a person to live in peace with others, engage others positively and intentionally influence their decisions and actions towards a desired direction. Different terms are used to describe people skills including soft skills, interpersonal skills, and human skills.

Understanding People Skills

The online Business dictionary defines people skills as "A set of skills enabling a person to get along with others, to communicate ideas effectively, to resolve conflicts, and to achieve personal or business goals."[5] They are also known as human skills, soft skills or interpersonal skills in management literature.

People skills are necessary for success in leadership since they enable a leader to understand, motivate and work with other people at a personal level or within group set-ups.

Good people skills are necessary for productive relationships in every area of life. In leadership, people skills are more important than technical competence and intellectual knowledge because[6] leaders with good people skills listen, communicate and relate to others in a positive way that influences them to support the leader's agenda.

According to the Portland business journal[7] leaders with people skills:

- Understand people, empathize with them and, communicate effectively.
- Promote respect, mutual understanding, and productive workplace relations.
- Develop a productive working relationship, minimize conflict

and maximize rapport.
- Moderate behaviors to avoid impulsiveness and enhance agreeableness.

Essential interpersonal skills

Research on people skills has identified many interpersonal skills, which affect leadership performance.[8] The most significant people skills in this regard are:
- Emotional intelligence,
- Communication,
- Ability to manage conflicts,
- Building and working with teams,
- Leading change,
- Motivating people and,
- Ability to facilitate meetings, among others.

The Role of Attitude in Developing People Skills

Developing good people skills begins with the right attitude towards yourself and others. "The people with whom you work reflect your attitude. If you are suspicious, unfriendly and condescending, you will find these unlovely traits echoed all about you. But if you are on your best behavior, you will bring out the best in the persons with whom you are going to spend most of your working hours." -Beatrice Vincent

Here are two attitudes to avoid as you work to develop your people skills,

1. Superiority complex

Superiority complex is an attitude of considering yourself more highly than you ought that conceals actual feelings of inferiority and failure.[9]]It is a psychological defense mechanism used to compensate for feelings of inadequacy and failure. Apostle Paul cautions against superiority complex in these words, "For I say, through the grace given to me, to everyone who is among you, not to think of himself more highly than he ought to think but to think soberly, as God has dealt with each one a measure of faith" (Romans 12:3).

Thinking of yourself more highly than you ought is a symptom of superiority complex. Superiority complex leads to arrogance causing you to look down on others. It turns the leader into a boss, who in turn ends up demotivating followers instead of inspiring them. A boss creates fear, a leader confidence. A boss fixes blame, a leader corrects mistakes. A boss knows all; a leader asks questions. A boss makes work drudgery; a leader makes it interesting. A boss is interested in himself or herself; a leader is interested in the group. -Russell H. Ewing

That, in turn, builds an emotional wall of resistance between you and other people, thus reducing your ability to influence them

2. **Inferiority complex**

Inferiority complex is a feeling of inadequacy. It makes you feel less capable, intelligent, and attractive, as compared to other people.[10] Leaders who suffer from inferiority complex often act aggressively to cover up for the feeling of inadequacy. Timothy seems to have struggled with inadequacy causing Paul to encourage him with these words, "Let no one despise your youth, but be an example to the believers in word, in conduct, in love, in spirit, in faith, in purity" (1 Tim 4:12).

Inferiority complex leads to insecurity, which makes the leader defensive and unapproachable. People with inferiority or superiority complex rarely take feedback kindly. Thinking too highly or too lowly of yourself are inappropriate attitudes to possess. The right attitude is to think soberly, according to the measure of faith God has given you. Acknowledge that you are still work in progress, with strengths and weaknesses that are being perfected to make you a better person.

Case Study 6. 1. The leader role modeled the right attitude

Christ the greatest leader that ever lived modeled for today's leader the words of Jim Rohn who said, "The challenge of leadership is to be strong, but not rude; be kind, but not weak; be bold, but not bully; be thoughtful, but not lazy; be humble, but not timid; be proud, but not arrogant; have humour but without folly."[11] Read Paul's description of Christ's mindset below and reflect on the questions that follow:

> In your relationships with one another, have the same mindset as Christ Jesus: Who, being in very nature God, did not consider equality with God something to be used to his advantage; rather, he made himself nothing by taking the very nature of a servant, being made in human likeness. And being found in appearance as a man, he humbled himself by

becoming obedient to death — even death on a cross! Therefore God exalted him to the highest place and gave him the name that is above every name, that at the name of Jesus every knee should bow, in heaven and on earth and under the earth, and every tongue acknowledge that Jesus Christ is Lord, to the glory of God the Father (Phi 3:5-11).

Reflection questions
a) What mindset did Christ have?
b) How did Christ's mindset or attitude affect his relationships with people
c) Is it practical to expect a leader to have an attitude of a servant? Discuss

Understanding Emotional Intelligence

Emotional intelligence (EI) is "the ability to manage ourselves and our relationships effectively."[12] It refers to a set of related abilities that empower leaders to "identify, understand, control and assess the emotions of the self and others."[13]

Emotional intelligence is an essential building block for people skills. Lack of emotional intelligence can be a liability in the leader's life. Leaders who lack emotional intelligence display one or more of the following behaviors.[14]

- Insensitivity: An uncaring attitude towards other people's needs and concerns. Insensitive leaders rarely inspire confidence and commitment in their followers.
- Volatility: Fits of explosive anger that scares and makes others feel threatened.
- Arrogance: A show of know it all attitude and an overbearing demeanor. Arrogant leaders arouse an attitude of indifference in their leaders.
- Selfishness: Putting a personal agenda over the well-being of others. Selfish leaders are poor conflict managers who careless about relationships and outcomes.
- Rigidity: – inflexible thinking, thinking their way is the only way.

At a personal level, how do you know when you lack emotional intelligence? Wilkins of the Harvard Business Review suggests the follow signs.[15]

- Feeling impatient and frustrated because others don't

appear to get your point,
- Getting surprised when others overreact to your comments or jokes,
- Taking the earliest opportunity to defend yourself and doing it with rigor. You think being liked at work is overrated,
- Having exceptionally high expectations for others as you hold for yourself or even higher,
- Blaming others for the problems in your organization,
- Getting annoyed when others expect you to understand how they feel.

Emotional Intelligence Abilities

Emotional intelligence comprises of four essential abilities namely: self-awareness, self-management, social awareness, and social skills. Below is a brief description of each:

1. Self-awareness

Self-awareness is the ability to monitor your own emotions and reactions.[16] It is a state of "knowing your motivations, emotions, and personality, what you enjoy and what you dislike, what comes easy and what poses challenges"[17] to you. Self-awareness is critical to your success as a leader.

Self-aware leaders share some common characteristics. They conscious of their feelings, and how their feelings and actions affect others. They can control their responses to achieve their intended reactions from others, and they are less impulsive, often thinking before acting. They possess a sincere desire to assist others in the pursuit of goals and can identify with the feelings and needs of others.

Increasing your self-awareness

You can increase your self-awareness by developing habits that relate to the following self-awareness domains:[18]

a. **Emotional awareness**
   - Assess your feelings at any given moment and why,
   - Establish the link between your feelings, your words, and your actions,
   - Reflect on the effect of your emotions on your performance and that of the people around you.

b. **Self-assessment**

- Identify your strengths and limits,
- Reflect your experiences and identify possible lessons,
- Seek candid feedback from close associates,
- Consider new perspectives and commit to continuous learning.

   a. **Self-confidence**
   - Develop confidence in your self-worth and capabilities.
   - Express your views that are unpopular and stand out for what you consider to be right; and
   - Learn sound decision-making skills and be decision even when you are uncertain or under pressure.

2. **Self-management**

Another term for self-management is self-regulation, which involves taking responsibility for your actions and well-being. It allows you to control your emotions, time, inner resources, and abilities to minimize unwanted impulsive reactions.

Self-management is an aspect of emotional intelligence that equips you to exercise self-control, demonstrate trustworthiness, conscientiousness, adaptability, and innovativeness. Self-control is an important part of self-management as it enables you to remain composed in spite of your emotional state.[19] It starts by recognizing and controlling your emotions, words, and actions appropriately rather than denying, hiding or masking them.

Leaders face many challenges and often work under pressure. Unrelenting pressure leads to stress under which lack of self-control manifests leaving a trail of damage behind. While leaders under pressure react differently, the emotional breakdown is a common consequence that shows in one or more of the ways listed below:

- Angry outbursts,
- Door slamming,
- Email-letter bomb,
- Withdrawal and isolation,
- Holding grudges and getting even,
- Criticizing,
- Sarcasm and inappropriate humor,

- Playing the victim and so on.

Steps to Gaining Self-Control

To enhance your self-management competence here are some actions you can take to fortify your Self-control

1. **Recognize and deal with emotional triggers,**

The first step in gaining self-control involves recognizing and dealing with emotional triggers. Emotional triggers are the factors that set off impulsive reactions that lead to loss of self-control. An emotional trigger acts as a catalyst that sets off the chain of reactions leading to a lack of self-control. Many factors can be emotional triggers, but for our purpose, we consider only three of them here:

   a. *Other people's moods and attitudes*

The mood and the attitudes of close associates can influence your emotions in a big way.[20] Your close associates may be your boss, your colleagues, a customer or any other person you closely work with. To deal with this trigger, first, identify whose emotions irritate you and why. Do not react in the same spirit to the person whose emotions affect yours. Do not take it personally either. Everyone is responsible for his or her emotions and attitudes. Choose not to help people carry their negative emotional baggage.

   a. *Hot buttons*

A Hot button any word or issue that causes unexpected bad reactions from a person. It may be something someone says or does which leaves you vulnerable to emotional breakdown. A hot button can be an issue in your life you do not like to talk about or, an issue that makes you lose your cool whenever raised.

The starting point for dealing with hot buttons in your life is to identify what they are and why you react the way you do whenever the buttons are pressed. Sometimes hot buttons are connected to issues you are struggling with which you are unaware of. It may be a sense of inadequacy, failure, or fear that drives us to overreact to the hot buttons.

It is okay to seek the help of a counselor, a therapist or someone you trust to uncover the underlying issues.

   b. **Criticism and blame**

Criticism and blame can easily cause a leader to lose self-control and react in unwanted ways. Unfortunately, leaders cannot run away from blame. It is easier to accept criticism and blame when you know you are guilty of the accusation, but when accused unfairly, that is a recipe for emotional breakdown.

How do you deal with criticism whether deserved or not? First, anticipate it. Eleanor Roosevelt once said, "Do what you feel in your heart to be right–for you'll be criticized anyway. You will be damned if you do and damned if you don't"[21] Anticipating criticism and blame may not take away the pain, but you are better prepared than if you never saw it coming.

Second, view criticism and blame as a form of feedback. That turns the attention from self-defense to identifying possible improvement issues in the situation.

2. Reflect on the source of your emotions

You are likely to react violently when your desire for something you hold dear is thwarted. Strong reactions related to human desires include the pursuit of power, wealth, acceptance, happiness, approval, security, and success among others. When we feel threatened with the opposite of these desires, a trigger goes off which leads to a loss of self-control

Strong fears will equally trigger strong emotional reactions likely to get out of control. For instance, fear of death, disapproval, rejection, loss of job, and uncertainty could easily trigger emotions beyond your control.

Reflection helps you understand better the cause of your expression of lack of self-control. Once you understand the cause, you can address it by yourself or with help from trusted people.

3. Reframe

To reframe is to change the way something is expressed or considered. The purpose of reframing is to alter your self-talk on the situation. If your natural reaction is to say, "I will kill someone" then you reframe by stating the opposite intended action. In this case, you could say, "I do not need to hurt anyone because of what has just happened. It is not worth it"

4. Rehearse

To rehearse is to practice before the real performance. By this time you have identified the underlying issues causing you to lose self-control. You know the triggers, and you have reframed. The last step is to take action, but before that, you need to practice mentally what and how you are going to do it. This way you are prepared psychologically to carry out the action step to reinforce your desired action.

The Christian leader has an extra resource to draw from in her effort to develop emotional intelligence. For her, all she needs has been supplied by the Holy Spirit. Hence, "The key to gaining self-control is yielding the self to the control of the Holy Spirit."[22] That is unlike the humanistic theories, which approach self-control from a pure discipline perspective. Paul lists self-control alongside the other character qualities produced by the indwelling presence of the Holy Spirit such as love, joy, peace, longsuffering, kindness, goodness, faithfulness and gentleness (Gal 5:22-23).

3. **Social awareness**

Social awareness refers to the ability to understand and respond appropriately to the needs of others. It awareness leads to stronger relationships, better work performance, and a better sense of fulfillment. It manifests through empathy, service orientation, and organizational awareness. Socially aware leaders understand how they react to different social situations, and effectively modify their interactions with other people to achieve the best results. The outcome of social awareness is the ongoing development of social skills. The following is a brief description of specific social awareness attributes necessary for effective leadership,

a. **Empathy**

Empathy is the ability to sense other people's feelings, see things from their perspective, and take an active interest in their concerns. Goleman calls it our social radar, which requires being able to read another's emotion and respond to a person's unspoken concerns.[23]

b. **Service orientation**

You are service oriented when you are consciously set to meet the needs of your customers. It involves being able to anticipate, identify, and meet the customers' needs to their satisfaction.

c. **Developing others**

Developing others is rooted in the ability to see the individual potential and the desire to see that potential realized. People with this skill are good at sensing the developmental needs of others and facilitating the needed growth.

4. Social skills

Social skills comprise a set of behaviors and a series of actions that people use to interact or communicate with one another.[24] Social intelligence, the ability to think and act wisely in social situations.[25] These skills manifest as we relate to other people verbally and non-verbally, through gestures, body language, and our appearance. Since human beings are social creatures, we employ social skills to communicate our messages, thoughts, and feelings with others. Possessing emotional and social skills is associated with higher quality social relationships and more supportive social support systems.[26] Table six below show five specific social skills necessary for effective leadership:

Table 6. 1. List of Social Skills

Skill	Description
Persuasion	Ability to influence others thoughts, words and action through convincing reasoning
Communication	Ability to send clear, convincing messages
Leadership	Motivating and guiding people towards goal attainment
Leading change	Ability to initiate and guide people through a change process
Conflict management	Handling conflicts constructively to arrive at an agreed solution

Conclusion

To become an effective leader you need to possess four categories of skills, including conceptual, technical, political, skills, and people skills. Without people skills, you will be unable to connect emotionally with your followers and therefore unable to inspire commitment.

Developing good people skills begins with the right attitude towards yourself and others. Superiority complex will make arrogant while inferiority complex will make you insecure. Both attitudes will sabotage your ability to lead. Avoid them.

Emotional intelligence a set of related abilities that will empower you to identify, understand, control and assess your emotions and the emotions of your followers. Your ability to develop people skills is dependent on your level of emotional intelligence.

References

1. Maxwell, J. C. (1998). The 21 Irrefutable Laws Of Leadership: Follow Them and the People Will Follow You. Nashville, TN: Thomas Publishers.
2. Katz, R.L. (1974, September-October). Skills of an effective administrator. Harvard Business School, pp. 90-102
3. Robbins, S. P. & Hunsaker, P. L. (2009). Training in Interpersonal Skills: Tips for managing people at work. Pearson International Edition. Hong Kong.
4. Braddy, P. & Campbell, M. (2014). Using Political Skill to Maximize and Leverage Work Relationships. White Paper. Centre for Creative Leadership. Retrieved from: http://www.ccl.org/wp-content/uploads/2015/04/UsingPoliticalSkill.pdf
5. http://www.businessdictionary.com/definition/people-skills.html
6. Zenger, J. & Folkman, J. (2014, July). The Skills Leaders Need at Every Level. Harvard Business Review
7. Rifkin, H. (2002, June 2). "Invest in people skills to boost the bottom line." http://www.bizjournals.com/portland/stories/2002/06/03/focus6.html. Retrieved 21/4/2017
8. AACSB, (1993). The Cultivation of Tomorrow's Leaders: Industry's Fundamental Challenge to Management Education. Newsline, V. 23, pp. 1-3
9. www.thefreedictionary.com/superiority+complex
10. Cambridge Dictionary. http://dictionary.cambridge.org/dictionary/english/inferiority-complex

11. Attributed to Jim Rohn in Stein, S. J. (2017). The EQ Leader: Instilling Passion, Creating Shared Goals, and Building Meaningful Organizations through Emotional Intelligence. Hoboken, New Jersey, Wiley & Sons Inc.
12. Golemann, D. (1998). Working with Emotional Intelligence, New York, Bantam Books.
13. Salovey, P. &Mayer, J. D. (1990). Emotional Intelligence: Imagination, Cognition, and Personality. Vol. 9, pp. 185-211.
14. Bisk Education. (2017). Emotional Intelligence in the Workplace: What It Is and Why it Matters. University of Florida Executive Education https://essentialsofbusiness.ufexec
15. Wilkins, M. M. (2014). Signs That You Lack Emotional Intelligence. Harvard Business Review. https://hbr.org/2014/12/signs-that-you-lack-emotional-intelligence
16. Fallon, N. (2014). Want to Be a Good Leader? Step One: Know Thyself. Business News Daily. http://www.businessnewsdaily.com/6097-self-awareness-in-leadership.html
17. Mannarelli, T. (2006, Dec.). Charismatic, Transformation Leadership through Reflection and Self-awareness. Accountancy Ireland. Vol.38. No. 6, pp. 46-48.
18. Serrat, O. (2009). Understanding and Developing Emotional Intelligence. Asian Development Bank. https://www.adb.org/
19. Mersino, A. (2013). Emotional Intelligence for Project Managers: The People Skills You Need to Achieve Outstanding Results. Broadway, NY: AMACOM
20. Lynn, A. B. (2004). The EQ Difference: A Powerful Plan for Putting Emotional Intelligence to Work. Broadway, NY: AMACOM.
21. Quoted in Carnagie, D. (2010). How to Enjoy Life and Your Job: Selections from How to Win Friends and Influence People. New York. Pocket Books

22. Kelley, R. H. (1995). Divine Discipline: How to How to Develop and Maintain Self-control. Gretna, Louisiana: Pelican Publishing House

23. Goleman, D. (Working with Emotional Intelligence. London: Bloomsbury Publishing PLC.

24. Sharon Sacks, Karen E. Wolffe (2006). Teaching Social Skills to Students with Visual Impairments: From Theory to Practice. New York: AFB Press.

25. Riggio, R. E. & Reichard, R. J. (2008). The emotional and social intelligence of effective leadership: An emotional and social skill approach. Journal of Managerial Psychology Vol. 23 No. 2, pp. 169-185

26. Riggio, R.E., Watring, K. and Throckmorton, B. (1993), "Social skills, social support, and psychosocial adjustment", Personality and Individual Differences, Vol. 15, pp. 275-80.

Chapter Seven

Improving Competence Though Feedback

Introduction

Communication is a key aspect of people skills, and effective communication involves giving and receiving feedback. The purpose of feedback is to draw people's attention to their behavior and its impact on other people's performance.

Effective leaders use feedback to motivate, inspire and improve the performance of their people. It is a necessary skill for every leader because:[1]

- It encourages doing the right things and the right way,
- It leads to better performance,
- It redirects behavior to the more productive activities,
- It leads learning, growth, and development of the recipients,
- It contributes to the ongoing process of staff development in organizational settings, and
- It is central to developing high-performance teams.

When handled well, feedback can be a powerful tool for increasing skills and motivation. It can add much value in terms of professional, personal and organizational development. The value of feedback is evaluated by its ability to [2]

- Clarify good performance,
- Facilitate self-assessment,
- Deliver high-quality information,
- Encourage dialogue,
- Encourage motivational belief and self-esteem,
- Provide opportunities to close the performance gap and,
- Provide information to leaders to improve their performance.

Giving feedback involves communicating in a way that encourages the recipient to accept, reflect, learn from, and make appropriate changes in response to the feedback.[3] Your feedback should leave your recipient nourished - after all, to 'feed' is to nourish. Your feedback will achieve its objective better if the recipient does not perceive it as a punishment.

Your aim of giving feedback is to help the recipient make positive changes that lead to better performance. You can achieve that objective by paying attention to the kind of feedback you wish to give and the way you do it. As you prepare to give feedback, keep in mind the words of Solomon in (Prov 15:1), "A soft answer turns away wrath, but a harsh word stirs up anger".

Giving Feedback Skillfully

Feedback can be a powerful tool for increasing skills and motivation, both at the professional and personal level when given and received well. Here are seven things you can do to help the recipient receive and act on your feedback:

1. Focus on specific improvement issues

Feedback works best when it is more specific rather than general. As you provide feedback, point out specific past actions that need attention. For instance, instead of saying "good report" Say, "The report you submitted yesterday was well-written, understandable, and made your points about the budget very effectively."

2. Pinpoint controllable behavior

Point out particular issues within the control of the person receiving your feedback. There is no point in providing feedback about something beyond of the recipient. Besides pointing out specific improvement issues, guides the recipient to identify the necessary action to improve the situation

3. Keep feedback impersonal

Effective feedback focuses on the actions of the person rather than their motives and intentions. Avoid passing judgment on the person's motives and intentions as you give feedback. Instead of saying "Your bad manners ruined the meeting" say, "When you held competing conversations during the meeting, you distracted the people in attendance."

4. Link feedback to the desired goal

Direct negative feedback towards the recipient's goals. Point out how the recipient's specific behavior hinders him or her from reaching their goals. This way make feedback helpful to the recipient.

5. Provide timely feedback

Feedback is most meaningful if given within the shortest interval between recipient's behavior and feedback delivery. However, there are occasions when delaying feedback may be the right thing to do. For instance, giving feedback when you are emotionally upset can backfire. The same is true when you do not have complete information.

6. Clarify your feedback

The purpose of communication is to transfer understanding and meaning. For maximum effectiveness, your feedback should be precise and complete. If necessary, cite specific examples where the recipient behaved inappropriately.

To assess how well you have given the feedback have the recipient rephrase the content of your feedback.

7. Customize the feedback to fit the recipient

Feedback should be relevant to the needs and within the performance capacity of the recipient. Do not ask more than the recipient can do or beyond what they have control over. Consider recipients actual performance and your estimation of his or her potential. Depending on the potential for growth, give feedback that will stretch the recipient's ability without getting overwhelmed.

Giving Feedback to Your "Boss"

Giving feedback to your boss requires careful thought depending on his or her disposition and the way you relate to each other. Nevertheless, it is worth trying. Giving feedback to your boss can help him see himself as other people see him and hence make the necessary adjustment in his behavior and approach. That is perhaps what Solomon, in Proverbs 25:15 had in mind when he said, "With patience, a ruler may be persuaded, and a soft tongue will break a bone."

Before giving unsolicited feedback to your boss, here are a few things you need to note:[4]

1. Work on your relationship first

Giving and receiving feedback is a trust issue. Without trust, it will be hard for your boss to receive your feedback. Take time to build and maintain trust with your boss at all times so that when giving negative feedback becomes necessary; you will already have built bridges to reach him or her.

2. Ask for permission to give feedback

Launching into unsolicited feedback can be risky. That is why you should wait to be invited or, ask to be invited. If your boss has asked for your opinion, is open-minded and secure, then you have a good opportunity to give your feedback. Go ahead and share your thoughts. If not, look for a way to seek his consent.

3. Choose your words carefully

Whether you know it or not, your words have a great impact on your audience. They can make or break relationships. Solomon, the proverbs writer, compared pleasant words are to a honeycomb that brings sweetness to the soul and health to the bones, (Prov 16:24). Choose your words deliberately that you may build up your boss and lead to improvement because, "Death and life are in the power of the tongue, and those who love it will eat its fruit," (Prov. 18:21).

Reckless words in the name of feedback can ruin relationships and make the workplace unbearable to you. As a matter of principle, sandwich every negative comment between five positive comments.

4. Focus on your perspective

Your feedback is not necessarily the exact representation of the whole picture. It only expresses the truth as you see it from your standpoint. From your boss's viewpoint, things may be very different. Therefore, limit your feedback to what you are seeing and hearing, not what you think the boss should do or what you would do if you were the boss. To help you focus on your perspective, take these steps:

- Open with affirmative feedback,
- Point out the gap between what is expected and reality,
- Provide constructive suggestions for improvement,
- Acknowledge the limitations of your standpoint and,
- Affirm what your leader is doing right.

Avoid unproven allegations unless you can provide details to support your feedback. Make it clear that you know you could be wrong and you are ready to take correction if your perspective is proven wrong.

5. Choose the right time to offer your feedback

Your timing is as important as the feedback itself. The timing should be good for you and your boss. If possible, choose the time when both of you are relaxed and in a jovial mood. Depending on your timing, your feedback will yield one of the outcomes below.[5]

- The Wrong Action at the Wrong Time = Disaster
- The Wrong Action at the Right Time = Mistake
- The Right Action at the Wrong Time = Resistance
- The Right Action at the Right Time = Success

Refrain from dealing with sensitive issues when you are sure the boss is not ready to listen. Instead, look for an opportunity to provide anonymous feedback, for instance during formal meetings.

Case Study 7. 1. Nathan: The man who gave his boss feedback

Nathan was a prophet whom God sent King David after he had taken Uriah's wife and plotted the murder of her husband (2 Sam 12:1-8, 13). Read the details of the case below and assess how well Nathan gave feedback to the king, his boss. When Nathan came to David, he said,

"There were two men in a certain town, one rich and the other poor. The rich man had a very large number of sheep and cattle, but the poor man had nothing except one little ewe lamb he had bought. He raised it, and it grew up with him and his children. It shared his food, drank from his cup and even slept in his arms. It was like a daughter to him. "Now a traveller came to the rich man, but the rich man refrained from taking one of his sheep or cattle to prepare a meal for the traveller who had come to him. Instead, he took the ewe lamb that belonged to the poor man and prepared it for the one who had come to him." David burned with anger against the man and said to Nathan, "As surely as the Lord lives, the man who did this must die! He must pay for that lamb four times over because he did such a thing and had no pity." Then Nathan said to David, "You are the man! This is what the Lord, the God of Israel, says: 'I anointed you king over Israel, and I delivered you from the hand of Saul. I gave your master's house to you, and your master's wives into your arms. I gave you all Israel and Judah. And if all this had been too little, I would have given you even more. Then David said to Nathan, "I have sinned against the Lord." Nathan replied, "The Lord has taken away your sin. You are not going to die.

Reflection questions
f. How can you describe Nathan's attitude towards David as he gave him feedback?
g. How did David respond to Nathan's feedback?
h. What did Nathan do that contributed to the positive response from David?

Receiving Feedback

Feedback is something you will receive whether you ask for it or not. Sometimes it will be obvious you are receiving feedback, but more often than not, it will not appear that way. Either way, be ready to listen and take positive measures to use it to improve the situation. Here are some measures you can adapt to make the most out of the feedback you receive from others:

1. Understand how it looks like

Feedback takes many shapes and formats. Sometimes it does not feel like feedback. For instance:

- Criticism,
- Complain,
- Correction,
- Counsel,
- Compliment,

A casual look at these five forms of communication reveal one unpleasant reality – only one out of five forms of feedback is pleasant! The fact is, whether it is criticism, complaint, correction or counsel, the message is one – there is room for improvement.

2. Own it and hone it

The most natural reaction to feedback is to resist and fight back. The temptation to justify yourself is real. Instead of fighting back, accept the feedback and make the necessary changes to improve the situation.[6] To own feedback is to receive and personalize it. To hone it is to refine and act on it. That was the significance of Solomon's advice to his son when he told him; "Listen to counsel and receive instruction, that you may be wise in your latter days" (Prov. 19:20). For "If you listen to constructive criticism, you will be at home among the wise." (Prov. 15:31, NLT)

3. Assume good intentions.

Do not jump to the conclusion that malicious motives drive the person criticizing you. Many times that is not the case. Even when that is the case, the feedback given can help you improve your performance. Similarly, do not take it personally – feedback is not about you as a person but your behavior. Focus on what you can do better, or what you can do differently to get a better reaction.

4. Seek clarification

People around you have expectations of your behavior and performance. When you fail to meet those expectations, they are disappointed and will seek to let you know so that you may make the necessary adjustments. Use negative feedback as a chance to clarify expectations and goals around your position. Ask the right questions like, 'Are you saying…,' and 'what would you have me to do about this situation?'

5. Use the opportunity to improve relationships

Your relationships will rise or fall based on your reaction to the feedback given to you. That will be true whether you are dealing with your children, parents, co-workers or fellow employees. Treat negative feedback as an opportunity to bond with your people. Schedule regular meetings with key people in your life to discuss your progress and goals.

6. Use feedback to reinforce accountability

Whether you know it or not, the person giving you feedback is attempting to hold you accountable for your actions. Instead of seeing him or her as your enemy, use the opportunity to strengthen your relationship. Appreciate the fact that he or she cares that much to draw your attention to the situation. That is a great opportunity to demonstrate that you are accountable.

7. Reflect on the feedback

Feedback helps you to identify areas of your behavior and attitude where you need to make changes. Instead of becoming defensive, use this opportunity to think of ways you can improve your behavior and attitude.

Maybe your boss, your parent or your co-worker mentioned only one negative thing! — Chances are, you are not otherwise perfect. Take it as a starting point to consider other related weak points that you could work on to become a better person and leader. Be sensitive to issues raised by more than one person. Remember:

"If one person says that you are a horse, Smile at them. If two people say that you are a horse, give it some thought. If three people say that you are a horse, Go out and buy a saddle."[7]

8. Maintain a positive attitude

It is not easy to remain positive when people complain and criticize your performance. What is natural is to focus on the negative aspect of what they said rather than what you can do to improve.

A positive attitude is choosing to dwell on the bright side of their feedback. Use it to show your co-workers that you are mature, cooperative, and able to make the necessary changes.

9. Focus on Self-improvement

Make self-improvement your lifelong goal. That will help you change the way you react to feedback. It will make you open to criticism and correction since you are looking for ways to become a better person. Remember even negative feedback is a sign that people want to help you do better. Use feedback as raw material for improvement. The case study below describes a king who mishandled feedback and paid dearly for it.

Case Study 7. 2. The man who mishandled feedback

After forty years or reigning over Solomon over all Israel, Solomon retired and handed over power to his son Rehoboam who succeeded him as king (1 Kings 11:42-43). So, Rehoboam went to Shechem, for all Israel had gone there to make him king. Then, the whole assembly of Israel said to Rehoboam: "Your father put a heavy yoke on us, but now lighten the harsh labor and the heavy yoke he put on us, and we will serve you." Rehoboam answered, "Go away for three days and then come back to me." So the people went away. Then king Rehoboam consulted the elders who had served his father, Solomon during his lifetime. "How would you advise me to answer these people?" he asked. They replied, "If today you will be a servant to these people and serve them and give them a favorable answer, they will always be your servants." But Rehoboam rejected the advice the elders gave him and consulted the young men who had grown up with him and were serving him. He asked them, "What is your advice? How should we answer these people who say to me, 'Lighten the yoke your father put on us'?" The young men who had grown up with him replied, "These people have said to you, 'Your father put a heavy yoke on us, but make our yoke lighter.' Now tell them, 'my little finger is thicker than my father's waist. My father laid on you a heavy yoke; I will make it even heavier. My father scourged you with whips; I will scourge you with scorpions.'" Three days later Jeroboam and all the people returned to Rehoboam, as the king had said, "Come back to me in three days." The king answered the people harshly. Rejecting the advice given him by the elders, he followed the advice of the young men and said, "my father made your yoke heavy; I will make it even heavier. My father scourged you with whips; I will scourge you with scorpions." So the king did not listen to the people. When all Israel saw that the king refused to listen to them, they answered the king: "What share do we have in David, what part in Jesse's son? To your tents, Israel! Look after your own house, David!" So the Israelites went home (1 Ki 12:3-16).

Consequently, the kingdom of Israel split into two. Rehoboam retained two tribes; the tribe of Judah and Benjamin. The other ten tribes revolted against him and went with Jeroboam.

Reflection questions

a) What feedback did the whole assembly of Israel give to Rehoboam when they went to Shechem to make him a king over Israel?
b) What feedback did the elders who had served his father Solomon give to Rehoboam?
c) When the people returned to Rehoboam three days later, what response did Rehoboam give?
d) What were the consequences of the way Rehoboam handled the feedback given by the people?
e) What do you learn from this case study that can help you improve your people skills?

Conclusion

Feedback is something you will receive whether you ask for it or not. Sometimes it will be obvious you are receiving feedback, but more often than not, it will not appear that way. Either way, be ready to listen and take positive measures to use it to improve the situation.

Effective leaders use feedback to motivate, inspire and improve the performance of their people. It is a necessary skill for every leader. Feedback will be a powerful tool for increasing your leadership skills and the motivation of your staff if you handle it well.

To handle feedback effectively you must know how it looks like, how to give it skillfully and above all, you use it to improve your performance.

References
1. HBS (2006). Giving Feedback: Expert solutions to everyday challenges. Harvard Business School Publishing Corporation
2. http://www.bradfordvts.co.uk/educational-supervision/feedback/
3. Robins, S. P. & Hunsaker, P. L. (2009). Training in Interpersonal Skills: Tips for managing people at Work. London, Prentice Hall.
4. Gallo, A. (2010, March 24). How to give your boss feedback. Harvard Business Review.
5. Maxwell, J. C. (1998). The 21 Irrefutable Laws Of Leadership: Follow Them and the People Will Follow You. Nashville, TN: Thomas Publishers.
6. Jacquelyn Smith (JAN 29, 2014) 8 Ways Negative Feedback Can Lead To Greater Success At Work.
7. The Little Black Book of Billionaire Secrets. https://www.forbes.com/
8. Adair, J. (2007). Developing Your Leadership Skills. Philadelphia, PA: Kogan Page.

Chapter Eight

Developing Your Leadership Style

Introduction

Leadership is the process by which one person influences the thoughts, attitudes, and behaviors of others"[1] to move them towards the achievement of predetermined desirable goals.

Gardner defines leadership as the "process of persuasion or example by which an individual (or leadership team) induces a group to pursue objectives held by the leader or shared by the leader and his or her followers.[2]" In this process, "The leader's role is to influence and provide direction to his followers and provide them needed support for theirs and the organization's success.[3]" The ultimate purpose of leadership is to persuade the people to pursue mutually beneficial goals shared between the leader and his people."[4]

Leadership style, on the other hand, is the way the leader leads. It is the method used by the leader to persuade people to commit to pursuing the mutually beneficial goals. It is the leader's most preferred method for influencing people to do what he or she wants.

Influence Techniques

Influence techniques are the methods, systems, and the procedures that leaders use to get people's cooperation. Every leader has a preferred technique which he or she uses to get people to take the desired course of action. Some methods yield positive results while others backfire on the leader and lead to disastrous results.

The leader's style is defined by the technique most frequently used. Here are some common techniques used by leaders to exert influence over their constituents.[5]

1. Positional Power

Positional power flows from the formal position held by the leader. Positional leaders use this power to remind people of their authority, especially when faced with resistance from their followers. For instance, at home, a husband is using positional power when he declares "I am the head of this family…" Similarly, a boss at the workplace may declare "I am the boss…" Some other times the leader will pose questions like "Do you know who I am?

All these are attempts to influence people based on positional power.

Positional leaders demand obedience based on the title or the position they hold within the organization. They make independent decisions and expect the followers to follow promptly. No questions, no discussion. No one else is allowed to make a decision or to suggest alternatives. It is either "my way or the highway!" Failure to do what the leader wants lands you in big trouble.

This technique works best in military type settings like the armed forces and prisons where the leader's orders the law. In ordinary organizational settings, this method will induce rebellion, resentment, and hatred towards the leader.

2. Political Scheming

Political scheming is a manipulative influence technique at gaining the people's support by appealing to their selfish partisan interests. Once the leader decides what she wants, she will use any means to get her way, which may include bribing, granting favors, giving gifts, making false promises, threatening, undermining, compromising and any other means likely to yield the desired results.

A political schemer will usually surround herself with cronies who do what the leader wants to be done and, isolate those perceived to be enemies.

Leaders who rely on political scheming as a means of gaining influence with people end up doing more harm than good, due to the deceptive and manipulative nature of the technique.

Case Study 8. 1. Abimelech's Conspiracy

Then Abimelech the son of Jerubbaal went to Shechem, to his mother's brothers, and spoke with them and with all the family of the house of his mother's father, saying, "Please speak in the hearing of all the men of Shechem: 'Which is better for you, that all seventy of the sons of Jerubbaal reign over you, or that one reign over you?' Remember that I am your flesh and bone." And his mother's brothers spoke all these words concerning him in the hearing of all the men of Shechem; and their heart was inclined to follow Abimelech, for they said, "He is our brother." So they gave him seventy shekels of silver from the temple of Baal-Berith, with which Abimelech hired worthless and reckless men; and they followed him. Then he went to his father's house at Ophrah and killed his brothers, the seventy sons of Jerubbaal, on one stone. But Jotham the youngest son of Jerubbaal was left because he hid. And all the men of Shechem gathered together, all of Beth Millo, and they went and made Abimelech king beside the terebinth tree at the pillar that was in Shechem (Judg 9:1-6)

Reflection questions

a. To whom did Abimelech go for political support
b. What did Abimelech rely on to gain the support of the people?
c. What did Abimelech do to consolidate his political power?
d. What are the benefits and dangers of relying on political scheming as an influence technique?

3. Relationships

Relationships provide a powerful means of gaining influence with people. Leaders who use this technique invest in building positive relationships with most of the people in the organization. Through those relationships, the leader can direct the followers towards his preferred direction. In this case, the people do what the leader wants not because of the task itself, but because they care for and respect the leader.

A Biblical example is David, who had developed such a good relationship with his soldiers that they were willing to risk their lives to get his wish done. David's case is given below for your consideration:

Case Study 8. 2. David's Mighty Men

These are the names of the mighty men whom David had: Josheb-Basshebeth the Tachmonite, chief among the captains. He was called Adino the Eznite because he had killed eight hundred men at one time. And after him was Eleazar the son of Dodo, the Ahohite, one of the three mighty men with David when they defied the Philistines who were gathered there for battle, and the men of Israel had retreated. He arose and attacked the Philistines until his hand was weary, and his hand stuck to the sword. The Lord brought about a great victory that day, and the people returned after him only to plunder. And after him was Shammah the son of Agee the Hararite. The Philistines had gathered together into a troop where there was a piece of ground full of lentils. So the people fled from the Philistines. But he stationed himself in the middle of the field, defended it, and killed the Philistines. So the Lord brought about a great victory. Then three of the thirty chief men went down at harvest time and came to David at the cave of Adullam. And the troop of Philistines encamped in the Valley of Rephaim. David was then in the stronghold, and the garrison of the Philistines was then in Bethlehem. And David said with longing, "Oh, that someone would give me a drink of the water from the well of Bethlehem, which is by the gate!" So the three mighty men broke through the camp of the Philistines, drew water from the well of Bethlehem that was by the gate, and took it and brought it to David. Nevertheless, he would not drink it but poured it out to the Lord. And he said, "Far be it from me, O Lord, that I should do this! Is this not the blood of the men who went in jeopardy of their lives?" Therefore he would not drink it. These things were done by the three mighty men (2 Sam 23:8-17).

Reflection Question
a) Did David ask his mighty men to go and get him water?
b) What do you think made the mighty men of David risk their lives to bring David the water which he much desired?

A relational leader does not need to demand or command. His wish is as strong as a command. That is possible only where the leader has built a strong relationship with his people that they feel obliged to satisfy his wants.

4. **Leading by Example**

The leader, who leads by example, gets things done by living the life he expects from the followers. The leader serves as a role model to his or her people. He or she does not have to command action or behavior change– instead, he implies or asks, and the people are ready to follow his or her example.

Case Study 8. 3. Apostle Paul the Role Model

A Biblical illustration of leading by example is Apostle Paul. Consider the following scripture passages taken from his address to his followers:

- Imitate me, just as I also imitate Christ. 1 Corinthians 11:1
- For though you might have ten thousand instructors in

Christ, yet you do not have many fathers; for in Christ Jesus I have begotten you through the gospel. Therefore I urge you, imitate me (1 Cor 4:15-16).

- And the things that you have heard from me among many witnesses commit these to faithful men who will be able to teach others also (2 Timothy 2:2).
- The things which you learned and received and heard and saw in me, these do, and the God of peace will be with you (Phi 4:9).

Reflection Questions
a) What was Paul doing that he wanted the Corinthian believers to do?
b) Can a leader afford to say "Do as I say and not as I do"? Why?

Whatever Paul was asking his followers to do, he had done in their presence. Therefore, he could ask them to imitate him with confidence. By setting an example for the followers, the leader earns the right to ask them to do likewise. Leading by examples makes it easier for the followers to follow what they have seen in their leader.

5. Persuasion

To persuade is to cause people to believe something after a sustained effort. Persuasive leaders' use various techniques including; argument, reasoning, selling techniques, and other credible methods to persuade people to support their initiatives. Paul used persuasion to influence others as often as was necessary. To the Corinthian Church, he said, "Therefore, knowing the fear of the Lord, we persuade others. But what we are is known to God, and I hope it is also known to your conscience" (2 Cor 5:11, ESV).

Case Study 8. 4. King Agrippa almost persuaded
Paul demonstrated his power of persuasion as he made his defense before King Agrippa. See the details in the case study below:

> Now as he thus made his defense, Festus said with a loud voice, "Paul, you are beside yourself! Much learning is driving you mad!" But he said, "I am not mad, most noble Festus, but speak the words of truth and reason. For the king, before whom I also speak freely, knows these things; for I am convinced that none of these things escapes his attention since this thing was not

done in a corner. King Agrippa, do you believe the prophets? I know that you do believe." Then Agrippa said to Paul, "You almost persuade me to become a Christian" (Acts 26:24-28).

Reflection questions
a) How did King Agrippa respond to Paul's defense? (v.28)
b) What did Paul do in his defense, which almost persuaded King Agrippa?

Persuasion is a powerful method for influencing skeptical people who need to be convinced by facts.

6. Power Sharing

Some leaders share power as an influence tool. They surrender some of their power to potential opponents in exchange for support and buy-in for their decisions. Power sharing is common in political contexts where leaders form political alliances and coalitions.

Political leaders often use power-sharing to silence their rivals by appointing them to prominent positions. In exchange, the promoted rivals feel obligated to support the leader's initiatives.

Power sharing takes different forms in organizational settings. It includes involving people in decision-making, consulting stakeholders and allowing people to have a greater say in the day-to-day running of the organization.

In the 21st century, power sharing has gained significance with people agitating for greater involvement in matters affecting their lives. Sometimes the people reject the leader's decision – not because it is bad, but because they were not consulted.

7. Character

Character is the greatest source of influence for leaders.[6] Character gives the leader a significant source of personal power. Influence based on people's perceptions of your character, including such elements of character as integrity, honesty, fairness, courage, kindness, modesty, prudence, and so on, has longer lasting impact than the other sources of influence.[7]

Without character, your role or position will not help you. Character helps us build trust and respect with people and, the more people trust us, the more our influence with them. We build trust through our integrity, authenticity and walking the talk. Your character is the expression of who you are. And influential character is built on a foundation of integrity.[8]

8. Charisma

Charisma is the special charm or appeal displayed by some leaders, which excites and attracts people to the leader. Charismatic leaders have pleasant personalities that inspire people to like and admire their style. Through this attractive personality, leaders can pull people to their side and move them to do as the leader wishes. Alexander the Great[9] was a great charismatic leader. Look at his profile:

> He was only 18 when he succeeded his murdered father as King of Macedonia and only 32 when he died, but he was able in the short time in between to conquer much of the known world. His magnetism was such that his soldiers - who knew him well and fought beside him - thought him immortal, and followed him for years through battle after battle and one unknown country after another. As he lay dying, his whole army - 50,000 men - filed past to say goodbye personally to the leader they loved and revered. That is charisma.

Charismatic leaders influence people in several ways including:

- Courageously confronting social evils and injustice committed by traditional authority structures,
- Displaying confidence in who they are and what they stand for,
- Challenging established limiting assumptions, beliefs, and traditions,
- Inspiring their followers to go beyond self-imposed limitations to reach their potential,
- Appealing to the followers' aspirations and desires to gain their loyalty, and
- Motivating their followers to fight for the promise of a brighter future.

Case Study 8. 5. Jesus Christ: The Charismatic leader

Jesus is a great leader who influenced people through charisma. Below are a few incidences when He influenced people through charisma:

a. Jesus displayed power and confidence

Then Jesus returned in the power of the Spirit to Galilee, and news of Him went out through all the surrounding region. And He taught in their synagogues, being glorified by all (Luk 4:14-15).

b. **Jesus taught with authority**
And many of the people believed in Him, and said, "When the Christ comes, will He do more signs than these which this man has done?" The Pharisees heard the crowd murmuring these things concerning Him, and the Pharisees and the chief priests sent officers to take Him. Then the officers came to the chief priests and Pharisees, who said to them, "Why have you not brought Him?" The officers answered, "No man ever spoke like this Man! (Jn 7:31-32, 40-41, 44-46).

Therefore many from the crowd, when they heard this saying, said, "Truly this is the Prophet." Others said, "This is the Christ." Now some of them wanted to take Him, but no one laid hands on Him.

c. **Jesus appeals to the followers' aspirations**
And seeing the multitudes, He went up on a mountain, and when He was seated His disciples came to Him. Then He opened His mouth and taught them, saying: Blessed are the poor in spirit, for theirs is the kingdom of heaven. Blessed are those who mourn, for they shall be comforted. Blessed are the meek, for they shall inherit the earth, (Mat 5:1-5).

d. **Jesus exposed unethical leadership**
Jesus confronted unethical leadership among the religious leaders of his day in these words;

Woe to you, scribes and Pharisees, hypocrites! For you pay tithe of mint and anise and cummin and have neglected the weightier matters of the law: justice and mercy and faith. These you ought to have done, without leaving the others undone. Blind guides, who strain out a gnat and swallow a camel! "Woe to you, scribes and Pharisees, hypocrites! For you cleanse the outside of the cup and dish, but inside they are full of extortion and self-indulgence, (Matt. 23:23-25).

Due to their appeal to the aspiration and desires of the followers, charismatic leaders attract a huge following and inspire unusual loyalty.[10]

Reflection question
Identify other cases in the scriptures when Jesus influenced people through His charisma.

9. Vision casting

Vision casting is merely communicating your vision in a simple but powerful way so that others embrace it and make it their own. Some leaders share their vision with followers in such a way that the followers buy into it and join in getting it done.

Leaders who know how to connect their vision with the people's aspirations help the followers to see the benefit of joining the leader to get the job done. This way the leader manages to influence the followers.

The leader's big vision, his passion, and belief in the goal easily convince the followers that it is doable, while the possibility of being part of such a big dream inspires them to give everything they have to pursue the dream.

Case Study 8. 6. Nehemiah the wall-builder

Nehemiah is a good example of a leader who shared his vision with the people so effectively that the wall of Jerusalem was built in a record 52 days: See the details below:

> It came to pass in the month of Chislev, in the twentieth year, as I was in Shushan the citadel, that Hanani one of my brethren came with men from Judah; and I asked them concerning the Jews who had escaped, who had survived the captivity, and concerning Jerusalem. And they said to me, "The survivors who are left from the captivity in the province are there in great distress and reproach. The wall of Jerusalem is also broken down, and its gates are burned with fire." So it was, when I heard these words, that I sat down and wept, and mourned for many days; I was fasting and praying before the God of heaven.

> So I came to Jerusalem and was there three days. Then I arose in the night, I and a few men with me; I told no one what my God had put in my heart to do at Jerusalem; nor was there any animal with me, except the one on which I rode. And I went out by night through the Valley Gate to the Serpent Well and the Refuse Gate and viewed the walls of Jerusalem which were broken down and its gates which were burned with fire.

Then I said to them, "You see the distress that we are in, how Jerusalem lies waste, and its gates are burned with fire. Come and let us build the wall of Jerusalem, that we may no longer be a reproach." And I told them of the hand of my God which had been good upon me, and also of the king's words that he had spoken to me. So they said, "Let us rise and build." Then they set their hands to this good work (Neh. 1:1-4, 2:11-13, 17-18).

Reflection question
a) How did the people respond when Nehemiah challenged them to build the wall of Jerusalem? (v.18)

b) What did Nehemiah do that convinced to rise and pursue his vision?

a. Spiritual Power
Some leaders depend on spiritual power influence followers. This divine power manifests through supernatural manifestations that cannot be explained scientifically or by logic. The Christian version of this power is the anointing or the spiritual gifts. Through spiritual power, the leader can declare things that are not, and they come to be. She can perform supernatural acts like miracles, healings, and revelation of hidden things in people's lives. Through this spiritual power, leaders can foretell the future as well as declare happenings in people's lives which come true.

The demonstration of spiritual power is a great source of influence for Christian leaders. Leaders who manifest spiritual gifts through the power of the Holy Spirit draw a huge following.

Case Study 8. 7. Elijah and the Prophets of Baal
The use of spiritual power to attract followers is not limited to Christians alone. A lot of non-Christians like the magicians, sorcerers, diviners, witch doctors, and fortune tellers influence a lot of people through the working of dark works. Look at the case of Elijah and the Prophets of Baal below:

> So Ahab sent for all the children of Israel and gathered the prophets together on Mount Carmel. And Elijah came to all the people, and said, "How long will you falter between two opinions? If the Lord is God, follow Him; but if Baal, follow him." But the people answered him not a word. Then Elijah

said to the people, "I alone am left a prophet of the Lord; but Baal's prophets are four hundred and fifty men. Therefore let them give us two bulls, and let them choose one bull for themselves, cut it in pieces, and lay it on the wood, but put no fire under it; and I will prepare the other bull, and lay it on the wood, but put no fire under it. Then you call on the name of your gods, and I will call on the name of the Lord; and the God who answers by fire, He is God." So all the people answered and said, "It is well spoken." Now Elijah said to the prophets of Baal, "Choose one bull for yourselves and prepare it first, for you are many; and call on the name of your God, but put no fire under it." And when midday was past, they prophesied until the time of the offering of the evening sacrifice. But there was no voice; no one answered, no one paid attention. And it came to pass, at the time of the offering of the evening sacrifice, that Elijah the prophet came near and said, "Lord God of Abraham, Isaac, and Israel, let it be known this day that You are God in Israel and I am Your servant and that I have done all these things at Your word. Hear me, O Lord, hear me, that these people may know that You are the Lord God and that You have turned their hearts back to You again."

Then the fire of the Lord fell and consumed the burnt sacrifice, and the wood and the stones and the dust, and it licked up the water that was in the trench. Now when all the people saw it, they fell on their faces; and they said, "The Lord, He is God! The Lord, He is God!" (1 Kings 18:20-25, 29, 36-39).

Reflection question

Why was Elijah involved in a battle with the prophets of Baal?
  a) What did Elijah propose as the solution to their conflict?
  b) How did the people respond to Elijah's proposal?
  c) How did the people react when Elijah prayed, and fire fell and consumed the burned sacrifice?

Elijah influenced the nation of Israel to follow Jehovah God instead of Baal through demonstration of power when he called fire down from heaven unlike the prophets of Baal, who were unable to do it. When the fire fell from heaven and consumed the sacrifice on the altar through Elijah's prayer, all the people fell face down on the ground and cried out "The Lord- he is God! Yes, the Lord is God!" (1 Ki 18:39).

The Bible has many cases of leaders using spiritual power to draw people towards God's agenda. When God called Moses to lead the children of Israel out of Egypt, He equipped him with the power to perform miracles to persuade the Pharaoh and the Egyptians to let the people of God free (Ex 4:1-9).

Acts 8 describes the case of a man called Simon, who "Everyone, from the least and the greatest, often spoke of him as the 'Great One – the Power of God.' They listened closely to him because for a long time he had astounded them with his magic" (Acts 8:10-11, NLT).

The way you sees yourself, your position and how you relate to your people has a great influence on your leadership style. Similarly, the performance of your people is affected by the leadership style you adopt in given circumstances.

The Different Leadership Styles

Every leader has a natural leadership style based on personality type and experience. However, since no one leadership style is suitable for all situations, wise leaders learn to choose the most appropriate style based on the prevailing circumstances and the desired outcome. Thankfully, there are many leadership styles to choose from depending to enhance your leadership ability.

In this section, we explore a wide range of available leadership styles and their effect on your relationship with your followers. We also look at the best situation to use each style and their impact on the organizational performance.

1. The Coercive leadership style

Leaders who use the coercive leadership style[11] rely on the use of power and authority to get things done. Such leaders often remind the people who the boss is. They threaten their followers with dire consequences to induce compliance.

At home, the coercive leader may use physical violence to force the spouse to do his or her will. In Church, coercive leaders employ manipulative means to force the members to submit to their will. For instance, the leader may threaten the followers with divine judgment if they disobey. Some leaders will go as far as cursing those who hesitate to take their orders. Scripture such as "Touch not mine anointed, and do my prophets no harm" (Ps 105:15, KJV), are used by coercive leaders to manipulate people.

When to use a coercive leadership style
Coercive power can produce results in the short-term; however, since it relies on intimidation to do so, it will backfire if used as the only means for exerting influence.[12] You should, therefore, use the coercive leadership style sparingly and only when necessary. Some of the circumstances that may force you to use this style include:

a. When the action is needed urgently
For instance, when faced with a deadline you may have to demand the followers to work extra hours to meet the deadline.

b. When you have no other option
After you have exhausted all other avenues for getting a necessary action, then it is to use coercion to induce compliance.

c. During crisis
A good example would be what the President of Kenya did in 2015. The problem of alcoholism had reached alarming rates in Kenya. Most young men in central Kenya among other places had become alcoholic. Consequently, some communities were at the risk of losing a whole generation. Hence, the president declared war on illegal brew and ordered all leaders to crack down on the makers, distributors, and sellers of the illicit alcohol.

d. When dealing with special categories of people
For instance, some level of coercion is necessary to discipline young children who do not see the reason for obeying their parent's instructions. Also when dealing with prisoners or criminals – coercion may be the only language the people understand.

Case Study 8. 8. When Jesus used a coercive leadership style
Is coercive leadership style ever justifiable? I doubt it! Nevertheless, some people will say yes and given an example of Jesus in the temple reproduced below:

The Passover of the Jews was at hand, and Jesus went up to Jerusalem. In the temple, he found those who were selling oxen and sheep and pigeons, and the money-changers sitting there. And making a whip of cords, he drove them all out of the temple, with the sheep and oxen. And he poured out the coins of the money-changers and overturned their tables. And he told those who sold the pigeons, "Take these things away; do not make my Father's house a house of trade." His disciples remembered that it was written, "Zeal for your house will consume me" (Jn 2:13-17, ESV).

Reflection questions
a) What did Jesus find happening in the temple?
b) What did Jesus do to the money-changers, sheep, and oxen?
c) Did Jesus beat the people with the whip? Underline your supporting statement from the scriptures

Before using this text as the basis for justifying coercive leadership style, note that this was an isolated incident and not the leadership style of Jesus. In fact, it is the only incident when Jesus made anyone to do anything against their wish.

2. The Autocratic leadership style

The autocratic leadership style is also known as the directive style, authoritative style, and the telling style.[13] "Autocratic leaders are usually rigid in their thinking and perceptions.[14] In this style, the leader does not consult the followers or even allow them to give their input towards organizational decisions. The leader makes the decision, announces it and expects the followers to adopt it without question.

In an autocratic leadership style, force may or may not be used or implied. To make it work, the leaders rely on rewards and punishments to induce compliance.

When to use an autocratic style

Autocratic leadership style should be used sparingly because of the negative reactions it elicits from the followers. A few situations where you may use it include when:

a. Dealing with New, untrained employees

When dealing with new workers who do not have the necessary skills and experience, it is logical that you will get the best results by telling the workers what is expected of them and holding them accountable to deliver.

b. Dealing with demotivated Employees

Autocratic leadership style may be the best option in the workplace, especially when dealing with indifferent employees who do not respond to any other leadership style. Employees tend to develop a culture of 'don't care' attitude towards the organization's objectives. In a situation where employees lack discipline, are ungrateful, make unrealistic demands and exert minimum efforts to reach the organization's goals, then you may result in an autocratic style to change the organizational culture.

Note: this will work where you have low-level employees and not volunteers. If you are dealing with experts and highly skilled workers, you should consider using other styles to address the problem.

c. **High-volume production needed**
Sometimes the organization may have a deadline to deliver goods or services within a very short time. Failure to do so may cost the organization dearly. In this case, the leader may not have the luxury of time to negotiate. He or she may have to set the expectations for the workers to follow

d. **You have limited time for decision-making**
Autocratic leadership style is acceptable where you have to make urgent decisions to save a critical situation. For instance, when an accident occurs in the organization, your first reaction should be to decide on the best cause of action, issue orders to be taken to save any injured people, prevent further damage and contain the situation and then other things can follow later.

e. **When the legitimacy of your authority is challenged**
Autocratic leadership style may be necessary to assert your authority when that authority is challenged or when some followers engage in sabotage and subversive actions.

f. **Under special situations**
In special circumstances like when dealing with young school children, military, emergency, and prisons, autocratic leadership style may be the most appropriate style unless you want to be run over by the people involved.

When to avoid an autocratic leadership style
For the best results you should avoid adopting the autocratic leadership style when:
- The atmosphere becomes tense, fearful, or resentful,
- Dealing with empowered people who expect their opinions to be heard,
- Your followers depend on you to make all their decisions,

- There is low morale or the members are leaving the group, and there is frequent absenteeism.

Impact of Authoritative leadership on the organization

On the one hand, autocratic leadership provides direction and decisive leadership to the organization, especially where change is urgently needed and where people's energy and efforts need to be focused towards a given direction. On the other hand, autocratic leaders often leave fear and mistrust in their wake.

As a result, the people will rarely perform beyond the commands issued by the leader. At best, the people will continue following autocratic leaders as long as it is convenient for them. Otherwise, they will use the earliest opportunity to harm you and the organization.

Due to its tendency towards command and control mechanisms to get people to perform, autocratic leadership style fails in building supportive personal relationships which are necessary to keep the people together. Thus, in the long-term, there is a high turnover when the best people leave the organization to join others where they can form meaningful relationships.

At its worst, autocratic leadership style can sacrifice initiative, new ideas, and the individual and group development of staff members. That may cost the organization missed opportunities for innovation where new ideas are withheld.

3. The Democratic leadership style.

The democratic leadership style is also known as the participatory leadership style. A democratic leader understands that there is no organization without its people. Hence, the leader gives the people a voice in decision-making. By so doing, "Democratic leaders build organizational flexibility and responsibility and help generate fresh ideas."[15] The democratic leadership style places a high value on people's ideas and their contribution towards the decision-making process.

A democratic leader looks at leadership positions in terms of responsibilities rather than status and often consults in decision-making. The democratic leader:
- Asks, values, and takes into account others' opinions, while retaining the ultimate responsibility for decision-making,
- Keeps the people informed,

- Shares decision-making and problem-solving responsibilities,
- Gathers information from the people and considers them before making decisions,
- Helps the people evaluate their performance,
- Encourages the people to set their goals,
- Encourages the people to grow in their jobs,
- Recognizes and inspires achievement,
- Aims at producing high quality and high quantity results in the long-term.

When to use a Democratic leadership style
Democratic leadership style works best where there is a need to keep group members informed. It will be an appropriate style when the leaders seek to encourage maximum participation from group members in decision-making and problem-solving. A wise leader will use the democratic style to provide opportunities for group members to develop a high sense of ownership, personal growth, and job satisfaction. It will also be an ideal style when the group is dealing with complex problems that require a lot of input from everyone and when the leader is seeking to encourage team building and participation.

When to avoid democratic leadership style
The democratic leadership style applies to many situations, but you may want to think twice before using it. The style may be suitable include when:
- Dealing with emergency or quick action is needed,
- The people involved do not have all the information to make a well-informed decision,
- The possibility of making mistakes would be too costly for and the and the organization,
- The matter under consideration involves classified and confidential information,
- Organizational safety is a critical concern.

Effects of the Democratic leadership
Democratic leadership can encourage friendships and good relationships throughout the organization since it helps people feel valued when their opinions are solicited. But, it leads to the best

decisions when the people concerned have a vested interest in the matter. It could also lead to a stalemate when two or more parties hold strongly to their chosen positions.

4. **The Bureaucratic leadership style**
You may want to call this style, leadership "by the book" since it involves doing everything according to the laid down rules and regulations of the organization.[16] The bureaucratic leader tends to be a well-organized person who will not make a decision or take a move that is not covered explicitly by the rules. He or she will refer to the immediate supervisor for wisdom on what to do regarding issues that are not provided for in the guidelines.[17]

Characteristics of bureaucratic leadership
- The leader relies on rules, regulations, or laws, to ensure absolute control over the organization,
- The organizations structured along the lines of specialties.
- People with like talents are grouped together,
- A strict vertical hierarchy of authority that is formalized by the leadership and strictly adhered to,
- Consistent focus on performance sometimes at the expense of members,
- Recruitment of members is based on talent, technical skills and superior ability to deliver results.

When to use bureaucratic
The bureaucratic leadership style works best where;
- The people involved are expected to carry out routine tasks,
- There is a need for standards and operating procedures,
- Group members use dangerous or delicate equipment which could easily lead to accidents,
- Safety or security procedures are involved,
- The situation involves military and law enforcement agencies,
- Handling of money is involved, for instance, detailed bookkeeping, requisition and accounting procedures are necessary.

When to avoid bureaucratic leadership
You may consider a better leadership style when

- You need to change negative work habits.
- The people involved are likely to lose interest in their tasks and fellow group members.
- You want to empower the people to do more than is expected of them.

Effect of bureaucratic leadership

Bureaucratic leadership style may lead to superior results where high accuracy and efficiency are priority considerations. However, the style is likely to discourage creativity and innovation. It can also lead to bored and unmotivated group members. Consequently, the organization may end up underperforming due to lack of motivation on the part of the group members.

5. The "Hands-off leadership style"

The 'hands-off' leadership style is also commonly known as the laissez-faire leadership style. It exists where the leader plays a passive role. The style is characterized by apparent indifference, non-involvement and a "leave alone" approach or neglect of responsibility.

The hands-off leader provides little or no direction to the group members. Instead, the leader gives the members as much unregulated freedom as possible. The leader gives all authority and power to the members to determine goals, make decisions, and resolve problems on their own.

A variation of the hands-off leadership style is the delegating leadership style, which is most appropriate where the followers are highly skilled and motivated to carry out their tasks without supervision. It is characterized by low involvement of the leader in the task performance and relationship with the group members. The leader delegates the responsibility for accomplishing the task to the followers and needs to be informed of the progress.

When to use the Hands-off leadership style

The hands-off leadership style may be used when:
- Dealing with experts who know their work well and are self-driven
- There is a system in place to hold group members accountable for desired outcomes
- Departmental leaders have full responsibility for running their departments

When not to use the Hands-off style
You should avoid this style when;
- People involved feel insecure in your absence,
- You are unable to provide regular feedback to the members' performance,
- The people need your affirmation and recognition for continued motivation,
- You are responsible and accountable for the performance of the organization,

Effect of Hands-off style
Hands-off leadership style could easily lead to confusion and frustration of stakeholders. Eventually, this may lead to negative behavior especially where the members lack self-motivation and direction. That may further lead to feelings of resentment towards the leader. In some extreme cases, the people may start to agitate for a replacement of the leader.

6. **The Transactional leadership style**
In simple terms, the transactional leader offers people what they need in exchange for he needs.[18] The leader relies on rewards to encourage the desired behavior and punishment to discourage undesirable behavior. The leader's influence is based on the premise that – doing what the leader wants, will get you what you want. The leader's influence in the long-term is therefore dependent on his or her continued ability to meet and respond to the changing needs of the members.[19]

When to use a transactional leadership style
The use of rewards and punishment yields results under certain circumstances like:
- When dealing with a crisis and prompt action needs to be carried out in a precise manner,
- When you want to motivate your followers to accomplish urgent goals,
- When you want to achieve short-term goals and objectives,
- When you have a clear organizational structure and specified rules, policies, and expectations, especially when the followers are aware of due rewards and punishments and for the system,
- When faced with punitive consequences for failure to meet

targets with fixed timelines.

When to avoid transactional leadership style

Transactional leadership style will not yield the desired results when:

- Long-term commitment to the vision and the long-term goals of the organization are more important,
- When you want to encourage creativity and innovation among the followers. Transactional leadership style thrives under adherence to strict rigid rules which hampers thinking outside the box,
- When employees job demands close interaction with customers. Punished employees tend to vent their frustrations on the customers as a way of getting even with transactional leaders.

The impact of transactional leadership on the organization

Transactional leadership can lead to short-term gains such as increased and motivation and productivity where efficiency is a priority. In the long-term, however, it will kill creativity and produce insensitive staff driven by what they can get from the organization.

Choosing the Right Leadership Style

Given the various leadership styles, how does the leader decide on the best leadership style to adopt in any given specific situation? Is there one leadership style, which is better than others at all times? According to Tannenbaum and Schmidt, there are three important forces to consider namely:

1. Factors related to the leader,
2. Workgroup related factors, and
3. Situational Factors.

Each of these three influencing is briefly discussed below:

1. The leader related factors

These include the leader's personality, background, education, and experience all of which influence the way the leader perceives their given leadership challenge. The leader related factors are often unconscious and should be evaluated to minimize the negative impact that might result from choosing the wrong style.

1. The leader's value system.

The leader's belief system about leadership will influence how much freedom the leader allows the group members to exercise. If the leader believes the group members should participate in making decisions that affect them and their work, then the leader will most likely allow much freedom and participation from the group members. On the other hand, if the leader believes that it is the leader's responsibility to make all decisions, which will be reflected in the leader's style, which characterized by more authoritative decision-making on the leader's part.

2. **Leader's confidence in the group members.**
The leader's confidence in the group members will depend on how much he trusts them to make the right decision. This trust depends on the reader's appreciation of the group members' knowledge, skills, and attitudes. The more confidence the leader has on the group members, the more freedom the leader is likely to allow the members to exercise in decision-making.

3. **The leader's natural inclinations.**
Depending on their temperaments, some leaders function more naturally as authoritative decision makers who like to issue orders and directives. Other leaders are more participative and tend to involve concerned parties in decision-making. A leader's natural leadership inclination will influence the style a leader adopts in any given situation.

4. **The leader's feelings in uncertain situations**
Some leaders have a greater need for predictability and stability of leadership outcomes. Others have a greater tolerance for ambiguity and uncertainty. A leader who wants to maintain control of the processes and outcomes of the group activity will most likely want to be at the center of the decision-making process thus allowing the group members limited if any leeway to contribute to the decision-making process. Feelings of insecurity in a leader's life may cause the leader to be threatened by the group members' ability and hence influence the leader's choice of leadership style towards a more directive approach.

1. **Workgroup related factors**
The most appropriate choice of leadership style will also be influenced by the characteristics of the group member(s). The group members' backgrounds, personality, education, and experience are key factors to consider since they will influence largely the way the group members will respond to the leader's

leadership style. A leader who understands, appreciates and deliberately takes those factors into consideration is most likely to settle for the style, which will optimize the group members' performance in response to his or her style.

A leader should settle for a style which allows the group members more discretion in decision-making where the group members;

- Have the necessary knowledge, skills, and attitudes,
- Have a higher need for freedom,
- Expect to be involved in decision-making,
- Are ready to assume more responsibility,
- Are capable of effective decision-making,
- Do not need clear-cut directives to perform their tasks effectively,
- Have bought into the organization's vision and attach high importance to the task,
- Have a clear understanding of the organizational goals and identify with them.

In situations where the above conditions do not exist, the leader should adopt a more directive style.

2. Situational factors

In addition to factors associated with the leader and group members, the choice of a suitable leadership style will also depend on the situational circumstances existing within which the leader and the group are operating. Some of the environmental factors that may require attention while choosing the best leadership style for a given situation include the

    a) Organizational factors,
    b) The nature of the task,
    c) The available time and
    d) The Group effectiveness.

A brief discussion on each of these factors is given below:

a. Organizational Factors

Organizational culture includes the values, beliefs, customs, norms, and the traditions deeply held and shared by the members of the organization. The organizational culture determines what is accepted as the right leadership behavior.

An abrupt and huge departure from the norms, traditions and

operating procedures of the organization especially by a new leader to the organization can render the leader ineffective even when the goals being pursued are noble.

Similarly, the type of the organization to some extent limits the appropriateness of some leadership styles. For instance, in prison or military barracks, a more directive approach is more expected as opposed to a more democratic style, which in some cases may lead to chaos.

b. The Nature of the Task

The nature of the task to be accomplished will influence the amount of discretion the leader allows the group members to have in decision-making. That is true in cases of high-risk tasks whose outcomes have the potential to cost the organization dearly in case of an error in judgment. In such cases, the leader is more likely to issue directives rather than delegating decision-making to the group members – after all, the buck stops with the leader who is answerable when things go wrong.

Consider for instance in case of war, the commander in chief does not have the luxury of delegating his authority to decide to declare war to the other commanders however senior in rank may be, simply because the future of the nation, the lives, and welfare of the citizens depend on that decision.

c. Available Time

The amount of time available for the completion of a given task exerts a lot of influence on the leadership style to be used. For instance, in case of an emergency like an accident, the leader does not have the time to consult with the concerned group regarding the best course of action. In that case, the leader adopts a directive style and if need be, consults the concerned parties afterward when the crisis has been managed.

On the other hand, if the leader has six months to decide on the best course of action to be taken, a more participatory approach may be the way to go where all the concerned group members are informed and involved in the decision-making process.

d. Group Effectiveness

Group effectiveness refers to the group members' ability to agree on the way forward and work together to deliver desired results.

Group effectiveness may be gauged by the level of cohesiveness, mutual acceptance and the extent to which they share a common purpose.

A leader's willingness to involve group members in decision-making will depend on the confidence the leader has on the group's ability to work together effectively. The more experience the group members have working together harmoniously, the more the likelihood of the leader involving the group members in the decision-making process.

Conclusion

Leadership style is the method used by the leader to persuade people to commit to pursuing mutually beneficial goals. Every leader has a most preferred style of influencing people to do what he or she wants; you can call it the default leadership style.

Influence techniques are the methods, systems, and the procedures that leaders use to get people's cooperation. Effective leaders know how and when to use the right technique in any given situation

There is no one leadership style suitable for all situations at all times. Different situations require different leadership styles. Your success as a leader will depend to a greater extent on your ability to use the right influence technique and leadership style at the right time and situation.

References
1. Mills, D. Q. (2005). Leadership: How to lead, how to live. MindEdge Press. Kindle Edition
2. Gardner, J. (1993). On Leadership. New York, NY: Free Press.
3. Goodnight, R. (2004). Laissez-Faire Leadership. Encyclopedia of leadership. Sage Publications 16
4. Gardner, J. (1990). On Leadership. New York. The Free Press
5. Community Tool Box (2015). Leadership Styles. Retrieved from: http://ctb.ku.edu/
6. Stoner, J. L. (2014). Your Greatest Source of Influence. Seapoint Centre for Collaborative leadership. Accessed on May 20, 2018. https://seapointcenter.com/greatest-source-of-influence/

7. Bacon, T. (2011). Elements of Influence: The Art of Getting Others to Follow Your Lead Special ed. Edition. AMA-COM;
8. Tredgold, G. (2016). How to Build Influence and Land That Leadership Role. https://www.huffingtonpost.com
9. Walbank, F. W. (1998). Alexander the Great: King of Macedonia. Encyclopedia Britannica.
10. Malina, B. J. (1984). Jesus as Charismatic Leader? Journal of Bible and Culture. Vol 14, Issue 2, pp. 55-62
11. Goleman, D. (2000). Leadership that Gets Results. Harvard Business Review. Product 4487
12. Rahat, T. (2015). Leadership Styles. AIOU Scholars. Retrieved from: http://aiouscholars1.blogspot.co.ke/2015/04/leadership-styles-by-tayyaba-rahat.html
13. Tannenbaum, R., & Schmidt, W. H. (1973). How to choose a leadership pattern: should a manager be autocratic or democratic – or something in between. Harvard Business Review, May-June Issue.
14. Goodnight, R. (2004). Laissez-Faire Leadership. Encyclopedia of leadership. Sage Publications
15. Goleman, D. (2000). Leadership that Gets Results. Harvard Business Review. Product 4487.
16. Maqsood, S.; Bilal, H.; Nazir, S. & Baig, R. (2013). Human and Social Science Research Vol. 1, No. 2, 139-144.
17. Spahr, P. (2015). What is Bureaucratic Leadership? How Rules Can Guide People. St. Thomas University online.
18. Kuhnert, K. W., & Lewis, P. (1987). Transactional and Transformational Leadership: A Constructive/ Developmental Analysis. Academy of Management Review, 12(4), 648-657.
19. Kellerman, B. (1984). Leadership: multidisciplinary perspectives. Eagle-wood Cliffs, NJ: Prentice Hall.

Chapter Nine

Developing Your Administrative Competence
Introduction

In this chapter, we focus on developing the administrative function of leadership. Leaders perform three inseparable, overlapping and complementary roles. First, leaders lead; a function distinct from management and administration. Notable scholars like Kouzes and Posner[1] and Kotter[2] have identified key functions that leaders carry out under the leading role. These include,

- Providing direction by clarifying the vision and mission,
- Aligning people to the vision and mission,
- Inspiring people,
- Challenging the process,
- Empowering people to act, and
- Modeling the way.

Second, leaders administer the organization through the efficient organization of people, information, and other resources to achieve organizational objectives.[3] That is the administrative function of leadership. It involves,

- Exercising full control over the activities of the organization to move towards a predetermined direction,
- Deciding what should be done, and when it should be done,
- Formulating plans, framing policies and setting objectives, and,
- Making the best possible allocation of limited resources.

Third, so doing they coordinate the leaders manage, and by resources of the organization through planning, organizing, directing and controlling to attain the goals and objectives of the organization.[4] By managing, leaders perform the executive function of leadership. Regarding hierarchy, managers work with the administrators to [5]

- Implement the policy that has been formulated through the administrative function,
- Putting plans and policies into action,

- Determine who is to do what and how, and,
- Create value for the organization.

Understanding the Administrative Function

Amadi defines administration as a "process of systematically arranging and coordinating the human and material resources available to any organization for the main purpose of achieving stipulated goals of that organization."[6] The purpose of administration is to coordinate the activities of individuals and groups to accomplish predetermined goals[7].

Effective leadership goes hand in hand with administration and management. Administration takes care of the day-to-day running of the organization while management deals with the execution of procedures, policies and the plans of the organization. The administrator is responsible for making the rules, regulations and standard operating procedures to govern the day-to-day running of the organization.

An effective administrator should, therefore,

- Apply the general concepts of Administration
- Plan and monitor work
- Facilitate productive meetings
- Manage workplace communications
- Empower the office staff's ability to manage and organize office effectively and professionally,
- Manage information effectively
- Develop an appropriate office management strategy
- Develop an appropriate assets management strategy
- Develop administrative procedures and,
- Plan and control administrative budget.

Effective administration is a key function associated with a high level of workplace productivity and efficiency. Without a good administration, the organization will flounder in its efforts to implement its goals and strategies. Below we explore some of the keys competencies the administrator should possess:

Setting Organizational Objectives

In chapter 5, we defined goals as broad statements indicating the major steps the organization intends to take in pursuit of its vision and mission. Here we define objectives as specific outcomes an individual, department or organizational group wants to pursue to achieve the organizational goals. Table 9.1 below highlights the major differences between goals and objectives.[8]

Table 9. 1. Differences between goals and objectives

Goals	Objectives
A goal is a purpose statement, which a person, group or an organization strives to achieve	Objectives are specific outcomes the department or organizational group wants to achieve the organizational goals
Goals are outcome statements that define what an organization is trying to accomplish	Objectives are the specific milestones which a person or a group plans to achieve in a within a given period
Goals describe the end-result	
Goals provide broad ideas	Objectives specify the Means to an end
Goals focus on the long-term period	Objectives provide tangible facts
Goals are comparatively hard to measure	Objectives focus on the Medium-term to Short term
	Objectives are easier to measure

Goals without objectives are unlikely to be accomplished while objectives without goals will never get you to where you want to be.

Characteristics of effective objectives

Objectives are effective depending on the way you write them. Effective objectives focus more on results than on activity. While activity is necessary for objective achievement, not every activity contributes to the achievement of a given objective. It is possible to have good activities that do not contribute towards the achievement of our objectives. With results-oriented goals, every activity is evaluated and structured to make it is necessary for the achievement of the desired outcome.

Effective objectives are written to ensure:
- There is no room for misunderstanding,
- The expected outcome is achievable,
- They are seen to be appropriate,

- Progress can be monitored to meet given standards,
- Everyone knows the expected results and their due date.

Objectives form a vital component in the planning process since they represent benchmarks, which indicate the organizational direction. An easier way to evaluate whether your goals are effective is to check whether they are SMART[9] where;

S- Specific
Objectives should be stated in a precisely to indicate exactly what needs to be done, with or for whom. Research has shown that more specific and ambitious goals lead to an increase in performance as compared to easy objectives.[10]

M- Measurable
Effective objectives are easy to measure. They indicate how much of the desired results should be expected by a given date. That makes it easy to tell when they have been achieved.

Achievable
Achievable objectives provide enough challenge but can get done in the proposed time frame given existing resources. For a Christian, existing resources include faith in God to accomplish what he has promised no matter how impossible it appears.

R- Relevant
Relevant objectives are appropriate and important to the organization and the individuals expected to pursue them. They are the right objectives for the organization. The organizational mission and the needs of the stakeholders determine the relevance of the objectives. In volunteer organizations, goals must matter to the stakeholders. Otherwise, they will not commit to pursuing the objectives fully.

T- Time-bound
Effective objectives have deadlines setting boundaries on the latest time desired results should be realized. Effective goals have a target date so that you have a deadline to focus on and something to work towards. Deadlines help to prevent routine tasks from taking priority over your longer-term goals.

You can make your objectives even SMARTER by ensuring they are **E**xciting and **R**ewarding. An objective is exciting if it resonates well with the individual's aspirations and dreams. It is rewarding if its fulfillment leaves the member with a sense of satisfaction. It is the Exciting and Rewarding element of the objectives that inspire members to go after them.

Achieving Organizational Objectives

Administrators are responsible for setting SMART objectives that lead to the realization of the organization. In chapter 4 we discussed setting and achieving goals as a key leadership function. In this chapter, we go to the next level and planning, allocating and monitoring work. Planning and monitoring work begins with setting clear objectives, followed by task performance, finally, monitoring, and controlling work performance.

Planning work

Proper planning is necessary for achieving individual and group objectives. Planning involves decision-making regarding what ought to be done. Good planning should be realistic about what can be achieved using the available resources.[11] Available resources include:

- Personnel,
- Machines and equipment,
- Materials and components,
- Finances.

While good planning does not guarantee success, lack of proper planning does guarantee failure. Good planning yields many benefits including:

- It facilitates orderly task completion. Many objectives require several activities to be completed.
- It ensures the effective use of time. Planning involves maximum utilization of resources by avoiding idle time,
- It minimizes costs by ensuring proper utilization of resources and waste avoidance,
- It helps identify resources that will be needed and making provision of them ahead of time,
- Planning involves identifying needed skills and which helps proper use of group members,
- It helps identify possible work interruption and measures to minimize such interruption,
- It helps meet customer requirements and identify

improvement issues,
- It helps identify health and safety issues.

Work planning techniques
There are many techniques and tools for planning work available out there. Different people have different preferences and so choose whatever works best for them. Among the most common work planning techniques include:

1. Checklists
The online Business dictionary defines a checklist is a "Comprehensive list of important or relevant actions or steps to be taken in a specific order." A good checklist is precise, efficient, practical and easy to use even in the most difficult situations. It provides critical reminders of the most critical and important steps likely to be skipped in the work process.[12] Preparing a checklist involves:

- Writing a list of all the activities to be done within a given time,
- Identifying the urgent or priority tasks, and,
- Keeping a continuous list of items by adding tasks and activities as you go on.

Using checklists to plan work can yield many benefits. Here we identify six of them as discussed by Andy Singer of Hartford Business Journal:

b. Organizing.
Checklists are an effective means of helping individuals stay more organized by ensuring workers do not skip critical steps in the process. A to-do-list is a form of a checklist, which allows you to quickly, and efficiently manage your various tasks.

c. Motivation:
Checklists motivate you to take action and complete tasks systematically and in an orderly manner. The joy of keeping a checklist comes from ticking each completed task, which inspires the individual to move to the next item with a sense of achievement.

d. Productivity:

People who use checklists are more likely to achieve more than those who do not. Using a checklist enables you to complete repetitive tasks more quickly and efficiently, and with fewer mistakes.

e. Creativity:

People who use checklists complete repetitive tasks faster leaving them with spare time to invest their brain-power in creative thinking and activities.

f. Delegation:

Checklists encourage leaders to delegate activities more by breaking down tasks into specific tasks. When leaders have confidence tasks will be done correctly, they delegate more which leads to more productivity.

g. Excellence

The use of checklists leads to better customer care as it minimizes careless omissions when dealing with the customer. Using checklists ensures that you do not forget anything. For instance, by keenly following through customer orders and concerns, employees provide superior customer service thereby achieving excellence in the eyes of the customer.

8. Scheduling

The Collins English dictionary defines a schedule as "A plan that gives a list of events or tasks and the times at which each one should happen or be done." In work, planning a schedule is used to set and control deadlines. A schedule sets up a timetable of a logical sequence of tasks, leading up to completion date.[13]

For effective scheduling,

- Give adequate notice of the schedules to all the persons involved in the work,
- Allocate realistic time for each task within the schedule, and,
- Give allowance for unexpected events and interruptions.

There are many scheduling tools and apps out there thanks to advanced technology. The most commonly used ones include the Schedule Planner, Google Calendar, and Microsoft Outlook among others. All you need to do is open your preferred tool and fill in the options such as the date, event, task and reminder slots.

Allocating Work

Allocating work involves deciding whom to assign a particular task or a sequence of tasks. Here are some factors to consider before allocating work to your staff members,

- **Priority**. Allocate the most important task first
- **Skills** - Depending on the work priority, allocate the task to the most skilled person
- **Availability** – Allocate the task to the most available person
- **Development** - Allocate the task to those willing and committed to personal development,
- **Interest** – Allocate the task to the most interested person

Staff briefings

Staff briefing is a meeting planned for leaders to meet with their staff on a face-to-face basis to deliver information, ask questions and collect feedback. A team briefing system is an excellent way to enable communication upwards, downwards and sideways throughout an organization.

Leaders who hold regular staff briefings enjoy many benefits including [14]

- Conveying new ideas,
- Improved communication – downwards, upwards and sideways,
- Clarity of information and direction from the top,
- Prevention of rumor mongering and 'grapevine.'
- Receive valuable feedback from questions and suggestions from all staff
- Increased awareness and involvement of the staff,
- Creation of an open communication culture
- Minimized misunderstandings
- Shared information on financial, commercial and strategic issues
- Shared mission, vision, goals, and objectives,
- Reduce assumptions and misperceptions,
- Team building

Case Study 9. 1. Nehemiah the Planner.

Nehemiah presents a good example of planning, allocating and monitoring work.

a. Preparation.

Nehemiah did not just wake up and walk to Jerusalem to rebuild the wall. A careful examination of the record of his work reveals a carefully planned and executed strategy. In Neh. 1:1-11 when Nehemiah received the news about the situation at Jerusalem from his brother Hanani, he spent many days in prayer and reflection. In Nehemiah 1:4, he testifies; so it was, when I heard these words, that I sat down and wept, and mourned for many days; I was fasting and praying before the God of heaven."

Prayer is a powerful means of preparation. It allows the leader access to the mind of God and provides an avenue for the revelation of God's view of the situation and the best way to address the situation. For instance,

b. Nehemiah identified the task in advance

Nehemiah knew beforehand what he needed to do. When the king asked him, "What do you request?" he replied without hesitation, "If it pleases the king, and if your servant has found favour in your sight, I ask that you send me to Judah, to the city of my fathers' tombs, that I may rebuild it" (Neh 2:5).

c. Nehemiah knew the kind of facilitation he needed

He asked the king for letters of authorization to facilitate:
- His travel, (Neh 2:7)
- Access to construction materials, and,
- His accommodation (Neh 2:8)

d. Nehemiah had a clear plan for work allocation

Chapter three of Nehemiah reveals a detailed work plan and duty allocation. Each household was assigned to work on the wall segment next to their homestead. Technical duties like repairs were allocated to suitable personnel like the goldsmiths and the merchants (Neh. 2:32)

e. Nehemiah monitored work progress

Nehemiah monitored work progress and addressed interruptions promptly. He took appropriate measures to protect the workers against threats from their enemies. For instance, he positioned men behind the lower parts of the wall, at the openings; and set the people according to their families, with their swords, their spears, and their bows, Neh 4:13) just in case Tobiah and Sanballat made good their threat to attack the workers.

f. Nehemiah provided motivation when needed
The enemies of Jerusalem were threatening and intimidating the people to discourage them from completing the work. This is how Nehemiah responded, he says, "And I looked, and arose and said to the nobles, to the leaders, and to the rest of the people, "Do not be afraid of them. Remember the Lord, great and awesome, and fight for your brethren, your sons, your daughters, your wives, and your houses," (Neh. 4:14).

Nehemiah presence and involvement with the people as they worked on the wall was a great motivation to the people. He was a good role model and that encouraged the workers to follow his example.

Reflection questions
- Identify two incidences when Nehemiah had staff briefings and each case identify the key agenda addressed

Facilitating Productive Meetings
Facilitating productive meetings involves planning, chairing, leading group discussions, following up on action points and evaluating the meeting effectiveness. Below we discuss each of these functions in that order.

Planning for the meetings
Have you ever been to a meeting that was not well planned? In such meetings there seems to be no agenda, the leader does not have the relevant information and, discussions seem to move to and from every direction without a clear focus. After the meeting, you feel like your time was wasted and wonder whether it was worth attending a meeting that is not taking you anywhere! Soon people lose interest in such meetings.

Effective meetings do not just happen; they are a result of careful preparation and deliberate execution. When meetings lack structure and a concise agenda, they can often be ineffective and unproductive. These types of meetings often run over a specified period, lack control, fail to move forward with their goals and participants may become frustrated and disenfranchised.

On the other hand, well-run meetings keep employees engaged and make them feel that their time and input is valued. Before you convene a meeting:

- Determine the purpose of the meeting,
- Decide on the agenda,
- Allocate time for each item of the agenda,
- Determine the expected outcome of each agenda,

To avoid wasting the members' time, you should:

a. Prepare the agenda

Agendas help streamline meetings and avoid wasting time. As the designated leader, you must prepare and think through the agenda for discussion before the time for the committee meetings. As Karen Leland and Keith Bailey, authors of the book *Time Management In An Instant*, point out, every meeting needs a "PAL"—Purpose, Agenda, and Limits.[15] During the meeting, present the agenda to the committee for adoption, deliberation, and decision-making. That does not mean you are the only one to come up with the agenda, but rather, you should provide clear direction. Once you have presented the agenda, allow other members room to raise any other business they may consider necessary for discussion during the meeting session.

The other members expect you to come prepared, to tell them what to do and guide them by considering alternative options for decision-making. Since you are the leader, you carry the mental load and responsibility for the group.

As you prepare and think through the agenda consider the following:

When preparing an agenda, consider the following:[16]

- *Topics*—what topics should be covered to meet the objective? What are the priorities?
- *Outcome*—what do we want to accomplish during the meeting?
- *Order*—what is the most logical order to discuss the topics?
- *Timing*—how much time should be allotted to each topic?

Total meeting time?
- *Attendees*—who should attend to ensure a successful meeting?
- *Time* and location—when and where will the meeting take place?

Thinking through the agenda before the meeting helps you in several ways. For instance it:

a. Helps save time; instead of coming to fumble trying to figure out what to discuss, the members can go straight to the business because the leader has already thought through it
b. Helps you look more organized; having thought through the agenda helps you to look more focused and organized. It communicates to your members that you take your role seriously
c. Helps you to provide needed guidance; having thought through the agenda, you can answer questions that may arise about the agenda, you can clarify issues and give more details where necessary

d. Chair executive committee meetings

The designated leader is expected to call for and chair the group meetings. That includes committee planning meetings and general meetings for all the members. If you do not call for the meeting, nobody else will, and since decisions are made and action steps taken during the meetings, you may end up accomplishing very little.

You need to discuss with the members how often you will be meeting and for how long. Once that decision has been made, follow up and ensure that the meetings take place as scheduled. Chairing meetings involves calling the meeting to order and coordinating the discussion by the members in an orderly and systematic order.

It is not a must that you always chair the meetings personally. In special circumstances, you may delegate that responsibility to another member. For instance when:

- Circumstances cannot allow you to be present at the meeting,
- The matter being discussed concerns you personally,
- You want to train other members to learn how to lead meetings.

e. Communicate the purpose of the meeting

People are busy and want to know what to expect in the meeting. Explain the purpose of the meeting clearly and be sure the meeting is necessary. Clear communication includes a statement of the expected outcome of the meeting. One way to ensure you are specific and clear about the purpose of the meeting is to answer the questions of what, why, when, and where. Your announcement about the meeting should answer these questions:

- What is the agenda for the meeting?
- Why is it necessary?
- Where is the meeting venue?
- When does the meeting start?
- How long will it take?

Planning helps you to think through the entire event more carefully. It calls for creative thinking and innovative ways of doing things. You can even involve your other leaders in brainstorming about how to make your meetings more relevant and interesting.

f. Keep the members informed

Communicate details related to the members. These could include the date, the venue and the duration. Members want to know particularly when the meeting will end. Although you are responsible for communicating this information to the members, the task can be delegated to the secretary or to any other member where necessary.

During the meeting stick to the starting and ending time. Nothing kills enthusiasm among group members like consistently starting meetings late and ending past the time indicated to the members. Overcome the temptation to start the meeting late while waiting for more people to come.

g. Notify key participants

Successful events require thorough advance preparation. That is true for business meetings, worship service, fundraising events, weddings and even simpler events like regular self-help groups and fellowship meeting. Notify the expected participants to the event their role in the meeting. For instance, the programmer, the speaker, the ushers and anyone else who will be playing a specific role in the meeting.

If there are guests, prepare them in advance. Let them what to expect and at what point they will be invited to play their part in the meeting. Develop a habit of reminding people about the event within two or three days to the event.

h. Take care of physical arrangements.

A successful group event takes various physical arrangements. That may include reserving the meeting venue, making sitting arrangements, Organising for any special equipment like instruments and notifying the security personnel to be aware you are expecting external guests. If you plan to serve refreshments to the guests and the members make sure those involved serving are ready for it. In short, you should make sure all the physical arrangements have been made in readiness for the meeting.

Chairing the meetings

The more busy people are, the more time conscious they are. To attract more members to group meetings and keep them involved, the leader must remain focused on the agenda and ensure the meetings are productive. That involves monitoring the group discussions and activities to ensure effective time management and desired results.

During the discussions, allow enough time to exhaust the agenda without spending too much time on the same issue when a decision can be made without further discussions. Below are some specific guidelines for making your discussions more productive;

a. Keep the discussion focused on the goal

Avoid digressions from the topic and the tendency to change the topic. While a certain level of digression is normal, sometimes the discussion can get off the topic, thereby wasting much precious time. Sometimes the discussion can move to and from one agenda to another until members are not sure which agenda they are discussing. That is common when dealing with closely related agenda. One way to avoid digression is to remind the members of the goal of the agenda constantly.

b. Summarize key decisions

During the group discussions, many ideas will be floated as ways to solve the problem. Some ideas will be contrary to each other while others will be complementary. For instance, during Bible study discussions two members may give contradictory answers to the same question which leaves participants wondering which of the two the correct one? Before you move to the next agenda, conclude and confirm the decisions made and the action tasks to be followed up.

You can ask the secretary to read what he or she captured during the discussion, and the major decision made. That will help members keep track of the progress and to mark the transition from one agenda to the next.

c. Keep track of the time

Members can get engrossed in the debate until they forget time is passing. Especially where the discussion centers on an interesting topic or a sensitive issue. You are responsible for keeping the members informed about how much time is remaining, compared to the agenda yet to be addressed. It is also important to prioritize the agenda so the most important and urgent business comes before what can wait. You do not want to run out of time only to find out something needs urgent that cannot wait until the next meeting. The main thing a leader does is to help the group get organized.

d. Bring the discussion to a definite close

Close the meeting at the planned time unless the members agree to extend it. As you wind up, review the key conclusions and decisions agreed upon, the action steps to be taken before the next meeting and the people tasked to undertake the specific actions. If there are persons tasked to carry out certain assignments that are not in the meeting then agree who will inform them. Consider also whether there is anything else to be done before your next meeting.

e. Ensure equal opportunity for participation

Most likely, your group will comprise people with different personalities. Some people prefer to think before they speak while others think loudly. It is not unusual to have a scenario where the discussion is dominated by two or three people while the rest act as observers. It is your responsibilities as a leader to ensure each member has an equal opportunity to contribute to whatever is going on. The following are some guidelines to help you equalize participation:

f. Direct your comments to the group

Address the whole group unless you are responding to a question by an individual or, you are asking a specific person a question. Maintain eye contact with everyone in the group, particularly the usually quiet ones. While it is natural to pay attention to the more talkative members, make everyone feel their presence is important to the success of the meeting.

g. Control the dominating or long-winded speakers

Sometimes you have a member who monopolies the discussion, so other members have no chance to contribute to the debate. It is even worse when such members talk as if their idea is the only way to go. Look for a diplomatic way to slow such members without discouraging them. Here are some suggestions you can try to slow them down

- Establish rules on how frequently and how long one should speak,
- Sit where you can naturally overlook them when you ask a question to the group,
- Avoid direct eye contact with them unless you want them to talk,
- Cut in tactfully, for instance by asking, "How do the rest of you feel about this issue?"

In the extreme cases talk with this member outside the meeting and encourage him or her to give others time to speak also.

h. Encourage the less talkative members to participate

Some of the best ideas come from the quiet people because they have thought through the issue thoroughly. Unfortunately, before they have time to think, other people have already spoken, and the discussion has been closed! Quiet members may feel overwhelmed by the more talkative ones or even irritated by them. Such members may choose to withdraw from the discussions and switch their attention to other things. Unless you take action, you may eventually lose such members as they eventually stop attending the meetings.

You can encourage less talkative members to participate by:

- Scanning through the entire group for non-verbal signs of irritation, disagreement or even indicators that someone wants to say something.
- Tactfully asking specific individuals to comment, e.g., "Mary,

you have not said much about this issue, what you think?"
- Asking the less talkative person to investigate the matter and report her findings to the group at the next meeting.

Your role is to draw out the ideas of everyone. Remember, group success may be defined as the maximum utilization of everyone's ideas.

i. Avoid commenting on everyone's remarks
Commenting on everyone's response is time wasting besides portraying a superior patronizing attitude. Once the members learn to expect you to respond to everyone, they will wait for your comment before the next person can make their contribution.

View your role in the discussion as that of a facilitator of the discussion. Your goal is to ensure a web of verbal interaction, where members are responding spontaneously to each other's ideas. It is prudent not to repeat or interpret what others have said unless it is necessary.

j. Guide the group to make the best decision
The leader's opinion is often considered final and could easily discourage contrary views. Hold your ideas till everyone has spoken and then allow members to react to what you have said. Wise leaders know how to make group members own the decisions made by leading them to come up with the best decisions. They do this by bouncing questions of interpretation back to the members and allowing them to process different views before a decision can be made.

k. Remain neutral in arguments
Sometimes discussions will lead to heated arguments where all or, some few members take opposing sides. In such cases, it is prudent for you to remain neutral position. When you take sides, you lose the objectivity to see valid points from the opposing side while still encouraging members from the other side to participate. You also trigger feelings of resentment from members from the side you are not supporting. You do not want to be seen as partisan in such cases. You want everyone to go out feeling they can trust you to support them even if you do not agree with their ideas.

Leading group discussions
Group discussion is a systematic and purposeful interactive oral

process, where the exchange of ideas, thoughts, and feelings take place through oral communication.

Group discussions are a normal administrative function in any organization. Discussions facilitate making important decisions that guide organizational day-to-day operations. They happen in board meetings, school committees and Church group meetings among many other settings. Productive group discussions do not happen by accident. They are well planned and facilitated.

Leading group discussions involve starting the discussions on a positive note, ensuring discussions proceed in an organized manner, stimulating creative ideas and stirring critical thinking among members. Effective leaders monitor the agenda to ensure what is not accomplished in one meeting can be addressed at the next meeting. Let us examine these functions in more detail:

a. **Start on a positive note**
Your opening remarks are very important since they set the tone for the rest of the meeting. To ensure a productive meeting, here are guidelines you can follow to make sure the meeting gets started on the right footing:

b. **Help members feel comfortable**
Help reduce tension among members. You can do this by starting with a prayer, an icebreaker, introducing new members if there are any, or by sharing some relevant information. Appreciating members for attendance and encouraging continued participation is also important. Do not take members involvement for granted. People like being noticed and appreciated.

c. **Communicate expected outcomes**
Briefly review the purpose of the meeting, the expected outcomes and any limitations the members may need to remember during the discussions. That information should have been communicated in advance but even then, reviewing it helps to refresh the members' memory.

Reviewing the purpose and expected outcomes of the meeting helps members to remain focused. Without a clear goal for the meeting in mind, the discussion is likely to veer off the track and digress to unrelated issues that may consume time unnecessarily.

d. **Provide the information in advance**

Group members need background information to help them make informed decisions. Background information includes copies of previous minutes, information sheets, list of the agenda, reports budgets and any other form of information necessary to help members make informed decisions.

e. **Established special roles**
In regular group meetings, special roles include the recorder, timekeeper, and a substitute chair should the leader step aside briefly. Let the members decide whether those roles will be rotational or whether one person will serve in that capacity for the entire term of service for the committee.

f. **Agree on the procedures to be followed**
Guide the members agree on the procedures to be used in making decisions. Are they going to vote? Are they going to decide by consensus? How about participation? Are they going to make contributions in any order or anyone can talk at any time? Are members going to address the chair or address each other directly? At least make sure the procedure is clear to all members and that it is followed.

How you facilitate the discussions will determine the outcome of the meeting and how much will be accomplished. Think through every agenda and decide what you want to achieve by the discussion.

Reserve your opinion until you have heard what the other members think before you can share yours. That will encourage the free flow of ideas which you can draw from as you summarize the discussion and the final decision.

Following up on action points
One purpose of meetings is to make decisions that lead to the realization of the organizational goals. As a result, some members are given tasks to act on before the following meeting. Follow up on meeting action points involves reminding people of the actions steps they were assigned during the meeting and reporting to relevant authorities. Between the meetings, the leader undertakes these administrative duties:

a. **Ensure action points carried out.**
Keep track of the assignments given to the members of the

previous meeting and remind the members when their action is due. Also, keep in touch with the members either by phone or by email to monitor their progress.

b. Serve as spokesperson for the group
At the departmental, your administrative duties involve representing your group at a higher organizational level where you may have to respond to questions regarding your department's activities. Be ready to give a report regarding your department's progress.

Prepare also to raise any concerns affecting members of your department. That regards matters where you lack adequate authority or resources to facilitate.

Evaluating meeting effectiveness
One famous quote attributed to Albert Einstein compares insanity to "Doing the same thing over and over again and expecting different results."[17] Effective leaders evaluate the outcomes of meetings to discover ways of improving the group's effectiveness. Leaders who do not evaluate their performance regularly end up making poor decisions, which eventually affect their performance. Good leaders adjust their behavior from one meeting to the next to get better results.

By evaluating meeting effectiveness, you want to answer these questions:
What went well about the meeting? What did not go so well and can be improved? What do we do differently to get better results? The more you involve your group members in answering these questions, the more you are likely to arrive at an objective assessment of the meeting effectiveness. The following are some useful guidelines to follow as you evaluate the effectiveness of your meetings:

a. Review your notes of the meeting
Even when you have a secretary recording the minutes, it wise to jot down some brief notes of the key happenings during the meeting. After the meeting, use those notes to help you answer some key questions such as:

- Did the meeting accomplish its purpose?
- Did every member participate?

- Did I manage time well?
- Were the members creative and critical enough?

b. Identify improvement issues

Based on your answers to the above questions, come up with specific adjustments to improve the last meeting's performance. People love progress and signs of success. They love to see something new and positive about their performance. Use that knowledge to cultivate enthusiasm in your group members and to promote a culture of continuous improvement.

c. Set goals for improving the next meeting

After identifying the improvement issues, establish specific goals for improving the performance of your next meeting. For instance, you decide that the next meeting can be improved through the balanced contribution of each member; you can set a goal to ensure that everyone participates by tactfully limiting the number of times one member can contribute before everyone else has spoken. If you feel like the members were not creative enough during the previous meeting, you can set a goal to familiarize the members with the brainstorming procedure.

d. Facilitate behavior change

The key to improvement is changing the way we do things. For those who talk too much, relevant behavior change will involve learning to hold their thoughts to allow other members to participate while for those who rarely volunteer to speak it may involve taking the risk of sharing their thoughts more often.

To facilitate behavior change, you need to take the group through a self-assessment process by addressing the question; 'how can we do this better?' Behavior change comes easy when each can verbalize what they must change and even suggest what they can do to bring about the desired change.

Managing Written Communication

Effective leadership requires effective communication. Leadership is both built on and conveyed through language.[18] Effective communication determines the extent to which the followers understand, buy into and commit to pursue the organization's vision and goals.

To become a good leader, you have to become a good

communicator, and that's not all; you have to ensure effective communication is sustained at all the levels of the organization. If you do not manage communication well, no one else will. That is true whether you have a public relations department or not.

Effective leaders therefore intentionally ensure their message is received understood, accepted, and, the desired action is taken in response to their message.

The need for clear records

While much of the communication within the organization is oral, there is a need to maintain written communication. Effective leaders manage written communication well for three purposes:

a. **Reference.**

Keep written records to serve as a reference point of what happened in past. Clear records provide a history of past events. That helps new leaders to make informed decisions today because they know where the organization has come from.

For instance, with clear records, new leaders can familiarize themselves with the organization's mission, goals, strategies, and other important facts so they need not start afresh.

b. **Information.**

With clear written and well-kept records, new leaders can retrieve the records and familiarize themselves with the organization past as much as possible. Written records help preserve institutional memory. They preserve the history of the organization to allow new leaders to have access to the information they need to carry on with their work more effectively.

Clear records inform other stakeholders of the organization's activities. For instance, written reports keep the authorities updated on what is happening at the lower levels of the organization.

Clear records inform members of the organization's assets and obligations. That provides the basis for accountability and good stewardship which are important effective leadership.

c. **Coordination.**

Written communication serves to coordinate activities with other groups that work together towards the same broad objective. They help remind people of plans, their responsibilities, and accountabilities.

Though your role as a leader is not necessarily to do the writing, you are responsible for ensuring proper records maintained. You, therefore, must ensure someone is charged with that responsibility and they know and are doing what is expected.

Forms of written communication
Organizations use various forms of written communication including:
a. Personal notes
b. Minutes
c. Notices
d. Reports

a. Personal notes
These are brief sketches you jot down as the meeting is ongoing to capture the key points of the deliberations. This way you can focus on what is important about the ongoing discussions. Personal notes may include:

- Ideas or issues to follow up about after the meeting,
- Assignments you and others have been allocated,
- Proposed ideas and action steps,
- Interpretations made by the others,
- Important dates and events,
- Key decisions made and,
- Ideas triggered in your mind by the discussion.

Later after the meeting, you should review your notes to clarify and elaborate on them as you plan action steps to consider as you implement your ideas.

b. Minutes
Minutes comprise formal notes of what happens during formal deliberations. As a leader, you are responsible for ensuring an accurate record of what happens during your meetings is taken and kept for future reference. Distribute this information to members before the next meeting to help them refresh their minds as they prepare to attend the next meeting. That saves time during the meeting and prepares the members to be more productive since they have already reflected on the proceedings of the previous meeting.

The role of taking minutes is usually assigned to the secretary to the committee though; in other cases, someone else may be appointed to record the meeting proceedings. For a small group meeting the minutes should contain a summary of the deliberations including the following:

- The date and venue of the meeting,
- A record of attendance and absences and any apologies,
- The agenda,
- All the ideas considered by the members,
- Any criteria agreed upon in making decisions,
- All decisions,
- All assignments,
- Any plans and procedures for future action,

It is common practice to provide for signing space, usually done by the chairperson and the secretary in the next meeting. After the minutes have been signed, they become the official record of the organization and may be as authoritative evidence in a court of law.

Encourage members to express themselves freely and protect confidentiality by handling sensitive information with care, especially where minutes are to be distributed to members. Do not include sensitive information in the record for circulation where a breach of confidentiality is at stake.

Handle information such as, details of who proposed what cause of action, who voted for or against what, and who provided what information with care. In such cases, it is safe to include the conclusions, summaries and the assignments

After the meeting, the person taking the minutes should sign the copy and, in consultation with the leader have them distributed to the members shortly. Below are samples of the same Minutes for a small group in two formats.

c. Reports

Best practice organizations require preparation of regular reports of activities and progress towards set goals. That enhances accountability besides helping maintain the group's focus on the organization's vision, mission and goals. The leader is expected to submit reports by the set date.

If you wish to prepare the report personally, that is okay, however with your many responsibilities you may not have the time and energy to do everything. A better way is to equip one or two other members of your committee to take up this responsibility.

A common practice is to prepare a draft and then circulate it to the members for their input. Once the input by other members is added, you can call a meeting for the members to adopt it before submitting it as the official report from the committee.

In your report, you may include:
- Plans, goals, and objectives,
- Activity report showing previous activities,
- Achievements,
- Challenges faced,
- Attendance record,
- Any other relevant information,

The administrative leadership role requires the ability to manage a range of details and functions and the list covered in this book is not exhaustive. Space and time did not allow us to cover every detail. Nevertheless, by developing your ability in the areas covered in this text, you will have taken a step towards becoming a better leader.

d. Written Notices and Visuals

Written Notices and Visuals represent another form of written communication the leader should manage. These are the common forms of meeting notifications sent to concerned individuals to notify them of a forthcoming meeting. Avoid impromptu meeting announcements common in some organizations where members are summoned without notice.

To maximize on the use of written notices, evaluate your notices against the criteria given in below. Effective Notices and Visuals should contain this information;

- The target audience - indicate the person or the group the message is meant for.
- The sender -include the name of the person sending out the notice or calling the meeting.
- The venue - show where the event will take place.

- The time - include the starting and ending time for the meeting,
- The purpose - State the expected outcome of the meeting,
- The agenda - indicate the objective of the meeting and if there will be room for other business,
- Expectations – indicate what is expected of the members e.g. what they are expected to bring.

Ensure notices contain enough information to help those concerned act as required. Take for instance this announcement:

"Members of the welfare committee will meet immediately after this meeting."

What do you think are the shortcomings of this notice?
You probably thought about some of the following shortfalls:

- Short notice
- Venue not indicate
- Assumes people have nothing else to do but wait to be called for a meeting
- Exact time not indicated
- No indication of the purpose of the meeting etc.

Regular impromptu call for meetings sends across the message that you do not respect the time of those concerned, you are disorganized, and you are not forward-looking. You do not want to paint that picture to your followers!

Meeting notifications should go out to each concerned member early enough to allow them time to plan and prepare for the meeting.

Written notices may take different formats. For instance, memos posted on the notice board, emails and short text messages (SMS) among others. Visuals include a combination of text, symbols, graphics, and pictures. They include posters, overhead projector, transparencies, PowerPoint slides, and videos.

Many organizations have adopted visuals as a way of making notices due to their richness and ability to capture the attention of the audience. Churches are particularly prone to ignoring conventional communication. I, therefore, use the church as a reference point in the following illustration:

Sample written notice

Date: Tuesday, May 26, 2015

To: Local Church council (Alphonse Mwatela, Maina Warui, Michael Onyango, Stephen Wanyoike, Paul Malusi, Martin Mudaki, Adonina Mutua, Eunice Matere)

From: Rev. Etemesi Omar (Pastor, Springs of Life Church)

Re: Local Church Council Meeting
Our next Local Church Council Meeting is scheduled to take place on Saturday, June 6th, 2015 at 11.00 am, in the Boardroom

The Purpose:
To: 1) Approve this year's audited report, 2) Set a date for this Year's AGM, 3) Prepare a schedule of worship service speakers for June- Dec period and 4) Evaluate the Church performance for the first half of this year.

Bring: Your dairy, Bible and a pen
Where detailed reports involving figures and graphs are part of the agenda, circulate those handouts in advance. For instance, where annual general meeting when financial reports are to be tabled, providing members with an opportunity to peruse copies of the financial statements in advance prepares them to be more engaged in discussing the report

Essentials of Effective Written Communication

Whether you are dealing with meetings minutes, notices, reports or letters, written communication strive to have your written communication meet the 5C criteria given below.

Good written communication should be:[19]

a. **Clear**
A message is unclear when it does not convey the message you intended it to deliver. Avoid sending ambiguous messages that can be interpreted to mean different things to different people. Use simple language that is appropriate for your intended recipients. Avoid complicated jargon and terms that do not add value to your message. Keep it simple and avoid abbreviations as much as possible unless their full meaning is known to recipients of your message.

b. **Concise.** Limit your message to what the recipient needs to know and do. Use short sentences and justify unpleasant or difficult messages where necessary.

c. **Complete.** Provide complete information to help the recipient take the intended action. Include all the facts, evidence and conclusions that the reader needs to act.
d. **Correct.** Ensure your information is factual, and that your conclusions and recommendations are justified. Have your message checked for grammatical typos and spelling mistakes.
e. **Courteous.** Be courteous. People dislike rude language and are offended by unkind words.

Case Study 9. 2. The Trinity and leadership

The doctrine of the Holy Trinity is central to understanding the Christian faith.[20] According to this doctrine, there are three persons in the Godhead; God the Father, God the Son, and God the Holy Spirit. These three are one God and three different expressions of the same God. According to Zscheile, "The way in which we understand the nature of God and the way in which we envision and enact leadership within Christian communities are inexorably linked, whether recognized or not."[21]

While recognizing the limits of the analogy between the Trinity and human behavior, there is much we can learn about leadership from the way the three persons of the Trinity operate.

The use of the term 'God the Father' points to the first person of the Trinity, God as creator and supreme authority.[22] First, we see God the Father in the Bible as the ultimate leader, the vision bearer and the initiator of everything. Many scriptures attest to this function of God the Father, for instance, "In the beginning, God created the heavens and the earth (Gen 1:1)."

The vision of man as God's delegated authority flows from the heart of God the Father. God the Father expresses His vision in these words; "Then God said, "Let us make mankind in our image, in our likeness, so that they may rule over the fish in the sea and the birds in the sky, over the livestock and all the wild animals, and over all the creatures that move along the ground" (Gen 1:26)

Throughout the creation story, the words "And God said..." are used repeatedly, indicating the Father's leadership role. God the Father is, therefore, the expression of the Triune nature of God as He relates to His creation.

Second, Jesus Christ, the second person of the Godhead carries out the administrative role. His role as the Administrator of God's estate comes alive as you read the Gospels. A case in point is Mark 6:7-14, which says,

> Calling the Twelve to him, he began to send them out two by two and gave them authority over impure spirits. These were his instructions: "Take nothing for the journey except a staff—no bread, no bag, no money in your belts. Wear sandals but not an extra shirt. Whenever you enter a house, stay there until you leave that town. And if any place will not welcome you or listen to you, leave that place and shake the dust off your feet as a testimony against them." They went out and preached that people should repent. They drove out many demons and anointed many sick people with oil and healed them.

In the above scripture, we see Jesus sending the disciples, giving them the authority and the power to act. That is the administrative role.

Third, the Holy Spirit, the third person of the Godhead, and plays the role of the Executive or the managerial role of the Godhead. He is God, actively involved in the world and with humanity. Jesus, describing the role of the Holy Spirit to the disciples used these words, "But when he, the Spirit of truth, comes, he will guide you into all the truth. He will not speak on his own; he will speak only what he hears, and he will tell you what is yet to come" (Jn 16:13).

Reflection questions
a) Identify the three functional roles of leadership
b) Compare the three functional roles of leadership to God's triune nature. What differences and similarities can you draw from this analogy?
c) Which one of the three functional roles of leadership represents your greatest strengths?

Conclusion

Effective administration is a key function associated with a high level of workplace productivity and efficiency. It involves setting goals, planning and allocating work, monitoring performance, facilitating productive meetings, and managing workplace communication.

Effective leadership goes hand in hand with administration and management. Administration takes care of the day-to-day running of the organization while management deals with the execution of procedures, policies and the plans of the organization. The administrator is responsible for making the rules, regulations and standard operating procedures to govern the day-to-day running of the organization. Effective leaders understand the need for administration and make sure it is taken care of.

References

1. Kouzes, J. M., & Posner, B. Z. (1995). The leadership challenge: how to keep getting extraordinary things done in organizations. San Francisco: Jossey-Bass Publishers
2. Kotter, J. P. (2000). What leaders really do. Harvard Business Review. Product number 3820.
3. Mills, D. Q. (2005). Leadership: How to lead, how to live. Walham, MA: MindEdge Press. Kindle Edition
4. Mescon M., Albert M., Khedouri F. (1988). Management, Third Edition Harper-Row, Publishers, N.Y., pag.464.
5. Surbhi, S. (2015). Difference between Management and Administration. Key differences. https://keydifferences.com
6. Amadi-Eric, C. (2008). Introduction to Educational Administration: A Module. Port Harcourt. Harey Publications
7. Simon, H. A., Smithborg, D. W., & Thompson, V. A. (1950). Public Administration, New York: Alfred A. Knopf.
8. Trent, R. J. (2007). Strategic Supply Management: Creating the next source of Competitive Advantage. Andrews Way, Lauderdale: J. Ross Publishing.
9. Meyer, J. P. (2003). Attitude Is Everything: If You Want to Succeed Above and Beyond. The Leading Edge Publishing
10. Locke, E. A., & Latham, G. P. (2002). Building a practically useful theory of goal setting and task motivation: A 35-year odyssey. American Psychologist, 57(9), 705-717.
11. BPP Learning Media (2012). Planning and Monitoring Work. ILM Level 2 Leading Series 2013.London, BPP Learning Media Ltd.
12. Gawande, A. (2010). The Checklist Manifesto: How to Get Things Right. London, Profile Books Ltd.
13. BPP Learning Media (2012). Planning and Allocating Work. ILM Leading Series 2013 Level 3. London, BPP Learning

Media Ltd.
14. BPP Learning Media (2012). Giving Briefings and Making Presentations. ILM Leading Series 2013 Level 3. Lon-don, BPP Learning Media Ltd.
15. Leland, K. & Bailey, K. (2008). Time Management In an Instant: 60 Ways to Make the Most of Your Day, CGAV9; 1 edition
16. Simoneaux, S. L &. Stroud, C. L. (2015). A Meeting of the Minds: The Art of Planning Productive Meetings. Journal of Pension Benefits, pp. 94-97
17. Brown, R. M. (1983). Sudden Death New York: Bantam Books. p. 68.
18. Griffin, J. (2010). How to Say it for First-Time Managers: Winning Words and Strategies for earning your Team's Confidence. New York. Prentice Hall Press.
19. Williams, K. (2006). Introducing Management: A Development Guide: Burlington, M: E. Butterworth-Heinemann.
20. Moltmann, J. (1993). The Trinity and the Kingdom: The Doctrine of God, 1st Fortress Press ed. Minneapolis: Fortress Press,
21. Zscheile, D. J. (fall, 2007). The Trinity, Leadership, and Power. Journal of Religious Leadership, Vol. 6, No. 2,
22. Kimbrough, L. (2006). Contemplating God the Father B&H Publishing.

Chapter Ten

Take It Home

Introduction

The objective of this chapter is to guide you to apply the principles and lessons taught in this book to improve your character and competence. It is not what you know what changes your life, rather, it is what you do about what you know that brings life transformation. That is a universal principle repeated by great minds through human history. Albert Einstein described insanity as doing the same thing over and over again and expecting different results. Jesus told his disciples; "If you know these things, blessed are you if you do them" (Jn 13:17).

It does not matter how many books you read, how many academic degrees you earn and how many leadership seminars you attend; if you do not apply what you learn, it will all be lost. After all, "Education is what remains after you have forgotten everything you learned in school."[1]

In chapter one we looked at the six ways people learn leadership. We discussed learning techniques including observation, lectures, experiential learning, case study analyses, group discussions and action learning. In this chapter, I present the key principles, concepts, and lessons presented in each chapter and offer suggestions on specific action steps you can take to maximize your learning from the book. When everything is said and done, it is what you apply that will determine whether you grow your ability to lead or you remain the same.

1. Deepen your Understanding through Reflection

Reflection is a learning method that encourages deep thinking about your existing knowledge and experiences to engage in a process of continuous learning. Reflection is recognized as a powerful learning tool for leadership other professional disciplines.

The process of reflection involves a conscious exploration, examination, and understanding of what you are feeling, thinking and learning. It involves a "thoughtful consideration of the negative and positive emotions triggered by an experience."[2]

Two things you can do to become a reflective learner:

a. Keep a leadership reflection journal

A leadership journal is a daily record of ideas and events related to your leadership journey. It is similar to a diary, only that you write your thoughts, ideas, feelings, and events as they occur.[3]

The main purpose of keeping a reflective journal is to challenge you to become more aware of what you do, how you do it, why you do it. Leaders often act unconsciously without careful consideration of their motives, impact and the consequences of their actions. A leadership reflection journal will help you identify useful problem-solving strategies and recognize your strengths and weaknesses.

One way to keep a leadership journal is to take a few minutes at the end of each day and reflect on the happenings of the day. If you are just beginning, you may use the questions in table 10.1 to guide you:

Table 10. 1. Leadership journal reflection questions

- What happened?
- What did I do?
- How did I do it?
- Why did I do it?
- What did I learn?
- How did I feel? Why?
- What does it mean
- Which aspects were successful?
- What should I have done differently?
- What do I need to do next time?
- What specific areas do I need to improve or extend?

Keeping a leadership journal will benefit you in at least two ways; first, you will expand your self-awareness. You will become more conscious of your strengths, energizers, and challenges. Second, it will help you manage your stress. As you process stressful events through entries into your leadership journal, you will release the negative emotions, and ultimately enable learning.[4]

b. Reflect on the principles learned from this book

As a Man Thinketh, so is he.[5] Reflecting on the key principles, lessons, and concepts taught in this book will greatly influence your basic assumptions and what you believe about leadership. Eventually, your leadership beliefs will influence your leadership practice.

The section below presents the key concepts and principles to help with your reflections. You can choose to focus on one chapter per day, week, month or as long as it takes to internalize the key takeaways.

Chapter 1. Ideas for Reflection
- We live and work in a constantly changing world
- Leaders need to ensure their knowledge, skills, and experiences are evolving with changing demands
- Commit to continuous learning and development crucial
- Leadership is about who you are as well as what you do
- Who you are determines what you do and greatly influences your leadership style.
- The key to becoming an effective leader is to focus on becoming the kind of leader people want to follow
- Having a leadership position or title does not guarantee people will follow you. Growing your leadership ability will.
- Developing your leadership ability will help you understand what leaders do and equip you with the skills you need to deliver on your mandate
- Effective leadership development rests on three pillars: character competence, and commitment.
- Leadership is not an exclusive club for those born with leadership qualities, but is a skill that can be developed,
- Successful leadership development produces authentic leaders who:
  - ✓ Know who they are and what they believe in;
  - ✓ Show consistency between their values, ethical reasoning, and actions;
  - ✓ Develop positive psychological states such as confidence, optimism, hope, and resilience in themselves and their associates;
  - ✓ Are widely known and respected for their integrity.

Chapter 2. Ideas for Reflection
- Character is a complex combination of moral, mental and emotional qualities that influence everything you do.

- Leadership character is the most effective means of persuasion.
- Research findings on leadership indicate that many failures in leadership are character related.
- Your character affects your leadership ability in both direct and indirect ways. It determines the quality and the degree of your influence.
- Your character will either reinforce or weaken your influence with people.
- Character is what makes a person unique from others.
- Your character is a complex combination of moral mental and emotional qualities.
- A person of integrity does what is right even when it is not convenient.
- The word temperament does not appear in the Bible. However, the concept appears in several places using different terms such as the natural man, the old man, and the flesh.

Chapter 3. Ideas for Reflection
- Leadership character does not happen accidentally. It is an intentional effort cultivated and nurtured through hardship and trials.
- Character building is a lifelong process that begins in our infancy and continues until death.
- Many factors work together to shape your character including; your temperament, early childhood experiences, training, and, religious faith.
- Your temperament works like the manufacturer's default settings; it determines why you act the way you do.
- Instruction from parents, teachers, and peers in the formative years play a major role in shaping one's character.
- The first step in character development is to identify specific character deficiencies and then develop an action plan for growth.
- Developing moral reasoning ability marks an important step towards character development.
- There is power in the written word. Reading has a similar

effect on a person's character as watching value loaded movies.

Chapter 4. Ideas for Reflection
- Your leadership journey begins when you discover God's purpose for your life.
- Your mission and vision, which are critical factors in your leadership flow out of your purpose.
- After discovering your life purpose, your next step is to write your mission statement articulating what you do to fulfill your purpose.
- A well-written mission statement is a powerful tool for understanding, developing, and communicating important organizational objectives.
- A vision statement is a future-oriented declaration of the organization's purpose and aspirations.
- The purpose of a vision statement is to motivate, inspire and energies the members of your organization to rise and pursue the organization's desired future.
- Many Christian leaders can't clearly state their vision. Approximately, only 3-5% of pastors have a compelling vision,
- Leadership as the capacity to translate vision into reality,
- Leaders translate vision into reality by sharing their vision with their followers until they buy into and commit to pursuing it,
- Every genuine vision comes from God and is birthed in prayer,

Chapter 5. Ideas for Reflection
- The purpose of goal setting and planning is to make you a proactive leader who takes advance action to facilitate desired results.
- Great achievements rarely happen by chance. They are a result of deliberate efforts carefully planned and executed by those who desire to make a difference.
- Effective leadership begins with a clear sense of purpose, mission, and vision followed by goal setting.
- Research has established a close relationship between setting goals and success in life.

Facts about goal setting:
- ✓ People with written goals are 50% more likely to achieve their goals

- ✓ A whopping 92% of New Year's goals fail by January 15th
- ✓ Only 3% of adults write down their goals on paper
- ✓ Setting a goal is the first and crucial step in turning the invisible into the visible
- Effective goals focus more on results than on activity. While activity is necessary for objective achievement, not every activity contributes to the achievement of a given objective.
- Many leaders with big, hairy, audacious goals get frustrated because they are unable to make their goals materialize.
- You can make your goals even SMARTER by ensuring they are **E**xciting and **R**ewarding. A goal is exciting if it resonates well with the individual members' aspirations and dreams.
- Many planning and goal setting attempts fail because of poor implementation.
- Operating below your set goals and standards is an indication that you are underperforming.
- Setting unrealistic goals can have a negative impact on your followers and the organizational performance.
- Regular goal evaluation events help to keep goal implementation on track.

Chapter 6. Ideas for Reflection
- People skills are relational abilities that enable a person to live in peace with others, engage others positively and intentionally influence their decisions and actions towards a desired direction.
- Without people skills, the leader is unable to connect emotionally with the people and therefore unable to inspire commitment.
- Effective leaders possess four categories of skills, which set them apart from their peers, including conceptual, technical, political, skills, and people skills.
- Different terms used to describe people skills include soft skills, interpersonal skills, and human skills.
- Developing good people skills begins with the right attitude towards yourself and others.
- Emotional intelligence refers to a set of related abilities that empower leaders to identify, understand, control and assess the

emotions of the self and others.
- Emotional intelligence is an essential building block for people skills.
- Emotional triggers are the factors that set off impulsive reactions leading to loss of self-control.

Chapter 7. Ideas for Reflection
- Communication is a key aspect of people skills, and effective communication involves giving and receiving feedback,
- Giving feedback involves communicating in a way that encourages the recipient to accept, reflect, learn from, and make appropriate changes in response to the feedback,
- When handled well, feedback can be a powerful tool for increasing skills and motivation.

Chapter 8. Ideas for Reflection
- Leadership style is the method used by the leader to persuade people to commit to pursuing mutually beneficial goals.
- Every leader has a most preferred style of influencing people to do what he or she wants; you can call it the default leadership style.
- Influence techniques are the methods, systems, and the procedures that leaders use to get people's cooperation.
- No one leadership style is suitable for all situations at all times. Different situations require different leadership styles.
- The leader who desires to become more effective will commit to developing his or her ability to adopt the most suitable style in different situations and circumstances.

Chapter 9. Ideas for Reflection
- Leaders perform three inseparable, overlapping and complementary roles. They lead, administer and manage.
- Effective leadership goes hand in hand with administration and management.
- The leadership function involves providing direction, clarifying the vision and mission, aligning people with the vision, inspiring and empowering others to act.
- Effective administration is a key function associated with a high level of workplace productivity and efficiency. It involves setting goals, planning and allocating work, monitoring

performance, facilitating productive meetings, and managing workplace communication.
- Without a good administration, the organization will flounder in its efforts to implement its goals and strategies
- Planning and monitoring work begins with setting clear objectives, followed by task performance, finally, monitoring, and controlling work performance.

Develop Your Character through Discipline

Leadership character does not happen accidentally. It is an intentional effort cultivated and nurtured through hardship and trials. John Luther once said, "Good character is more to be praised than outstanding talent. Most talents are, to some extent, a gift. Good character, by contrast, is not given to us. We have to build it piece by piece by thought, choice, courage, and determination."[6]

Developing leadership character is not an easy task. On the contrary, it is a challenging endeavor as Phil Eastman rightly observes:

> It would be nice if becoming an effective leader were easy— and if all the ideas and techniques you read about or experience in workshops were simple to use. However, the real world is something else. Becoming a great leader is hard work." and "Like any long-term process, it is fraught with pain and exhilaration. To complicate the process, the development of leadership ability does not even begin with leadership— the ability to lead is built on character."[7]

The good news about the character is that anyone can develop his or hers. It, however, takes a conscious effort and a positive attitude ready to take advantage of different situations, experiences, and opportunities that life presents us with to exercise, apply and develop our character.[8]

As Nin pointed out:
> What we call our destiny is truly our character, and that character can be altered. The knowledge that we are responsible for our actions and attitudes does not need to be discouraging, because it also means that we are free to change this destiny.[9]

Benjamin Disraeli echoed Nin's thoughts using these words: Characters do not change. Opinions alter, but characters are only developed."[10] That was the essence of Jesus' message, "Either make the tree good, and its fruit good, or else make the tree bad and its fruit bad; for a tree is known by its fruit."

The great temptation for leaders is to try to appear good rather than be good. They are as the religious leaders during the days of Jesus who were more concerned about their outward conduct than the inner character. Jesus compared their excessive obsession with the outward appearance to washing the outside of a cup while the inside was full of dirt. He challenged them, "Now you Pharisees make the outside of the cup and dish clean, but your inward part is full of greed and wickedness. Foolish ones! Did not He who made the outside make the inside also? Luke 11:39-40.

Jesus did not have any problem with cups that were clean on the outside. He had an issue with the Pharisees' tendency to worry about their outside appearance while their hearts were full of greed and wickedness.

Leaders of weak character like the Pharisees conduct their public life to appear as if they have a strong character while that is not the case. Such leaders spend more energy and time covering their weaknesses instead of taking steps to correct their character flaws.

Studies on leadership character have identified several attributes associated with leadership effectiveness.[11] By developing these attributes, any leader stands a better chance of increasing the capacity to influence other people to collaborate. Table 2.5 below identifies these essential leadership character attributes.

Table 2. 1. Leadership character attributes

Accountability	Extroversion
Agreeableness	Humanity
Conscientiousness	Inspiration
Courage	Integrity
Credibility	Justice
Drive	Openness
Emotional intelligence	Respect

The following are steps you can take to develop your character

1. Identify the character qualities for improvement

The first step in character development is to identify specific character deficiencies and then develop an action plan for growth.

Practice the desired behavior.

Many leaders who are natural introverts have learned to behave like extroverts. After identifying the character attributes that you need to cultivate to build your leadership ability, the next step is to identify the action steps you can take to reinforce those attributes.

The Bible places much emphasis on doing what we know to be right regardless of how we feel. That is walking by faith as opposed to walking by sight. Every time you take a step to do what you believe to be the right thing, you strengthen your character to that extent.

2. Develop your moral reasoning ability

Developing moral reasoning ability marks an important step towards character development. Moral reasoning is a systematic process of thinking to determine what is right or wrong in a given situation.[12] Also referred to as moral judgment, it deals with the aspect of moral development that focuses on the thinking ability of the individual to understand what is right in the context of the situation.[13]

For the Christian leader, the Holy Scripture is a vital resource for developing moral reasoning. It provides a higher standard for choosing what is right and wrong. In the sermon on the mountain, Jesus provides universal guiding principles for thinking and acting when faced with tough ethical dilemmas. The Psalmist relied on the scriptures to determine the right course of action. He said, "Your word is a lamp to my feet and a light to my path" (Ps 119:105).

Uncertainty is the rule in the 21st Century knowledge economy. Leaders frequently faced with shifting values, interests and ethical dilemmas where it is not clear what is right and wrong. As such, developing moral reasoning ability becomes a useful mechanism for discerning the best course of action.

To develop moral reasoning, the leader must become a student of the Word of God. He must be willing to take the time to read, study, reflect and act on the Word of God on a regular basis. Like the Psalmist, he or she must be able to say, "Your word I have hidden in my heart, which I might not sin against you" (Psa 119:11)

3. Develop a disciplined lifestyle

A disciplined lifestyle plays a major role in shaping one's character. Self-discipline is the ability to control your feelings, overcome your weaknesses and, pursue what you think is right despite temptations to abandon it.[14]

A spiritual discipline is "a repeated bodily practice, done over and over again, in dependence on the Holy Spirit and under the direction of Jesus and wise teachers in his way, to enable one to get good at certain things in life that one cannot learn to do by direct effort."[15]

You become what you repeatedly do.[16] By identifying healthy actions to counter your weaknesses and disciplining yourself to do them daily, you can shape your character. Apostle Paul understood the value of self-discipline in life. He wrote, "But I discipline my body and keep it under control, lest after preaching to others I should be disqualified." (1 Cor 9:27)

Effective leaders embrace discipline and train themselves to do what they ought to despite the unpleasantness, which comes with it. They engage in regular physical exercises to remain physically fit, practice spiritual disciplines and know when to say no to self-indulgence, which may cost them their influence.

4. Read good books

Reading is a powerful tool for shaping a leader's character. Charlie Jones once said, "Five years from today, *you* will be the same person that you are today, except for the books you read and the people you meet."[17] The books you read influence your mind and thoughts for better or for worse. Your feelings follow your thoughts closely to fuel them into action.

Leaders are readers. Moreover, wise leaders understand the power of the written word and carefully select what they read. They believe in the words of Mark Twain who once said: The man who does not read has no advantage over the man who cannot read.

When was the last time you read a good book? Reading is the spark behind creative minds and is one of the most predominant traits of great leaders. Reading opens your mind to new ideas, perspectives and ways of dealing with issues. You can tell a leader who reads by listening to him or her. Such leaders have fresh and progressive ideas. They are always ahead of their followers. No wonder their followers are keen every time receive new revelation.

Get the most out of your reading

Reading can be a challenge, especially if you are beginning. But, once you get used, it turns out to be a powerful habit that keeps you on the growth trail for a long time. Here are a few suggestions to help you get the most out of your reading:

First, start with your area of interest. Identify your life themes and read related books. If you love cooking, get a cooking book and read it. If you love teaching, find something on communication and start there. If you start with a topic you do not care about, it will discourage you, and before long you will close the book and do other things

Second, identify your favorite role models and read their books. These may be public speakers like preachers, leaders or writers. Get their books and start reading them. Since you already like them, you will find it is to flow with their ideas and thoughts. Reading biographies of great leaders is a very educative experience. You may want to start from there.

Third, Take note of key ideas, thoughts or lessons. Some people write notes as they read. Others underline their books; others keep a journal of their thoughts as they read. The key thing is, find a way to capture and retain striking ideas that you come across.

Fourth, develop an action plan for applying what you read. There is a popular saying that goes like this: 'If you do not use it, you lose it.' Do not just read for entertainment alone. Look for avenues to share what you are learning with others. Do not keep your ideas to yourself. It is a known fact that we learn most what we teach others. Read to learn, and maximum learning comes from applying your lessons.

Finally, read challenging books. Reading challenging books stretches your mind, which is your most powerful asset. Great ideas and innovations arise from stretched minds. Jim Rohn once said, "Don't just read the easy stuff. It may entertain you, but you will never grow out of it."[18] Train your mind to wrestle with challenging ideas and new ways of looking at things. That is the realm of personal growth, which is what you are looking for anyway.

Developing Competence through Training

Every leader has a default leadership style that he or she tends to rely on in most circumstances. Unfortunately, no one style fits all situations. The leader who desires to become more effective will commit to developing his or her ability to adopt the most suitable style in different situations and circumstances. The following is a list of various steps the leader can take to cultivate effectiveness in adopting the most appropriate leadership style.

1. Study

Training is the most direct approach to learning any skill. It involves acquiring knowledge and applying principles learned through study. Leaders are readers and, any leader who wants to become better must commit to continuous growth through reading and studying leadership related stuff. You can cultivate your leadership skill by;

- Enrolling in a leadership program or course,
- Reading books and articles on leadership,
- Attending seminars or workshops on leadership,
- Reading biographies of great leaders.

2. Observation

You can learn a lot about leadership by keenly observing the behavior of both effective and ineffective leaders around you. At any given time you are surrounded by leaders who can serve as objects of your learning. Effective leaders cultivate a curious attitude as they related to leaders around them. They take time to observe and discover what it is that makes others effective or ineffective leaders.

3. Experiential learning

Experiential learning involves practice and personalization of leadership behavior through case studies, role-plays, and self-assessment quizzes. Self-quizzes and experiential exercise provide an effective method of helping the leader personalize the information learned, and thus connecting conceptual information to the leader's life. Practicing leaders can maximize their experiential learning by keeping a leadership reflection journal as discussed in this chapter.

4. Feedback from others

Good learners make use of feedback to help them identify and improve on areas of their shortcomings. A leader who wants to become better will intentionally seek feedback from fellow leaders and followers on his or her performance. By soliciting feedback from different people, a leader can learn of areas that need action and possible ways of addressing identified shortcomings.

For more structured feedback, you may consider using available tools such as the 360^0 feedback questionnaire designed to collect objective information about your performance from different people whom you interact with on a day-to-day basis. Seek feedback from people above you, your peers and your juniors who report to you. Let them know you desire to improve and you will get valuable feedback from people who know your weaknesses but are afraid to tell you.

5. Practice in natural settings

Like any other behavioral change, growth comes from practicing what you learn about a given skill or behavior. Dubrin[19] points out that it takes practicing a given leadership behavior at least six times in live settings before one can master it.

A wise leader uses their current leadership situation as a learning opportunity. Instead of complaining about the prevailing challenges, the leader uses the situation to apply what he or she is learning and hence grows from good to better.

References

1. Attributed to Thwing, C. F. (1892 August). The Ohio Educational Monthly and the National Teacher, Volume 41, Number 8, Relation of Ohio Schools to Ohio Colleges.
2. Boud, D. & Walker, D. (1998). Promoting reflection in professional courses: The challenge of context. Stud High Educ: 23:191-206.
3. Inam, H. (2017). To Be An Effective Leader Keep A Leadership Journal. Forbes Leadership Journal.
4. https://www.forbes.com/sites/hennainam/2017/04/02/to-be-an-effective-leader-keep-a-leadership-journal/#76c40c933b4d

5. Allen, J. (2006). As A Man Thinketh. New York. CreateSpace Independent Publishing Platform

6. Attributed to John Luther, quoted by John C. Maxwell. (n.d.). AZQuotes.com. Retrieved March 22, 2017, from AZQuotes.com, http://www.azquotes.com/quote/789297

7. Eastman, P. (2010). Character of Leadership. Leadership Excellence. www.characterofleadership.com.

8. Crossan, M., Gandz, J., Seijts, G. (2016). Developing Leadership Character. New York, NY. Routledge, Taylor & Francis.

9. Nin, A. (1931-1934). The Diary of Anaïs Nin, Vol. 1

10. Benjamin Disraeli (1804-1881) British politician and author.

11. Barker, C. and Coy, R. (2003). The 7 Heavenly Virtues of Leadership, Management Today Series, McGraw-Hill, Sydney.

12. Rest, J. R., Narvaez, DDIT2: Devising and testing a revised instrument of moral judgment. Journal of Educational Psychology, 91(4), 644-659.

13. Mensch, K. G. (2009). Belief and moral judgment: Considering implications of a religious paradox in neo-Kohlbergian moral reasoning. Unpublished doctoral dissertation, Regent University, Virginia Beach, VA.; Rose, D. J. (2012). Development of Moral Reasoning at a Higher Education Institution in Nigeria. Emerging Leadership Journeys, Vol. 5 Iss. 1, pp. 81- 101

14. https://www.google.com/webhp?sourceid=chrome-instant&ion=1&espv=2&ie=UTF-8#q=self+discipline+definition&*

15. Moreland, J. (2006). The Lost Virtue of Happiness: Discovering the Disciplines of the Good Life. NavPress.

16. Covey, S. (1998). The 7 Habits of Highly Effective Teens: The Ultimate Teenage Success Guide. Fireside; 1 edition

17. Jones, E. C. (1985). The People You Meet and The Books you Read. Executive

18. Rohn, J. Quoted in Lyseight, L. (2010). Don't read for exams: Keys for unlocking your potential: Xlibris Corporation.

19. DuBrin, A. (2010). Principles of Leadership. Cengage Learning, Canada: Nelson Education, Ltd.

About the Author

Dr. Katulwa is a senior lecturer in the School of Professional Studies at Scott Christian University, Kenya. Prior to this, he served in the Business and Leadership Departments of the Pan Africa Christian University as the Director of the MA in Leadership Program for eight years.

He earned his (BA) degree from the University of Nairobi; Bachelor of Theology (B.Th.) from Christian Life School of Theology; Master of Arts in Leadership degree from Pan Africa Christian University; A Doctorate in Business Administration (DBA) from the Swiss Management Centre University (Switzerland) and, a Doctor of Philosophy in Business Administration (PhD) from University of Central Nicaragua.

Dr. Katulwa is Pastor with Christian Church International (CCI) Kenya. He is a long-serving Executive Director of the Centre for Christian Discipleship (CCD) and Leadership Training Institute (LTI), which are leadership development ministries under the Christian Church International.

The author has a wide experience in teaching, training and supervising Research graduate students in leadership and business fields. He is a founder member of the Global Lead Alliance (GLA), which promotes networking of organizations involved in leadership development around the world. He has been involved in training leaders in Kenya, India, Malawi, and the Democratic Republic of Congo.

He is married to Anne Muteti and blessed with three children, Mumo, Kyama, and Mbete. They live in Thika, Kenya

www.ingramcontent.com/pod-product-compliance
Lightning Source LLC
Chambersburg PA
CBHW021357210526
45463CB00001B/127